D0778542

MOZART´S REQUIEM

Christoph Wolff

MOZART'S REQUIEM

Historical and Analytical Studies

Documents · Score

TRANSLATED BY MARY WHITTALL

WITH REVISIONS AND ADDITIONS BY THE AUTHOR

UNIVERSITY OF CALIFORNIA PRESS   BERKELEY   LOS ANGELES

The publisher gratefully acknowledges the contribution provided by
the General Endowment Fund of the Associates of the University of
California Press and a generous translation grant from Inter Nationes,
Bonn.

Originally published in German as *Mozarts Requiem: Geschichte—
Musik—Dokumente—Partitur des Fragments*, © 1991 Deutscher
Taschenbuch Verlag GmbH & Co. KG, München, and Bärenreiter-
Verlag Karl Vötterle GmbH & Co. KG, Kassel.

Credits: Fig. 1, Staatsbibliothek zu Berlin (Stiftung Preussischer
Kulturbesitz), Musikabteilung; Figs. 2–9, Österreichische National-
bibliothek, Vienna (Musik-Sammlung), by permission; Fig. 10,
Fotostudio Fasching, Wilhelmsburg, courtesy of Bundesdenkmalamt
(Abteilung für Klangdenkmale), Vienna. Musical examples (Parts
I–II) and Requiem score (Part IV), Bärenreiter-Verlag, Kassel, by
permission.

The following publishers have generously given permission to use
extended quotations from copyrighted works: From *Mozart: A
Documentary Biography*, edited by Otto Erich Deutsch, translated by
Eric Blom, Peter Branscombe, and Jeremy Noble, reprinted by
permission of A. & C. Black, Ltd. From *E.T.A. Hoffmann's Musical
Writings*, edited by D. Charlton, translated by M. Clarke, reprinted
by permission of Cambridge University Press. From *A Mozart
Pilgrimage*, by Vincent Novello and Mary Novello, edited by Nerina
Medici and Rosemary Hughes, copyright 1955 by Novello & Co.,
Ltd. From *The Life of Mozart*, by F. X. Niemetschek, copyright 1956
by George Allen & Unwin. From *1791: Mozart's Last Year*, by H. C.
Robbins Landon, reprinted by permission of Thames and Hudson,
Ltd. From *The Letters of Mozart and His Family*, 3d ed., translated by
E. Anderson, copyright 1985 by The Macmillan Press Ltd.

University of California Press
Berkeley and Los Angeles, California

Library of Congress Cataloging-in-Publication Data follows the
index.

Printed in the United States of America
1 2 3 4 5 6 7 8 9

The paper used in this publication meets the minimum requirements
of American National Standard for Information Sciences—
Permanence of Paper for Printed Library Materials, ANSI Z39.48-
1984. ∞

In memory of my mother and father

CONTENTS

There is hardly a more eloquent document to be linked with Mozart's musical biography than his unfinished Requiem. A work that has long been shrouded in legend and mystery, a work whose artistic merit, and even its authenticity, has been the subject of heated and acrimonious debate almost from the moment of Mozart's death, the Requiem follows the composer to his end. It creates the awareness of an irretrievable loss—a loss clearly extending beyond the Requiem fragment as such and casting a light on the much larger fragment of a tragically abbreviated life's work. There have been innumerable performances of the Requiem in the past, and the future will bring countless more, but none—no matter how convincing its efforts at completion—can ever convey a true impression of the state of the work at the time of the composer's death. In this regard nothing will ever match, let alone replace, the powerful statement that only Mozart's incomplete Requiem score can make.

The Requiem fragment at the center of this book provides a focus rarely emphasized in the work's performance history or recognized elsewhere. For this reason a newly edited version of Mozart's fragmentary score has been included here, supplemented by crucial excerpts from Süssmayr's 1792 Requiem completion, which represent the only material extant that may include traces and elements of original Mozart. The historical and analytical studies included here do not deal with every conceivable aspect of the Mozart Requiem. None of the chapters claim to be comprehensive, let alone definitive. Some arguments in Part I remain preliminary, owing to the lack of historical evidence and missing musical sources; the analytical commentaries in Part II hardly do justice to the musical work of art. And the documents selected for Part III, which by themselves make for some fascinating reading, give anything but a conclusive narrative. One must simply recognize that the nature of the subject matter itself—the complexity and obstinacy of the musical, literary, and archival sources combined with the extraordinary stylistic, technical, and aesthetic claims of Mozart's swan song—presents a set of ultimately insoluble problems and insurmountable challenges.

The present volume aspires not only to reflect the current state of research on Mozart's Requiem but also to provide some new perspectives concerning essential aspects of the work. Here I mention in particular two theses: (1) that Mozart's Requiem along with other works from 1791 and before represent points of departure in several musical genres—conceptually, stylistically, technically, and aesthetically—its character as "late work" being entirely coincidental; (2) that the compositional concept of the Requiem stresses the primacy of vocal (choral) structures vis-à-vis instrumental (orchestral) elements—the four-part vocal score almost exclusively carrying the musical substance of the work.

This book owes its origin to a graduate seminar, taught in 1982 at Harvard University, which explored in considerable depth many of the Requiem problems and their often paradigmatic character. It seems worth noting that Mozart's Requiem was actually the first work to be subjected in our modern sense to a rigorous scrutiny of both sources and style. The far-ranging discussions of the 1820s and 1830s, which involved individuals as lofty as Beethoven and Goethe, played an essential role in the development of musical scholarship. Indeed these discussions are intriguing examples of genuine source studies and stylistic evaluation that took place long before musicology constituted itself as an academic discipline. After all, Abbé Maximilian Stadler, the learned friend of the Mozart family, suggested as early as 1826 that "a *fac simile* be made of Mozart's original" in order to settle the authenticity dispute; and in 1838–39 Ignaz von Mosel, custodian of the Music Collection of the Imperial Library in Vienna, conducted graphological investigations into Mozart's and Süssmayr's handwritings. Finally, the first substantial historical-critical biography of any musician, Otto Jahn's four-volume Mozart biography (1856–59), which devoted a particularly large section to the Requiem problems, laid the decisive foundation for musicological research in which composers and their works are subjected to new and powerful scholarly exploration and analysis. Well over a century later, Requiem research makes one intensely aware of how intimately related to the origins of our discipline—and to the continuing excitement that musical scholarship entails—is the study of the sources and music of Mozart's last work.

This book is for the most part a translation of the original German version published in the fall of 1991, but it includes a few modifications and additions. The Mozart anniversary year produced a number of pertinent scholarly publications necessitating the addition of a few new references and the expansion of the Bibliography for the English edition. The most important and relevant recent material concerns the documentation of a requiem mass for Mozart held a few days after his death (see Docs. 4 and 5). Whereas the German version could accommodate this matter only in an appendix, the English version has integrated it into the main text. For this reason the numbering of the documents in Part III differs from that in the German version.

I wish to record my gratitude to a number of colleagues and friends who have generously provided me with helpful suggestions, important information, and constructive criticism, among them particularly Dietrich Berke, Robert Levin, Wolfgang Plath, Wolfgang Rehm, and Alan Tyson. Moreover, my research benefited considerably from the scholarship of Leopold Nowak (1904–91), editor of the Requiem score for the Neue Mozart-Ausgabe (1965); just a few years before his death I respectfully took over from him, or, rather, for him, the still outstanding critical report. Special thanks go to Mary Whittall, who competently and elegantly translated the main parts of my German manuscript, where she also spotted some snags and inconsistencies; it was a great pleasure to cooperate with her. Finally, I am most grateful to Doris Kretschmer of the University of California Press for undertaking this project with vigor and encouragement and for providing much needed guidance along the way; and to David Severtson for his vigilant and expert copy editing.

C.W.
Cambridge, Massachusetts

CHAPTER ONE

Historical Perspectives

The Composition, Completion, and Early Reception of Mozart's Requiem

Fiction, Facts, and Open Questions

The circumstances of Mozart's death have from the beginning provided fertile ground for mysterious fantasies and romantic fairy tales. Here was one of the greatest geniuses of all time writing, on his deathbed, a mass for the dead that he would leave unfinished. The first legends sprang up immediately after the composer's death, commingling into a single narrative the events surrounding the Requiem's genesis and the circumstances of Mozart's illness and death. These accounts are colored by mystery and characterized by the often bizarre traits found in popular and pseudo-scholarly versions of the tale. Familiar anecdotes cling to the history of the Requiem: for example, that of the "unknown messenger" (Doc. 9). This figure has a basis in the historical facts but has acquired a romantic aura as the "Grey Messenger" who, in bringing Mozart the anonymous commission to write a requiem for the dead, conveyed a warning of the composer's own impending death.[1] There are tales of remarkable documents which came to light and vanished just as mysteriously, such as a patently fictitious letter in Italian that Mozart is supposed to have written to Lorenzo da Ponte, saying that he could not rid himself of the image of the unknown man who incessantly importuned him, that he now knew his last hour was upon him, and that he must finish his funeral hymn ("il mio canto funebre"), for he could not leave it uncompleted.[2] The rumor that Mozart was poisoned by his jealous rival, Antonio

---

1. See Deutsch, "Der Graue Bote," and below, n. 10.
2. Bauer-Deutsch IV, No. 1190; comment in Eibl VI, p. 423. The "original" letter, said to belong to a private collector in England, was first published in 1877. It is now wholly discredited and its whereabouts are unknown.

Salieri, began to circulate at an early date.[3] Our own time has seen the fabrication of other fairy tales—for there is no better term to describe such absurd speculations—such as that Mozart's wife, Constanze, and his pupil Franz Xaver Süssmayr had a love affair (of which Franz Xaver Mozart, born in July 1791, is supposed to have been the fruit),[4] or that Constanze Mozart's financial wheeling and dealing in connection with the Requiem prove her to have been an adept and unscrupulous businesswoman.[5]

The early anecdotes may well have been motivated by the search for more or less plausible answers to the mystery of Mozart's deplorably early death, as a means of easing the sense of tragic loss, but those of recent date tend toward sensationalism. Biographical embroidering of the events surrounding Mozart's death, inseparable as they are from the genesis of his Requiem, will probably never cease altogether.

The essential elements of the actual story were already known by around 1800, and—with the aid of the few additional details that have since come to light—it has always been possible to construct an entirely down-to-earth narrative. The young Countess Anna von Walsegg, born von Flammberg in 1770, died on 14 February 1791. Her husband, Franz Count von Walsegg (1763–1827), of Schloss Stuppach (on the Semmering Pass, some fifty miles southwest of Vienna and about half that distance from the nearest sizeable town, Wiener Neustadt), wanted to commemorate her worthily, and to this end he turned to Vienna. From the sculptor Johann Martin Fischer he commissioned a marble and granite monument at a cost of over 3,000 florins (Doc. 14),[6] and from Mozart a setting of the requiem mass for the comparatively modest fee of 50 ducats[7]—that is, 225 florins (Docs. 9, 11, 16b, 16h, 20).[8] The count was an enthusiastic but dilettante musician with a taste for dressing himself in borrowed plumage from time to time, in that he would put on private performances of music he claimed as his own when it was in fact the work of other hands (Doc. 14). He intended to do the same with Mozart's Requiem, which is why the commission was transmitted in writing and

3. On the various versions of the poisoning legend, see Braunbehrens, *Mozart in Wien*, 429–35.

4. Cf. Schickling, "Einige ungeklärte Fragen"; comment in Eibl 1976–77.

5. Gärtner, *Mozart's Requiem und Constanze Mozart*, 11; cf. Wolf-Dieter Seiffert's review of Gärtner, *MJb* (1987–88): 289–92.

6. Wurzbach, *Biographisches Lexikon*, 4:245.

7. In setting the fee, Mozart was clearly guided by what he received for an opera (450 florins each for *Die Entführung*, *Figaro*, and *Tito*) and put a relatively high price on the Requiem: half as much as for an opera. On Mozart's income see Steptoe, "Mozart and Poverty," and Steptoe, "Mozart's Finances," in *Mozart Compendium*, 127–30.

8. The sum of 100 ducats (= 450 fl.) cited in some documents is erroneous.

with such discretion (Doc. 9).[9] It reached Mozart in the summer of 1791, anonymously, and very probably carried by a clerk employed by Walsegg's Viennese lawyer, Johann Nepomuk Sortschan.[10]

Mozart died on 5 December 1791, leaving the Requiem unfinished. The larger part of it had been written, however, and in order to honor the commission and collect the rest of the fee—an advance had been paid, and the whole represented a substantial sum to the young widow with two small children to support— Constanze Mozart arranged for its completion by several musicians from her husband's immediate circle. The score was finished by Franz Xaver Süssmayr (who had assisted Mozart in the last months of his life with the operas *Die Zauber-flöte* and *La clemenza di Tito*) and duly delivered to the unknown client, whose name Constanze learned only in 1800 (Doc. 19). The count had the work performed on 14 December 1793 in the parish church, the Neuklosterkirche, in Wiener Neustadt, within the liturgical framework of a mass for the soul of his late wife. The score used on this occasion was a copy in the count's own hand, giving his own name, "Fr. C[omte]. de Wallsegg," as the composer.[11] But the first performance of the completed Requiem had already been given, probably without the count's knowledge, on 2 January 1793 in the Jahn-Saal in Vienna, at a concert arranged by Baron Gottfried van Swieten for the benefit of Constanze Mozart and her children.[12]

Mozart's fragment had been performed even earlier, just a few days after his death and burial. The almost universally accepted notion that Mozart was quietly buried in a mass grave with no mourners present conveniently buttressed the prevailing view that the financially strapped composer had increasingly become alienated from his friends, supporters, and wider audience—a misinterpretation that was finally put to rest by Volkmar Braunbehrens, who showed that the burial ritual followed exactly the Josephine regulations observed in Vienna at the time.[13]

---

9. Constanze Mozart referred later (Doc. 16g) to the wax seal from the letter commissioning the Requiem. Niemetschek had also seen the letter (Doc. 9, Niemetschek's note).

10. Cf. Deutsch, "Der Graue Bote"; Deutsch, "Geschichte von Mozarts Requiem." For quite a long time the "Grey Messenger" was identified as Franz Anton Leitgeb (cf. Doc. 14, n. 17); however, as Deutsch argues convincingly, Leitgeb was not a stranger to either Mozart or his wife. Since the commission to Johann Martin Fischer for the tomb was sent via Walsegg's lawyer in Vienna, it is likely that the Requiem commission traveled by the same route and that a clerk from Sortschan's office would have been the carrier of this intentionally anonymous letter. On the Walsegg family, see Requiem Catalog, 237–42.

11. Cf. Biba, "Par Monsieur de Walsegg."

12. *Mozart-Dokumente*, 409; *Mozart DB*, 467. See also below, n. 26.

13. Braunbehrens, *Mozart in Vienna*, 413–18.

Further details have come to light regarding Mozart's funeral, which was paid for by Baron van Swieten, prefect of the Imperial Library and one of Mozart's staunchest patrons. For instance, on 6 December 1791 the funeral procession from Mozart's apartment to St. Stephen's Cathedral was led by a crossbearer, four pallbearers, and four choirboys with candle lamps. The identity of those who followed him also seems quite clear: the widow, Constanze; her sisters and other members of the Weber family; Baron van Swieten; Mozart's students Franz Jakob Freystädtler, Franz Xaver Süssmayr, and Otto Hatwig; then Mozart's colleagues and friends Johann Georg Albrechtsberger, Anselm Hüttenbrenner, and Antonio Salieri. However, of particular importance is what hitherto unknown church records, only recently discovered, have revealed: on 10 December 1791 a requiem mass was held for Mozart at St. Michael's, the parish church of the Hofburg (Mozart held the appointment of court composer) and chapel of the Caecilien-kongregation (the association of court musicians, of which Mozart was a member; Docs. 4 and 5). The memorial service was organized by Emanuel Schikaneder (impresario, librettist, and the first singer to play Papageno in *Die Zauberflöte*) and his colleague Joseph von Bauernfeld on behalf of Vienna's court and theater musicians. Moreover, a newspaper report of 16 December 1791 states that "the Requiem, which he composed in his last illness, was executed" (Doc. 5)—an unmistakable reference to an actual performance of Mozart's Requiem as part of a liturgical requiem mass.

This performance within less than a week of Mozart's death must have been confined to the finished part of the Requiem. The only completely finished and indeed performable section was the Introit, the first movement, but it seems that the Kyrie was included in the performance as well.[14] The extant documents reveal no concrete details regarding the performance of Mozart's Requiem fragment. Hence we can only speculate whether the remainder of the liturgical requiem was presented as plainchant or, perhaps, in combination with the finished portions of Mozart's four-part short score of the Sequence and the Offertory, with organ instead of orchestral accompaniment.

But there is no need to ponder why musical Vienna neglected to pay Mozart an appropriate tribute: it didn't. Mozart's friends not only held a memorial service soon after his death, they also chose the most fitting music. They clearly understood that when the dying composer put aside the Requiem score, he knew that he had been writing a requiem for himself.

14. For Mozart's funeral and memorial service, see Brauneis, "Unveröffentliche Nachrichten"; Brauneis, "Exequien für Mozart"; Wolff, Review of *Mozart: Requiem.*

The various anecdotes and legends that have accumulated around the Requiem's genesis can be related to the objective core of the story as set out above, if the crucial data are kept in sight. But we are on less certain ground when it comes to the essential details of the actual process of composition, beginning with Mozart's plan and conception of the work, and his execution of a substantial part of it, and continuing to its posthumous completion by a number of other composers. This, however, is precisely the area of greatest interest to those who wish to understand the Requiem as a musical work of art.

The voluminous specialist literature on the subject of Mozart's Requiem (see the Bibliography) has until now paid less attention to the fascinating way in which the various aspects of the history of the work's composition interlock with the history of its early reception than it has to a series of important individual questions. Foremost among these has been the fraught, complex question of authenticity, the exact relationship, that is, between that part of the unfinished work that is known to be by Mozart and the remainder, to which the extent of his contribution is problematical.

Friedrich Blume summarized the state of knowledge in the early 1960s in an article first published in English translation under the title "Requiem but No Peace."[15] This title expresses the patent resignation of one contemplating the host of open questions that still surround Mozart's last, unfinished work—in particular the question of authenticity. Blume acknowledged that Mozart scholarship found itself powerless to reduce the innumerable controversial statements and opinions that had been aired for nearly two centuries to a common denominator, let alone bring them to a final and conclusive resolution. The situation has scarcely changed in the three decades since Blume wrote. What is to follow on these pages will not affect our understanding fundamentally, but perhaps it will make a difference at the level of detail. One unhappy result of past discussion—as Blume noted— has been the polarization of source studies and stylistic criticism. The present study hopes to avoid giving primacy to either of these approaches; rather, the two aspects should be allowed to complement each other.

Some progress has been made, as can be seen above all from Wolfgang Plath's work on sketches he himself discovered and on the voluminous historical correspondence about the Requiem, or from Ernst Hess's stylistic analyses of Süssmayr's contributions to the work.[16] Last but not least, Leopold Nowak's edition,

15. *Musical Quarterly* 47 (1961): 147–69 (the English title was suggested by Paul Henry Lang).
16. Plath, "Über Skizzen zum Requiem"; "Requiem-Briefe"; "Noch ein Requiem-Brief"; Hess, "Zur Ergänzung des Requiems"; supplemented by the sensitive observations in Beyer's edition of the Requiem (1971; 1979); cf. also Beyer, "Zur Neuinstrumentation."

published in the Neue Mozart-Ausgabe, played a decisive role in illuminating the darkness that surrounds the Requiem by placing the accent firmly on the study of primary musical and archival sources, which proved to be far from exhausted.[17] H. C. Robbins Landon, on the other hand, presented a work of compilation rather than one that broke new ground;[18] other additions to the literature, in their concentration on the roles possibly played by Constanze Mozart and Franz Xaver Süssmayr, have tended toward the speculative, sensationalist, and/or polemical.[19]

The central questions remain the same as they have always been.[20] Everything starts from, and returns to, one fact: Mozart, having received the commission to write his Requiem in 1791, was unable to complete it because death took the pen from his hand. This truth is indisputable, although it was consciously and persistently concealed as far as possible by members of Mozart's family and intimate circle.[21] On the other hand, uncertainty has always clouded attempts to establish the exact amount of the surviving musical text of the Requiem that can be attributed to Mozart. The decisive role played by his pupil and assistant Süssmayr in completing the work is well known, and the parts of the score that survive in autograph permit, up to a point, exact differentiation of what is in Mozart's hand and what in the hands of others.[22] But we still do not know exactly how much of the music Mozart had worked out, the overall formal disposition or the form of what remained to be done. Further questions hang upon this point: what is the chronology of the composition and completion of the Requiem in 1791–92? When did Mozart start, and how did he proceed? What happened in the weeks immediately before and after his death? When was the score ready? And, further, what were the decisive technical and stylistic premises for the work,

17. NMA I/2, vols. 1–2 (1965). The Internationale Bachakademie Stuttgart organized a symposium on Mozart's Requiem in the autumn of 1987, with contributions from Franz Beyer, Robert Levin, Wolfgang Plath, and the present author (English version: Wolff, "Composition and Completion of Mozart's Requiem"). Moseley, "Mozart's Requiem," presents a recent, more detailed discussion of the sources.

18. Landon, 1791.

19. Schickling, "Einige ungeklärte Fragen"; Gärtner, *Mozarts Requiem und Constanze Mozart;* Hildesheimer, *Mozart;* in particular, Peter Shaffer's play *Amadeus* (later filmed).

20. The questions centering on the ominous "Grey Messenger" and the commissioning of the work by Count Walsegg must now be regarded as essentially settled. See Anton Herzog's "True and Detailed History of the Requiem by W. A. Mozart" (Doc. 14), discovered in the early 1960s; Deutsch, "Der Graue Bote"; "Geschichte von Mozarts Requiem"; Biba, "Par Monsieur de Walsegg."

21. Nissen, *Wolfgang Mozart's Biographie,* 1:571f., and 2:168–75, does not once allude to additions to the score made by other hands.

22. Cf. also Günter Brosche's commentary in his facsimile edition of the Requiem (1990).

and to what extent were those who worked on its completion after Mozart's death aware of them and able to implement them?

If we are to answer these questions, it can only be by reference to the whole complex of historical, archival, textual, and analytical factors. We cannot afford to neglect any one of these aspects, even though there is no hope that Mozart scholarship will ever be able to lay the question to rest. The attempt will be made in the following pages to organize the daunting quantities of intractable material into groups of compatible content while keeping the questions posed above in sight in at least some form. But there is no escaping the fact that some things can be treated only summarily and that some aspects will be favored above others: more emphasis will fall, understandably, on those of central importance, but those that promise to open new perspectives will also be explored.

The Requiem Controversy (1825–39)

The so-called "Requiem-Streit," or Requiem controversy, was kindled by a polemical article, "Über die Echtheit des Mozartschen Requiem" (On the Authenticity of Mozart's Requiem), published in 1825 by Gottfried Weber.[23] It caused a furor, for it raised the question of Mozart's authorship of the entire work. Weber began as follows:

> Of all the works by our glorious Mozart, there is hardly one that enjoys as much general admiration, even veneration, as his Requiem.
> This is, however, very remarkable—one might almost say amazing—for of all his works this is the one that can be described, bluntly, as the least perfect, the least finished: indeed, it is scarcely worthy to be called a work of Mozart's at all.

Jacob Gottfried Weber (1779–1839) was a lawyer by profession and an official of the court of appeals in Darmstadt at the time, but he was well read in music theory, and his article was written in a serious attempt to shed light on the contradictions that had been apparent for the previous twenty-five years. For the story of the work's genesis was generally seen as "threaded through with a certain mystical, almost romantic obscurity."[24]

23. Weber, "Über die Echtheit"; "Weitere Nachrichten über die Echtheit"; "Nachtrag zur Vertheidigung der Echtheit." On Weber's life and writings, see *MGG*, vol. 14, cols. 333–36, and *New Grove*, 20:267f.
24. Weber, "Über die Echtheit," 205.

In the course of that quarter-century, Mozart's Requiem had become well known to the musical public through numerous performances in many places as well as through the publication of a full score (Leipzig, 1800), a vocal score (Offenbach, 1801), and the parts (Vienna, 1812). But from a very early date, too, anecdotal reports had drawn a veil of mystery about the work. In connection with the appearance of the Leipzig first edition, Franz Xaver Süssmayr wrote a letter to Breitkopf & Härtel, setting out his crucial part in the work's final form. The letter was published in 1801 in the *Allgemeine musikalische Zeitung* (Doc. 17).[25] In spite of that, his name was not mentioned in any of the editions of the work. Since no documentary evidence or original source material was available, the question was inevitably asked: Had the Requiem been left unfinished, or had Mozart in fact finished it?

On the one hand, there was the plain statement in the first full-length biography of the composer, by Franz Xaver Niemetschek (Prague, 1798), that the messenger from the person who had commissioned the Requiem "arrived and asked for the composition in its incomplete state, and it was given him" (Doc. 9).[26] On the other hand, Friedrich Rochlitz's far more elaborate account, also published in 1798, declared that Mozart had believed that he was "writing this piece for his own funeral. He could not be shaken in this belief; he worked, therefore, like Raphael at his *Transfiguration,* with the constant sense that his own death was near, and, like Raphael, what he created was the transfiguration of himself."[27] Furthermore, Mozart believed that his client

25. The letter was published in vol. 4, p. 1; it was reprinted in Weber, "Über die Echtheit," 208f.

26. The brief reference to the Requiem in the first biography of Mozart, that of Schlichtegroll, also mentions its being unfinished. The reference is introduced by a quotation of Haydn's testimony to Leopold Mozart. " 'I tell you before God, and as an honest man, that I acknowledge your son as the greatest composer of whom I have ever heard; he has taste and possesses the most thorough-going knowledge of the art of composition.' This verdict from one better qualified than any other to judge was confirmed yet again by the Mass for the Dead, the so-called Requiem, which Mozart composed in the last days of his life but was unable to finish altogether. The solemn pathos of expression, which we find most aptly combined there with the highest degree of art, moved every heart at the performance given in aid of the composer's widow and children, and earned the admiration of all connoisseurs" (Schlichtegroll, "Mozarts Leben" [1793], 29).

27. In the *Allgemeine musikalische Zeitung* 1 (1798): 150. Rochlitz later told Weber that during Constanze Mozart's visit to Leipzig for the performance of the Requiem given there in 1796 (Doc. 15), he had "laid siege to her" to ask her questions "about everything that I was then capable of esteeming and taking interest in; among other things, about the genesis of the Requiem, and everything to do with it. From everything that I learned then, and at once made a note of, without any purpose in mind, other than not to forget it" (*Cäcilia* 4 [1826]: 287f.). See Solomon, "The Rochlitz Anecdotes," 32 (anecdote 20).

had been sent to him to warn him of his end. He was therefore all the more earnestly resolved to set up a worthy memorial to his name. He worked on in these beliefs, and it is no wonder that the outcome was so perfect a piece. He often sank in utter exhaustion and unconsciousness as he labored on. Before the four weeks were at an end he had finished but also—fallen asleep.[28]

The general public's confusion can only have been increased by the authors' claims to have based these differing accounts on the testimony of Mozart's widow.

Weber published a series of papers, setting out his grounds for doubting the Requiem's authorship, but his arguments were generally viewed in a negative light in later Mozart scholarship. An exception was Otto Jahn, who not only provided the first comprehensive discussion of the whole Requiem controversy, in his biography of Mozart, but also went so far as to credit Weber with an "honest endeavor," even if his criticisms of the Requiem were often unjustified and marred by polemical exaggeration.[29] Weber had based his case on the following premises.

We may . . . accept with Rochlitz that before his death Mozart had completed his swan song (but for a few small details, perhaps). We may further accept, with Gerber,[30] that after Mozart's death the manuscript of the work—complete but for a few small details, perhaps—was delivered to the unknown client. We further accept as well known that the identity of the unknown client was not discovered and that the original manuscript handed over to him has not come to light since then: no one has ever yet made any such claim. . . .

But it is common knowledge that before the author of an extensive work commits it to paper in the form of an orderly and complete manuscript, it is customary for him first of all to set down quick drafts: outlines, sketches, *ébauches, croquis,* call them what you will. In the case of vocal compositions, especially, there will be places in his rough draft where the composer may

---

28. Rochlitz, in the *Allgemeine musikalische Zeitung* 1 (1798): 178. See Solomon, "The Rochlitz Anecdotes," 33 (anecdote 22).

29. Jahn's discussion is found in his *W. A. Mozart* (1867), 800–814 ("Die Kontroverse über das Requiem"). Remarkably, Gruber, *Mozart und die Nachwelt,* treats the Requiem's reception history and the whole Requiem controversy only peripherally. See, however, the extensive documentation in Requiem Catalog, 271–92. The quotation is from Jahn, *W. A. Mozart* (1867), 804.

30. Ernst Ludwig Gerber, in *Neues historisch-biographisches Lexicon der Tonkünstler,* (Leipzig, 1814), s.v. "Mozart," col. 481: "Immediately after his death, the messenger called again, and asked for the work, and was given it in its incomplete state."

well write out only the parts for the four voices in full, on two or more staves; he will then have them copied out, in full score as it were, with the copyist leaving blank the staves on which the composer then writes out the instrumental parts. In short, before elaborating and writing down the complete score, the composer first executes sketches and other preparatory work of all kinds, according as circumstances, need, and convenience dictate.

It was no doubt sketches of such a nature, left behind among Mozart's papers, perhaps mixed up with other snippets of paper, that were given by his widow to Herr Süssmayr and used by the latter in the composition of the Requiem which we now possess.

An explanation on these lines serves not only, as may be seen, to resolve the apparent contradiction between Süssmayr's and Rochlitz's accounts, and between Rochlitz's and that of the truth-loving Gerber; but also to solve the riddle of how it came about that the Requiem was given to the unknown client and yet remained among Mozart's papers to be found by Süssmayr. . . . The upshot is that, in place of the above-mentioned, very well-founded suspicions concerning the authenticity of the Requiem as we know it, we now confront the sad but scarcely debatable certainty that this same Requiem, exactly as Süssmayr's letter to the publishers alleges, is largely Süssmayr's work, with not a movement in it purely by Mozart, while the authentic Requiem composed by Mozart has not—or at least not yet—seen the light of day.[31]

These premises underlay Weber's graver aesthetic doubts about the entire work, which led him to the conclusion that, contrary to Süssmayr's own testimony (Doc. 17), less of the original material of such movements as the Kyrie, the "Tuba mirum," the "Confutatis," or the "Quam olim Abrahae" fugue was by Mozart than alleged, while he must have had a substantially greater share in the movements that Süssmayr had claimed were by himself (Sanctus to Agnus Dei). Thus Weber cast serious doubt on the authenticity of the complete score that had been published by Breitkopf & Härtel in 1800, and widely distributed in the following twenty-five years, under the name of Mozart alone.

Weber's detailed criticism of the music was often both pedantic and unjustifiedly harsh, as his comments on the Kyrie illustrate:

It would distress me to be obliged to believe, for example, that it was Mozart who inflicted such warblings as the following upon the chorus [Kyrie,

31. Weber, "Über die Echtheit," 211–14.

mm. 18 ff.]. There would be howls of protest on all sides, from singers and critics alike, if such *gorgheggi* were offered under the name of Rossini, perhaps, or any other composer less highly respected than Mozart.[32]

This was not the first occasion on which Beethoven took umbrage at the man he called "Giftfried" Weber (translated "Gallfrey" as opposed to "Godfrey"): here he scribbled furiously in the margin, "O you arch-donkey" and "O you double donkey."[33] Nothing less, indeed, than the integrity of Mozart's genius was at stake, and the entire musical world was aroused to express a wide variety of views. The response that carried the most weight came from Abbé Maximilian Stadler, the long-established friend and adviser of the Mozart family, who wrote *Vertheidigung der Echtheit des Mozart'schen Requiem* (Defense of the Authenticity of Mozart's Requiem) and two supplementary statements.[34] Stadler was the first to refer to the original source material in his rebuttal of Weber's arguments (Docs. 22, 26a). At the same time, he threw new fuel on the fire with his remark that the Requiem also contained some motives of Handel.[35] Weber's reaction was to surmise that the movements in question could therefore only be studies by Mozart. Weber's opinions gained wide and enduring credence: even Robert Schumann regarded Mozart's Requiem as "not merely corrupt but wholly inauthentic except for a few numbers."[36]

The 1827 edition of the Requiem, *Neue nach Mozart's und Süßmayr's Handschriften berichtigte Ausgabe* (new edition, corrected on the basis of Mozart's and Süssmayr's manuscripts), published by Johann Anton André, the owner of Mozart's musical estate, was the first edition to name Süssmayr in connection with the work. In conjunction with his wish to present an improved edition, André

---

32. Weber, "Über die Echtheit," 216–18. The word Weber used for warblings was "Gurgeleyen," an allusion to Niemetschek's comment on Mozart's songs, in which the composer "dared to defy Italian singers, and banned all useless, characterless warblings, embellishments and trills!" (*Leben des Kapellmeisters Mozart* [1798], 49; the translation given here differs from the version on p. 58 of the English edition, *Life of Mozart*).

33. In Beethoven's copy of *Cäcilia* (see Krones, "Ein französisches Vorbild," 17). The Requiem controversy also reached the pages of Beethoven's conversation notebooks (cf. *Mozart-Dokumente*, Addenda et Corrigenda, 96f.).

34. Stadler, *Vertheidigung der Echtheit des Mozartischen Requiem; Nachtrag zur Vertheidigung; Zweyter und letzter Nachtrag.* On p. 46 of the last work, Stadler reproduced a letter sent him by Beethoven, dated 6 February 1826, saying: "You have done very well indeed in obtaining justice for Mozart's name through your truly masterly, penetrating essay."

35. See Part II, pp. 78–80.

36. K⁶, 730.

also sought to clarify the work's history and included a substantial introduction, which contained sober factual information but also found room for some fairly wild hypotheses, such as the attempt to connect the Requiem with another unfinished work, the Mass in C Minor K 427, and to prove that both dated from 1783 (Doc. 26a). The edition reveals plainly enough the difficulty of making a clean separation of Mozart's and Süssmayr's contributions and designating them appropriately. The problem becomes even clearer in the edition of the Sequence and Offertory published separately in 1829 ("as written by Mozart in his own hand, and copied exactly from Mozart's original by Abbé Stadler").[37] Nevertheless, André's editions of 1827 and 1829 constitute the first essential landmarks on the road toward an edition based on the best available sources.

In the early years of the Requiem controversy, none of the disputants could call on truly reliable evidence of Mozart's part in the composition. As Weber rightly bemoaned, the original manuscripts were not available. They remained unknown to the general public for as long as the owners—for whatever reason— withheld them. Abbé Stadler was the first to mention them (Doc. 22), but then, very quickly, one piece at a time, they came to light. Stadler himself gained possession of the autograph score of the Sequence, lacking only the "Lacrymosa," in 1826 and sold it to the Court Library in Vienna in or about 1829.[38] In 1826— and probably earlier—the "Lacrymosa," together with the Offertory, belonged to Joseph Eybler, one of Mozart's pupils and Salieri's successor as Capellmeister to the Court in Vienna;[39] he presented both manuscripts to the Court Library in 1833.[40] Neither Stadler nor Eybler gave any account, however, of how they came by these autographs. Stadler only mentioned a mysterious "friend," who gave him the material on 22 March 1826 (Docs. 23, 26a, 29).[41] Stadler's reference to the autograph material had an effect on the subsequent stages of the Requiem controversy, however, insofar as that material played an important part in un-

37. André's 1829 edition also includes a hypothetical "original score" of Mozart's "Requiem" and "Kyrie," reduced to the vocal parts and figured bass. See also below, pp. 17–22.

38. According to Nowak, "Die Erwerbung des Mozart-Requiems," this transaction took place in 1831. The diaries of Vincent and Mary Novello testify, on the other hand, that the manuscripts were already in the Court Library in July 1829 (Doc. 12).

39. He had been given them by Constanze Mozart, probably as early as 1792 (Doc. 25).

40. Cf. Nowak, "Die Erwerbung des Mozart-Requiem." Eybler suffered a stroke in 1833 and was given his pension. He had arranged that his Mozart Requiem manuscripts should go to the Court Library after his death (see Fig. 3). That they went there earlier was evidently connected in some way with the terms of his retirement.

41. Stadler's section of the manuscript (Codex b[1]; see pp. 21–22) was in Constanze Mozart's hands in 1800 (Doc. 16n) and was lent to André in Offenbach in 1801–2 (Bauer-Deutsch IV, 387).

derpinning the case that the "Lacrymosa" and the Offertory were indeed by Mozart, thus diminishing Süssmayr's role.

As the public debate about the Requiem continued,[42] it spread far beyond the circle of those most immediately concerned: the matter crops up, for example, in the correspondence between Goethe and Zelter.[43] But it took a completely new course when, to everyone's surprise, the complete "original" score was discovered in 1838, among music that had belonged, at the time of his death, to the late Count von Walsegg, who had commissioned the work in 1791. Through the agency of the count's former steward, Nowack, this score was in turn offered to the Court Library in Vienna and was purchased before the end of 1838 by the chief librarian, Moritz Count Dietrichstein, for the sum of 50 ducats (Mozart's original fee).[44] The curator of the music collection at that time, Hofrat Ignaz von Mosel, was very well aware of the significance that this unexpected find would have in the Requiem controversy and wasted no time in setting up a team of graphologists. Their professional conclusion, after comparing the score with some of the Süssmayr autographs in Budapest, was that it was the work of two hands, namely Mozart's and Süssmayr's.[45]

42. Cf. Jahn, *W. A. Mozart* (1867), 800ff. One of the most important participants in the discussion was the Berlin critic and theorist Adolf Bernhard Marx, who wrote about the matter several times in his *Berliner allgemeine musikalische Zeitung.*

43. "At last we have the score of Mozart's Requiem in our hands, corrected according to the original manuscripts and enhanced by so much discussion, and now we know what we always knew. You know the periodical *Cäcilia*, so you must have become familiar with Herr Weber of Darmstadt's bitter, sour, wordy polemic against the authenticity of this posthumous work. He has claimed, namely, that the Requiem is not by Mozart, to all intents and purposes, and if it is, it is the weakest, nay, the most sinful, thing that ever came from the pen of that celebrated man. In short, Mozart left the work unfinished, but after his death Süssmayer put his oar in, sullied Mozart's ideas, and the work was polluted, if not poisoned, by his imperfect understanding; since Mozart's death, the world has lived in a state of amazed—nay, amazing—delusion over this legacy, entirely due to the fairy tale of its composition, and no one yet has had the heart to drag the blemishes, patches, and flaws of a work of artistic forgery into the light. Such is Weber's fancy." Zelter's letter of 16 June 1827 to Goethe enlarges further on the subject of the Requiem. See Zelter and Goethe, *Briefwechsel*, 331.

44. Nowack, by then commissioner of justice in Schottwien, wrote to Dietrichstein and Mosel in October and November 1838, giving the names of those who had owned the manuscript since Walsegg's death (1827; the letters are reproduced in Nowak, "Die Erwerbung des Mozart-Requiem"; cf. also Doc. 14): Countess Sternberg, Walsegg's sister and residuary legatee; the manager of the Stuppach estate, Joseph Leitner, who bought Walsegg's musical manuscripts and instruments from the countess; the manorial secretary Karl Haag, formerly one of Walsegg's musicians, who bought the manuscript; finally, on Haag's death in 1837, his residuary legatee, Katharina Adelpoller.

45. The Süssmayr autographs included his horn concerto based on a Mozartian original (cataloged as K 514; see p. 45). On the Süssmayr manuscripts in the National Library in Budapest see Kecskeméti, "Süßmayr-Handschrifen in Budapest." Mosel, *Über die Original-Partitur des Requiem*, contains a circumstantial account of the investigation of the Requiem manuscript; cf. also the commentary in Plath, "Noch ein Requiem-Brief," 101.

Armed with this unanimous verdict, Mosel wrote to Constanze Nissen, Mozart's widow, on 7 February 1839, asking her bluntly to provide definitive information about Mozart's part in the composition of the Requiem (Doc. 31).[46] His sole concern was to obtain a more exact account of Süssmayr's contribution. Once again, however, Constanze avoided giving a direct answer: she replied briefly that Mozart often employed copyists and must have done so in the case of the Requiem—in short, Süssmayr had made no creative contribution to the work (Doc. 32).

Not once after Mozart's death did Constanze make an unequivocal statement about the Requiem, and yet it is impossible to accuse her of dishonest intentions. Like everyone else in the circle of those closest to Mozart, she was motivated primarily by the desire that the Requiem's reputation as Mozart's crowning masterpiece should not be tarnished. They all regarded the question of the work's completion as a matter of secondary importance. None of those who were asked to complete it, including Süssmayr (Doc. 17), wished to see their own names placed at the side of Mozart's—all of which demonstrates how inseparable the composition of the Requiem was from Mozart himself in their eyes and how much they identified the completed work with him.

Constanze died on 6 March 1842—a date that marks the end of the historical Requiem controversy, for she was the last survivor of those who had been directly involved in what happened after Mozart's death.[47] As the documents demonstrate, this small group—Mozart's closest intimates—had contrived repeatedly, and for honorable reasons, to draw all askers of unwelcome questions into an extraordinary game of blind-man's bluff. As a result, to some extent we remain in the dark to this day.

The First Edition and Süssmayr's Testimony

In considering how the Requiem controversy developed, it is important to recognize that what was known in the 1820s about the Requiem's genesis was not essentially different from what had already been established a quarter of a century earlier in connection with the preparation and printing of the first edition (1799–1800), but doubt had repeatedly been cast on that information in the interim. In 1800 the Leipzig company Breitkopf & Härtel lost the competition to acquire Mozart's musical estate to the enterprising publisher André of Offenbach, but it

---

46. Plath, "Noch ein Requiem-Brief."
47. Except for Joseph Eybler, who lived until 1846, but was disabled following his stroke in 1833.

brought off the coup of publishing the first edition of his Requiem in the same year.[48] Constanze knew of Breitkopf's plans and found herself faced with the need to secure permission to publish from the unknown person who had originally commissioned the work—a need made all the more pressing because publication would be to her benefit. Not knowing his identity, her first idea was to trace him by means of an advertisement in the newspapers (Doc. 16e), but in the end she did not carry out this plan.

For Breitkopf & Härtel, as the publishers, the question of whether Mozart actually completed the Requiem had become a pressing one before 1800. As their correspondence with Constanze shows, they felt obliged to get to the bottom of the matter in good time in order to avoid problems and embarrassment later. They had possessed a copy of the score, provided by Constanze, since the Leipzig performance of 1796 at the latest (Doc. 15), but it was in the hand of a copyist.[49] They also got in touch with Süssmayr, at Constanze's suggestion, and he responded in a letter, dated 8 February 1800 (Doc. 17), giving a more detailed description of his part in completing the Requiem. Finally, in the autumn of 1800, the pertinent sources were collated under notarial supervision—including the score that Constanze had had delivered to Count Walsegg in 1792 in fulfillment of his commission of 1791—for the count had intervened meanwhile, fearing that publication of the Requiem by Breitkopf & Härtel would affect his rights in the work and hoping, if he suffered a loss, at least to recover the fee he had paid Constanze in 1791 and 1792.[50]

A comparison of the first edition and the original score in Count Walsegg's possession took place in the office of the Viennese lawyer Sortschan. Constanze was represented in these proceedings by Nissen and Stadler. The Swedish diplomat Frederik Samuel Silverstolpe, then resident in Vienna, was also present and

48. It appeared before June 1800. The edition included a German version of unknown origin printed below the Latin text; in an appendix, it also included a poetic translation by C. A. H. Clodius (p. 179) and a German parody of the liturgical requiem text by Johann Adam Hiller (p. 180). Constanze could not include the Requiem in her sale of Mozart's musical estate to André, as she had no rights in the work.

49. The Leipzig performance was the first public performance of the completed Requiem outside Vienna (apart from the two given in Wiener Neustadt). It was given by the Leipzig Singakademie under Johann Gottfried Schicht, later Thomascantor, on 20 April 1796 (Doc. 15 and notes). An earlier performance is believed to have taken place in Leipzig, in the Thomas Schule, under Johann Adam Hiller, who also directed individual numbers from the Requiem in the Thomas Kirche. Two copies of the score were made during Constanze Mozart's stay in Leipzig, reportedly by a "Thomaner" called Jost (cf. Weber, "Weitere Nachrichten über die Echtheit," 297). The Breitkopf & Härtel first edition of the Requiem (Leipzig, 1800) was based on one of them.

50. A compromise was reached in that the count "offered to accept copies of several pieces of music in compensation" (Nissen, *Wolfgang Mozart's Biographie*, 2:170).

left an account of the circumstances of the collation (Doc. 18).[51] It fell to Stadler, with his special knowledge of Mozart's manuscripts, to mark all the material in the original score that was not in Mozart's hand, to the best of his ability. Wherever he identified a passage as having not originated with Mozart, he circled it in pencil (Fig. 3). On the basis of copies that Stadler made at the time as a record, these distinctions were adopted in the André editions of 1827 and 1829, where the letters M and S were used to denote the contributions of Mozart and Süssmayr respectively. Johannes Brahms used the same letters for the same purpose in 1877, in his edition of the Requiem for the old Mozart-Gesamtausgabe.[52]

In his letter of 8 February 1800 to Breitkopf & Härtel, Süssmayr had modestly described his work on the Requiem as "unworthy" of the name of Mozart (Doc. 17). The most important points he made were: (1) that Constanze had first asked "several masters" to complete the work, but these had been unable to undertake it for various reasons, or they were not prepared to put their own work at the side of Mozart's; (2) that the request was finally made to him because he had often played and sung through the music with Mozart during the last weeks of his life, and Mozart "had frequently talked to me about the detailed working of this composition and explained to me the how and the wherefore of his instrumentation"; (3) that "of the Requiem [i.e., Introit] with Kyrie, 'Dies irae' [i.e., Sequence], and 'Domine Jesu Christe' [i.e., Offertory], Mozart completed the four vocal parts and the figured bass" (except for the "Lacrymosa" after the line "qua resurget ex favilla"), while he "indicated only the motivic idea here and there" in the instrumentation; (4) that he, Süssmayr, had completed the Sequence, while the Sanctus, Benedictus, and Agnus Dei were entirely by himself; and (5) that "in order to give the work greater uniformity [*Einförmigkeit*]" he had taken the liberty of repeating the "Kyrie" fugue from the start, with the words "cum sanctis tuis," at the end of the work.

This letter has long been regarded, rightly, as the most important and most reliable testimony to Süssmayr's part in the Requiem.[53] But he died in 1803 and therefore could neither provide further enlightenment nor take part in the controversy of twenty-five years later. Thus the letter takes on something of the nature of a last testament. What it says, as well as what it does not say, must be measured against the extant primary sources. These in turn are still, remarkably

51. Stadler, *Zweyter und letzter Nachtrag*, 27–29, gives an account of the meeting and of his own role in it; further details of the written results of the collation appear in Moseley, "Mozart's Requiem," 227–29.

52. AMA 24/1.

53. Stadler believed Süssmayr's account was "perfectly correct" (Doc. 22).

enough, the very same cluster of manuscripts in which the key to the Requiem's genesis has lain from the first and which are still to be found in Vienna, where the whole story originally took place. The only new manuscripts that have come to light in nearly two centuries are the Requiem sketches in the Berlin Staatsbibliothek (Mus. ms. autogr. W. A. Mozart zu: KV 620; see Fig. 1).[54]

The Original Requiem Score

The sections of the Requiem score in Mozart's and Süssmayr's handwriting have been in the Court Library in Vienna (now the Österreichische Nationalbibliothek) since the late 1830s, sharing the shelf mark Mus. Hs. 17561. Since 1839 the manuscripts have been bound in two volumes, known as Codex a and Codex b.[55] This latter designation confuses and obscures the provenance and function of the various manuscripts, and, although it will be used in the following pages, it will be supplemented by bracketed numbers to allow the differentiation of Codex a[1] and a[2] and of Codex b[1] and b[2] (see Table 1 and the corresponding Diag. 1).

Codex a[1 + 2] contains the whole score that was delivered by Constanze Mozart to Count Walsegg in 1792 and reached the Court Library late in 1838 (Table 1, col. 3; Diag. 1: I/2 and III/3). Codex a[1] is essentially in Mozart's hand and, in accordance with the old numbering of the folios (fols. 1–10), originally formed the first part of the autograph score; Codex a[2], on the other hand, is entirely in Süssmayr's hand.

The first side of Codex a[1] gives the composer's name in the first person: "di me W: A: Mozart mppa. | 1792" (Fig. 2). This inscription was long regarded as autograph, and it was supposed that with "1792" Mozart was anticipating completing the work in that year. But closer scrutiny has shown that it is in the hand of Süssmayr and must be a deliberate forgery.[56] His handwriting is extraordinarily close to Mozart's in this particular instance (his ability to write in a hand deceptively similar to Mozart's was probably one of the reasons why Constanze asked him to finish the score that was to go to the unknown client). Indeed, the entire score of the Requiem, both the text and the music, shows Süssmayr taking pains to write in a hand resembling Mozart's, for his normal hand has traits that clearly distinguish it.[57]

54. Discovered there in 1960 and identified by Wolfgang Plath; cf. Plath, "Über Skizzen zu Mozarts Requiem"; Ziegler, *W. A. Mozart*, 40; and Konrad, *Mozarts Schaffensweise*, 201, 441–43.
55. Cf. the facsimile editions of 1913 and 1990.
56. Cf. Dalchow, Duda, and Kerner, *Mozarts Tod*.
57. Plath, "Noch ein Requiem-Brief," 101.

TABLE I.   The Manuscripts of Mozart's Requiem

Autograph Score *(state at 5 December 1791)*	*Intermediate Stages*	*Score for Count Walsegg* *(March 1792)*
Codex a[1] — — — — — — — — — — — — — >		Mus. Hs. 17561: Codex a[1][1]
	Additions to the Autograph	
	fol. 1: "di me W: A: Mozart mppa. | 1792." [Süssmayr]	
fols. 1–5′: Requiem		fols. 1–10: autograph
fols. 5′–9: Kyrie	Freystädtler and Süssmayr:	
fols. 9′–10: blank	instrumentation	
Mus. Hs. 17561: Codex b[1][1]		*Mus. Hs. 17561: Codex a[2][1]*
fols. 11–15′: Dies irae	Eybler: instrumentation	fols. 1–20′: copy and revision
fols. 16–19′: Tuba mirum	Eybler: instrumentation	of Eybler's instrumentation by
fols. 20–22 : Rex tremendae	Eybler: instrumentation	Süssmayr
fols. 22′–28′: Recordare	Eybler: instrumentation	
fols. 29–32: Confutatis	Eybler: instrumentation	
fol. 32′: blank	Eybler: instrumentation	
Mus. Hs. 17561: Codex b[2][1]		
fols. 33–33′: Lacrymosa	Eybler: bars 9–10	fols. 21–23: Süssmayr:
	(new composition)	instrumentation (bars 1–8) and
fol. 34: blank		new composition (bars 9–30)
		fol. 23′: blank

1. Österreichische Nationalbibliothek, Vienna. Codex a[1]–Codex b[1–2], brown ink = old continuous numbering (1–45). Codex a[2] = old numbering, new start for Sequence and Offertory (1–33) and for Sanctus and Agnus Dei (1–19). Codex a–b, red ink = continuous numbering (1–100) inserted by the Court Library at the time of its acquisition of Codex a (1838)

It is likely that the idea of passing off the authorial inscription as autograph goes back to Constanze's desire to place the seal of indubitable authenticity on the Requiem as wholly the work of Mozart. That was her intention from the very first—and she pursued her goal with single-minded consistency. The conspicuously emphatic formula "di me" (by me) is significant in this context: Mozart himself never used the phrase, but it occurs occasionally in works by Süssmayr.[58]

58. Brosche's facsimile edition (1990) contains illustrations of several examples of Süssmayr's signature (Preface, p. 14).

TABLE I (*continued*). The Manuscripts of Mozart's Requiem

Autograph Score (state at 5 December 1791)	Intermediate Stages	Score for Count Walsegg (March 1792)
Codex a[1]		*Mus. Hs. 17561: Codex a[1]*[1]

	Other Additions, Not on the Autograph	
	Mus. Hs. 4375 A[1]	
fols. 35–41: Domine Jesu	fols. 1–6: Stadler's	fols. 24–33′: Süssmayr's
fols. 41′–42: blank	instrumentation[2]	instrumentation[3]
fols. 43–45: Hostias	fols. 6′–8: Stadler's	
fols. 45′: blank	instrumentation	
[Sanctus-Hosanna-Benedictus][4]		fols. 1–19: Süssmayr: new
[Agnus Dei-Lux aeterna][4]		composition (fair copy)
		fol. 20: trumpet parts for
		Benedictus, remainder blank

Autograph Sketches

Mus. ms. autogr. W. A. Mozart zu: KV 620[5]

fol. 2r: (a) *Zauberflöte* Overture
      (b) Allegro (not identified)
      (c) Lacrymosa: "Amen" fugue—4-pt vocal score, 16 bars
      (d) "Rex tremendae," bars 7ff.—4-pt vocal score without text

2. Cannot be dated, perhaps early 1792
3. Possibly based on Stadler's work
4. Not in the autograph
5. Staatsbibliothek zu Berlin (Stiftung Preussischer Kulturbesitz) fol. 1r: melody sketch for closing chorus, *Zauberflöte* Act I finale, fol. 1v blank

Süssmayr's name is not to be found anywhere in the manuscript score of the Requiem—presumably by agreement, possibly supported by a financial inducement, but the reasons for this hypothetical arrangement are not likely ever to be fully explained.[59]

Süssmayr could sign the score in Mozart's name with a clear conscience because the Requiem *was* Mozart's work, ultimately, and he regarded his own role as a

59. The first edition (1800) also names Mozart alone as the composer.

DIAGRAM I. The Manuscripts of Mozart's Requiem

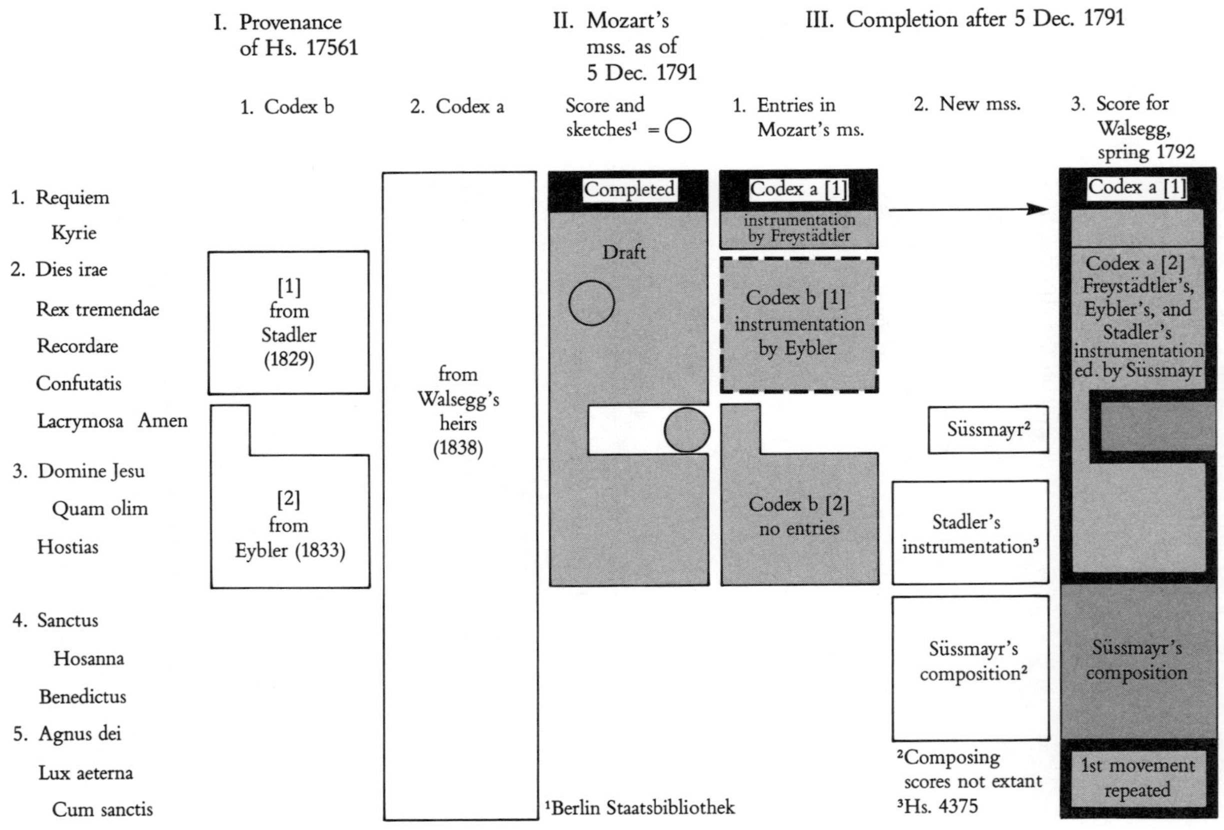

	I. Provenance of Hs. 17561		II. Mozart's mss. as of 5 Dec. 1791	III. Completion after 5 Dec. 1791		
	1. Codex b	2. Codex a	Score and sketches[1] = ◯	1. Entries in Mozart's ms.	2. New mss.	3. Score for Walsegg, spring 1792

1. Requiem
   Kyrie

2. Dies irae
   Rex tremendae
   Recordare
   Confutatis
   Lacrymosa   Amen

3. Domine Jesu
   Quam olim
   Hostias

4. Sanctus
   Hosanna
   Benedictus

5. Agnus dei
   Lux aeterna
   Cum sanctis

[1] from Stadler (1829)

[2] from Eybler (1833)

from Walsegg's heirs (1838)

Completed

Draft

Codex a [1]
instrumentation by Freystädtler

Codex b [1]
instrumentation by Eybler

Codex b [2]
no entries

Süssmayr[2]

Stadler's instrumentation[3]

Süssmayr's composition[2]

Codex a [1]

Codex a [2]
Freystädtler's, Eybler's, and Stadler's instrumentation ed. by Süssmayr

Süssmayr's composition

1st movement repeated

[1]Berlin Staatsbibliothek

[2]Composing scores not extant
[3]Hs. 4375

completely subordinate one. As he honestly declared to Breitkopf & Härtel, he felt his own work to be "unworthy of his great name" (Doc. 17). The date of 1792 was also nothing less than the truth. Everybody at the time knew that Mozart had not lived until that date. The only really untrue and deliberately misleading part of the inscription is the formula "mppa" ("manu propria"; in [my] own hand)—but even that can be interpreted as a sign of genuine devotion, in the service of which the deception appeared as an expedient: a white lie, not a black one.

Codex b[1] was originally the continuation (fols. 11–32) of Codex a[1]; that is, it was that part of the autograph score that, together with Süssmayr's manuscript, was intended to make up the score for Count Walsegg. Codex b[1] was separated from Codex a[1] early in 1792 and was presented to the Court Library in Vienna by Stadler in or around 1829 (Table 1, col. 1; Diag. 1: I/1), but it was available for the important collation that took place in the office of Walsegg's lawyer, Johann Nepomuk Sortschan, in 1800 (when it was in Constanze's ownership).[60] That is proved by the pencil marks encircling the non-Mozartian passages (Figs. 3 and 5).

Codex b[2] is the continuation (fols. 33–45) of Codex b[1] and, like it, was separated from Codex a[1] early in 1792. It passed from Joseph Eybler to the Court Library in 1833 (Table 1, col. 1; Diag. 1: I/1). This last section of the autograph score looks completely different from the rest: its pages hold nothing but four vocal parts and a bass, all in Mozart's hand—that is, without any material by another (Figs. 4, 6, 7). The only extraneous material is in the "Lacrymosa," where the soprano part in bars 9–10 contains Eybler's brief, and soon abandoned, attempt at a continuation.[61] This section of the score (Codex b[2]) therefore preserves the appearance of the score from the Kyrie to the Offertory, exactly as it existed at the time of Mozart's death (Diag. 1: II).

The overall impression of the autograph score (fols. 1–45 in the old numbering)[62] in its original 1791 state—that is, Codex a[1] and Codex b[1–2] together—confirms Süssmayr's description of those sections of the work written down by

60. Presumably this part of the manuscript had been returned to her by Süssmayr some time before (Doc. 16n).

61. A full edition of Eybler's continuation of the Sequence is to be found in NMA I/1, part 2, vol. 2, pp. 3–33.

62. The claim that the old numbering is autograph, which used to be generally accepted and is found as recently as Moseley ("Mozart's Requiem," 206) and the preface of Brosche's facsimile edition (1990), can no longer be sustained. (Communication to the author from Robert Levin, confirmed by Wolfgang Plath.)

Mozart. From the Kyrie to the "Domine Jesu," the vocal parts are fully worked out, and a figured bass and motivic ideas for the orchestral accompaniment are also present (Doc. 17). Significantly, Süssmayr does not omit the Introit and Kyrie from his list of the movements in autograph. These were long accepted as wholly autograph by Mozart scholars until Leopold Nowak discovered that the instrumental parts in the Kyrie were in the hand, not of Mozart himself, but of two others whose hands were easily confused with his.[63] Nowak made a plausible case for believing that the colla parte string and woodwind accompaniment (that is, what may fairly be termed the mechanical part of the scoring) is by Mozart's pupil Franz Jacob Freystädtler (Table 1, col. 2; Diag. 1: III/1), while the trumpet and timpani parts are by Süssmayr.

Folios 11–32 of the autograph (Codex b[1]) offer a completely different picture from that presented by folios 1–10 (Codex a[1]), for which Freystädtler and Süssmayr take the responsibility. The instrumentation on these folios is by Joseph Eybler, who did not take any pains over the visual appearance of his additions (Table 1, col. 2; Diag. 1: III/1; Fig. 3). Nowak described Eybler's instrumentation as the model for Süssmayr's work, but one may go further and assert that Süssmayr's score (fols. 1–20 of Codex a[2]) amounts to nothing more than a fair copy, with revisions, of Eybler's work. Here and there Süssmayr's changes make good worse and demonstrate that Eybler was, after all, the more experienced musician of the two. One example occurs in the opening bars of the Sequence, where Eybler's harmonically and rhythmically pointed treatment of the winds is toned down by Süssmayr's simplification (Exx. I.1 and I.2).[64] Writing later to Breitkopf and to André, Constanze expressly mentioned having observed that "in the copy retained by Süssmayr [Codex b[1]] . . . the inner parts . . . are wholly different" (Docs. 16m, 21). She did not know that they were nothing more nor less than Eybler's version.

In some respects the situation that pertains in Süssmayr's editing of Eybler's instrumentation is repeated in the two movements of the Offertory. The possibility that Maximilian Stadler may have had a hand in completing the Requiem

63. Nowak, "Wer hat die Instrumentalstimmen geschrieben?" (following an observation made by Franz Beyer about "incorrect transposition markings"; cf. the preface of Beyer's edition, 1971, p. 14; 1979, p. 14).

64. Nowak comments: "As early as the 'Dies irae' this is manifested in the relationship of the winds to the chorus. The way Eybler spans the choral rests with complementary rhythms in the wind, and thus carries on the chorus's 'block' rhythm as if in an echo, is wholly characteristic of his rhythmic sense. The procedure reinforces the chorus and intensifies its effect. Trumpets and trombones, too, are used more subtly to enhance the effect of the total sound than was done by Süssmayr. Eybler shows himself to be the more 'intelligent' of the two." See also other comments by Nowak (NMA I/1, part 2, vol. 2, Preface, pp. xii–xiv).

EXAMPLE I.I.   Dies irae, bars 1–4: winds (Eybler's instrumentation)

EXAMPLE I.2.   Dies irae, bars 1–4: winds (Süssmayr's instrumentation)

is supported by study of a manuscript in Stadler's hand (Mus. Hs. 4375A in the Österreichische Nationalbibliothek), for this contains the "Domine Jesu" and the "Hostias" with a scoring that represents a preliminary form of Süssmayr's version.[65] The unfinished state of the trombone part is one indication, among others, that Stadler's work is the earlier (Figs. 8 and 9; cf. Table 1, col. 2; Diag. 1: III/2). Admittedly, Stadler did not undertake to write his interventions on Mozart's

65. First suggested in a study of Stadler's role in sorting Mozart's musical estate (Senn, "Abbé Maximilian Stadler"); cf. also Stadler's autobiography (Croll, "Eine Autobiographie Stadlers").

own score, unlike Eybler, but first copied Mozart's draft and wrote his instrumentation on the copy. Finally, it appears that Süssmayr revised this draft version of the Offertory (fols. 24–33, Codex a[2]) exactly as he had Eybler's draft version of the Sequence.

In spite of their haste, the musicians involved organized their collaboration well, which suggests three things: (1) they must have been confident of their musical competence to carry out the task of completing the Requiem; (2) they had to meet the deadline for delivery of the commission, for which half the fee had already been paid; (3) the score needed to present the appearance of a uniform, "original" whole.

Regarding the first point, Constanze herself may not have been altogether competent to judge the musical abilities of Mozart's pupils in detail, but she wanted to find "masters" to complete the Requiem (it can scarcely be by chance that Süssmayr's letter of 8 February 1800 refers to "several masters").[66] Constanze's sister Sophie Haibl recalled in 1825 that, on his deathbed, Mozart mentioned Johann Georg Albrechtsberger, organist to the imperial court, whom he esteemed highly and to whom, in his opinion, "der Dienst" belonged "in the eyes of God and the world" (Doc. 10). The word "Dienst" (office or service) must be interpreted primarily as a reference to the post of nonstipendiary Capellmeister at St. Stephen's cathedral, yet it is not impossible that Mozart was thinking of the completion of his Requiem.[67] It seems likely, however, that Constanze turned first to Franz Jacob Freystädtler, whom she must have regarded as the most experienced of Mozart's Viennese pupils and who possessed, moreover, a handwriting similar to that of his teacher.[68] Sensibly, Freystädtler began with the easiest part, the colla parte accompaniment of the "Kyrie" fugue (strings and woodwinds), in preparation for the liturgical performance of the Requiem fragment on 10 December (Docs. 4 and 5). Since the first movement ended with a half cadence in the dominant, the next movement, the Kyrie, had to be included

66. The legend, in its heyday, drew in even Joseph Haydn; cf. the "Diary" of Placidus Scharl, quoted in *Mozart-Dokumente*, 441; *Mozart DB*, 512.

67. Albrechtsberger did, in fact, succeed Mozart as adjunct Capellmeister at St. Stephen's and Leopold Hofmann as principal Capellmeister in 1793.

68. On Freystädtler's relationship to Mozart, as his pupil, cf. the preface to NMA X/30, vol. 2: *Barbara Ployers und Franz Jakob Freystädtlers Theorie- und Kompositionsstudien bei Mozart*, ed. by Hellmut Federhofer and Alfred Mann (1989). The possibility that Freystädtler worked on the Kyrie while Mozart was still alive, and at the latter's request, is not at all likely (Moseley, "Mozart's Requiem," 210).

in order to round off the piece and end back in the tonic.[69] Freystädtler then abandoned the work for unknown reasons. We do not know if the problem was lack of time or if he took fright at the difficulty of the task. Both reasons— "pressure of work" and the reluctance of the "several masters" to have their talents measured against Mozart's—are cited by Süssmayr in his letter to Breitkopf (Doc. 17).

Constanze might have been observing the principle of seniority, for she turned next, after the thirty-year-old Freystädtler, to the twenty-six-year-old Joseph Eybler, another of Mozart's pupils.[70] Eybler applied himself to the task with greater diligence, but after orchestrating five sections of the Sequence he too gave up, again for reasons unknown. In Eybler's case there is a document dated 21 December 1791 (Doc. 6) in which he acknowledges the receipt of a commission to complete the Requiem: apart from the manuscripts themselves, this is the only documentary evidence that Constanze officially commissioned the completion from another composer.

It is conceivable that, after its abandonment by Eybler, the work next passed, not directly to Süssmayr, but to Abbé Maximilian Stadler. He may have completed the orchestration of the Offertory, where Mozart had already set down substantial indications of his intentions. Although not a pupil of Mozart, Stadler had been associated with him since the early 1780s. Later he played the major role in sorting through Mozart's musical estate[71] and had a hand in most of the posthumous undertakings to complete other unfinished work.[72] Stadler testified that he had "followed the entire course of events closely" (Doc. 22) and had

---

69. Since Freystädtler limited his instrumentation of the Kyrie to strings and woodwinds, the performance on 10 December 1791 apparently took place without trumpets and timpani.

70. Mozart wrote him a glowing reference on 30 May 1790: "I testify as his preceptor that I have found Herr Joseph Eybler to be a worthy pupil of his celebrated master Albrechtsberger, a well-grounded composer, equally skilled in chamber and church music, an experienced singer, a complete organ and keyboard player; in short, a young musician about whom one's only regret can be that there are so few like him." (Bauer-Deutsch IV, No. 1126; facsimile: Requiem Catalog, 252). In his autobiography Eybler wrote: "I had the good fortune to keep his [Mozart's] friendship unalloyed until his death, so that even in his painful last illness I was at hand to lift him, lay him down, and help wait on him" (Allgemeine musikalische Zeitung 28, no. 21 [1826]: col. 338).

71. See above, n. 66. Moseley casts doubt on Stadler's having had any part in completing the Requiem, but he does not take the evidence of the manuscripts fully into account (Moseley, "Mozart's Requiem," 213, 222–23). Stadler had been appointed an honorary member of the consistory in Linz in January 1791 and had to attend weekly meetings. But he sought a permanent position in Vienna and therefore went there frequently, eventually settled there, and lived on his private means until 1803, when he was appointed to the suburban parish of Altlerchenfeld (Croll, "Ein Autobiographie Stadlers," 179f.).

72. Plath, "Über Skizzen zu Mozarts Requiem," 451.

copied the Introit, the Kyrie, and the whole Sequence up to the "Lacrymosa" from the original manuscript, not long after Mozart's death (Docs. 25 and 27). Stadler may even have exerted an influence over the method adopted in completing the score. He did not write directly on Mozart's autograph, as Eybler did, when he was working on the Offertory but first made a faithful copy of it, which served thereafter as the basis for later work (cf. Fig. 8). One reason for this procedure may have been Eybler's often crude and unlovely-looking additions to the Sequence in Mozart's score. In any event, the autograph drafts of the sections of the Offertory were left free of insertions in other hands.

While the manuscript Mus. Hs. 4375A strongly indicates that Stadler had a hand in completing the Requiem, the only evidence to the contrary is the absence of any mention of the fact by Stadler during the Requiem controversy. It may be that he did not want to remind the world of it, much as Eybler had declined to mention it in his autobiography.[73] Oddly enough, by 1827 even Constanze had forgotten how Eybler came to be involved (Docs. 6 and 28). Finally, Stadler's contribution to the collation in Sortschan's office betrays a detailed knowledge of the original manuscripts, permitting him to distinguish Mozart's and Eybler's contributions with confidence (Docs. 18 and 27; Figs. 3 and 5).

Whatever Stadler's exact function may have been, there is no doubt that Süssmayr's was the really crucial role in finishing the Requiem. He had acted as Mozart's assistant during the last months of the latter's life, copying and carrying out certain compositional work as well, especially on *Die Zauberflöte* and *La clemenza di Tito*.[74] Thus Süssmayr took on the major part of the work on the concluding movement of the Sequence as well as what remained to be done on the rest of the Requiem, beginning at the Sanctus—that is, those movements that existed in the form of "fragments" (Doc. 28) or "scraps of paper" (Doc. 22).[75] Additionally, he had to collate and (where necessary) revise the contributions of his predecessors and finally produce a fair copy of the whole score for the client, to a standard that would meet the requirement for a manuscript that looked authentic (see above, p. 17).

---

73. *Allgemeine musikalische Zeitung* 28, no. 21 (1826): cols. 337ff.

74. On Süssmayr's part in preparing *Die Zauberflöte*, cf. NMA II/5, vol. 19, Preface, p. viii; on 3 July 1791 Mozart wrote to Constanze: "I hope Süssmayer won't forget to write what I set out for him straightaway" (Bauer-Deutsch IV, 145). In the case of *Tito*, "it is generally supposed" that Mozart left the composition of the secco recitatives to Süssmayer (who accompanied him to Prague), although the supposition, which is based on stylistic criteria, cannot be confirmed in the absence of surviving sources. Cf. Giegling, "Zu den Rezitativen von 'Titus,' " and NMA II/5, vol. 20, Preface, p. x.

75. See below, p. 42.

It remains a remarkable fact that none of the people who are revealed by the autograph[76] to have had a hand in completing the Requiem (in addition to Süssmayr)—that is, the "several masters" mentioned by Süssmayr—are named, either on the manuscript itself or in other sources. No one but Süssmayr—that is, neither Freystädtler, Eybler, nor Stadler—ever admitted having made a contribution, even though they had plenty of opportunity to do so during the years of the Requiem controversy, which was conducted in public. Apart from Eybler's receipt (Doc. 6), all the evidence is indirect. There is only one plausible explanation for the silence of all concerned: absolute loyalty to Constanze, combined with unrestrained reverence for Mozart's genius. They were at one in regarding the Requiem as Mozart's work and Süssmayr's leading role as subordinate; none of the other collaborators were worthy even of mention.

The second of the three points listed above is the need to meet the client's deadline. The fact that time was very short must have been a spur to everyone involved. The Requiem had been commissioned, and Constanze badly needed the outstanding 25 ducats. There must have been good reason for her to stipulate "the middle of the coming Lent" as the date by which Eybler should finish his work (Doc. 6).[77] It is reasonable to assume, in any event, that the date was set by the client. There is no direct evidence of the date on which the score was delivered to Count Walsegg, but on 4 March 1792 Constanze delivered a number of scores to the Prussian ambassador in Vienna for King Friedrich Wilhelm II of Prussia. These included a copy of the Requiem for which she was paid 450 florins (100 ducats; Doc. 7).[78] Thus not only was the score ready for Count Walsegg by the beginning of March, but at least two copies had also been made of it—one for Berlin and another for Constanze herself to keep.[79]

According to the date in his own handwriting, Süssmayr finished the Horn Rondo in D Major K 514, based on a Mozart draft, on 6 April 1792—a further indication that the Requiem was completed by then.[80] Süssmayr must also have

76. Codex a[1] and Codex b[1]; cf. Table 1.

77. Ash Wednesday fell on 21 February in 1792. The first anniversary of Countess Walsegg's death (14 February) may have played a part in fixing the deadline.

78. Constanze Mozart had obtained the anonymous patron's permission to present copies to royalty (Doc. 16c). In addition to giving the King of Prussia a copy, she later (1796) gave a copy to the Elector of Saxony for 200 friedrichs d'or (cf. Weber, "Weitere Nachrichten über die Echtheit," 297).

79. Süssmayr is also believed to have kept a copy for himself (Doc. 16f). "Of Süssmayr's score, two copies were made immediately" (Stadler, *Zweyter und letzter Nachtrag*, 28).

80. "Venerdi Santo [Good Friday] li 6 Aprile 1792"; cf. Tyson, *Mozart*, 253ff., and the discussion below on p. 45.

been hard at work to prepare his opera *Moses oder der Auszug aus Ägypten* for its premiere, which was due to take place on 4 May 1792.[81] The commission for this came from Schikaneder's company, and it left the composer with no spare time in March and April. All in all, it is reasonably certain that the team effort to finish the Requiem was concluded by about the end of February—that is, within three months of Mozart's death.[82] This raises another aspect of the work of completing the Requiem, especially Süssmayr's part in it: in view of the haste in which he was forced to work, his achievement is astonishing. There are, it is true, all kinds of infelicities, technical solecisms, and an absence of contrapuntal facility and inspired ideas, but these are features of other work by Süssmayr, and completing the Requiem presented demands and difficulties far outside the normal range of his activity.[83]

Mozart's Composition

It is time to look at the history of the Requiem *before* Mozart's death on 5 December 1791, for it must yield important information about the planning and structure of the work. Recent research into the paper the autograph is written on has confirmed a statement by Constanze that was previously doubted by many: namely, that Mozart did not begin to write the Requiem down until after his return from Prague in the middle of September 1791 (Doc. 9).[84] It was therefore

81. Lehner, "Franz Xaver Süßmayr."

82. Hitherto it has always been assumed by writers on Mozart—especially in view of the date of the first Vienna performance of the Requiem, early in 1793 (Deutsch, "Geschichte von Requiem")—that Süssmayr finished his score of the work late in 1792. As recent a writer as Moseley cites the date of the Vienna performance as suggesting that Süssmayr may not have finished "until quite late in 1792" (Moseley, "Mozart's Requiem," 213).

83. See below, p. 44, the discussion of Süssmayr's work on K 514, and the overly positive estimation in general of Süssmayr in Wlcek, *Franz Xaver Süßmayr*, 41–72.

84. See, in particular, Tyson, *Mozart*, 35, 252f. The autograph score of the Requiem uses two types of paper—paper type 1: fols. 1–8 ("Requiem" to "Kyrie," bar 45) and fols. 11–22 ("Dies irae" up to "Recordare," bar 10); paper type 2: fols 9–10 ("Kyrie," bars 46ff.) and fols. 23–45 ("Recordare," bars 11ff., up to "Hostias"). Cf. Table 1; the water marks are illustrated in the prefaces of the facsimile editions by Schnerich (1913) and Brosche (1990). Schnerich's hypothesis that the two different types of paper indicated two stages in the Requiem composition (before and after the visit to Prague) was adopted by many writers, but Tyson's researches have disproved it. According to Tyson, none of the Requiem sources were written before the Prague trip.

Paper type 2 occurs in several of Mozart's autographs from March 1791 on, including K 612, 614, 616, 620 (*Die Zauberflöte*), and 623 (the "Masonic" Cantata). Paper type 1, on the other hand, first occurs in those parts of *Die Zauberflöte* that were composed after Mozart's return from Prague: the overture, the Three Boys' trio "Seid uns zum zweiten Mal willkommen," Pamina's G-minor aria, and the trio "Soll ich dich, Teurer, nicht mehr sehn?"; it is also found in the sheet of Requiem sketches (which also has sketches for the *Zauberflöte* overture) and in the "Masonic" Cantata. See Alan Tyson, *Wasserzeichen-Katalog*, NMA X/33, vol. 2 (1992), nos. 62 and 102.

scarcely more than two months until the date on which he took to his bed (20 November 1791) and after which, if he could work at all, it was only with very great difficulty.[85] Mozart was moreover exceptionally busy during that autumn of 1791: the most immediately pressing task was to finish *Die Zauberflöte,* the first performance of which took place on 30 September, but then there were other projects, up to and including the "Masonic" Cantata K 623, which is the last work Mozart entered in his catalog, on 15 November.[86]

He did not start to work continuously on the Requiem until after the *Zauberflöte* premiere—that is, not before 1 October. His customary methods of working allow us to assume that he did not begin to write down the full score until he had a clear mental conception of the entire work; the vocal particello (Figs. 2–7), which is largely complete, represented nothing other than the foundations of the final score. "In his mind the work was already complete before he sat down at his desk," wrote Niemetschek; and, according to Nissen, "he finished whole pieces of music in his head and kept them there until he had a cause to write them down, or until he had reasons of his own to release them. He was then able to write them down very quickly."[87] If he worked on the Requiem in his head, as seems likely, he must have been in a position to write it all down, essentially movement by movement, in their proper order. This requires a few comments.

In all the relevant literature,[88] the "Lacrymosa" is generally regarded as the last movement composed by Mozart, because the autograph short score breaks off abruptly after eight bars—unlike the sections of the Offertory that follow later in the order of the work. Eybler's inscription on fol. 33 of Codex b[2] is also taken as evidence: "Last manuscript of Mozart. | Bequeathed to the Imperial and Royal Court Library after my death | by Joseph Eybler mpa" (Fig. 4). But the material Eybler left the library consisted of thirteen folios in all, and the inscription in

85. "He began to feel ill while still in Prague, before he had started the Requiem. . . . His fatal illness, from the time when he took to his bed, lasted fifteen days. It began with a swelling of the hands and feet, and near paralysis of the same, followed later by sudden vomiting: this condition was called a hot miliary fever. Up until two hours before his demise he remained perfectly lucid" (Nissen, *Wolfgang Mozart's Biographie,* 2:571f.). Lühning, "Entstehungsgeschichte von 'Titus,' " includes an analysis of the legends that grew up to connect Mozart's early symptoms with his stay in Prague and the completion of *La clemenza di Tito.* On Mozart's final illness, see in particular Bär, *Mozart,* 2d. ed., and Davies, "Mozart's Illnesses."

86. The other projects included the Horn Concerto K 412 (Tyson, *Mozart,* 246ff.) and the Clarinet Concerto K 622 (exact date of composition uncertain, but entered by Mozart in his catalog of works between 28 September and 15 November 1791). For other works see K⁶.

87. Niemetschek, *Leben des Kapellmeisters Mozart,* 54; *Life of Mozart,* 62; Nissen, *Wolfgang Mozart's Biographie,* 2:647.

88. For example, Landon, *1791,* 150.

question belongs to the fascicle that includes the Offertory (fols. 33–45) and therefore should not be regarded as referring only to the first sheet, which bears the "Lacrymosa." There is no further reason to assume that bars 1–8 of the "Lacrymosa" were composed later than the two sections of the Offertory.

But why did Mozart break off this movement after eight bars, unlike any of the others?[89] There are two likely reasons. First, the "Lacrymosa" stanza in the Sequence ends with the same words as those that end the Introit and Agnus Dei—the invocation "dona eis requiem." It would therefore make sense for the composer to create musical connections between these identical lines of text. But that would make it necessary to bring forward the composition of the Agnus Dei so as to be able to assess the nature of the correspondences (the Introit was already written). Second, Mozart intended to conclude the "Lacrymosa" with an

EXAMPLE 1.3. Sketch: Amen fugue (Lacrymosa)

89. Not after six bars, as Süssmayr wrongly wrote in his letter to Breitkopf & Härtel (Doc. 17).

"Amen" fugue, according to the sketch (Ex. I.3). The sketch maps out the exposition of the fugue in some detail, but there are no grounds for leaping to the conclusion that Mozart necessarily planned an extensive fugue on the basis of a sixteen-bar exposition. The old numbering of the folios (fols. 33–34) would indicate that only four sides were reserved for completing the "Lacrymosa," leaving enough space for about twenty-four bars—scarcely enough for a fugue, let alone an extensive one. If for no other reason than this, we can assume that the old folio numbering has no bearing on Mozart's plan for his work. The proportions of an "Amen" fugue would have called for at least two more folios.

It is certain, in the context of the overall layout he planned for the Sequence, that Mozart had intended the "Lacrymosa" to be a short movement. Süssmayr made it twenty-eight bars long, and that would not have been far wide of the mark. Admittedly, Süssmayr contented himself with a two-bar plagal cadence for his "Amen" instead of a fugue. This was probably not because he did not know what Mozart had intended—after all, Mozart had often discussed the work with him (Doc. 17)—but because he lacked confidence in his own ability to write strict polyphony to the necessary standard, especially if he had seen Mozart's sketch, which envisages inversion, diminution, and possibly even retrograde, among other things. According to Mozart's sketch (see Ex. I.3 and Fig. 1), the first subject of the "Amen" fugue is an exact inversion of the first subject of the Introit, which had already served with some additional ornamentation in the countersubject of the "Kyrie" fugue (Ex. I.4).[90]

EXAMPLE I.4.   The principal Requiem theme and its inversions

90. First pointed out in Levin, *Unfinished Works of Mozart*.

The theme of the "Amen" also relates to the opening bars of the "Lacrymosa," which in turn clearly relate to the Introit in both harmonic and melodic material. What may fairly be called a double correspondence seems to suggest, however, that the abandonment of the "Lacrymosa" after eight bars had less to do with the ebbing of Mozart's strength than with the recognition that he had reached a strategically significant moment and needed to reflect on the textual and musical associations that should be emphasized. The "Lacrymosa" is the last section of the Sequence, the longest part of the Requiem; it also marks the approximate middle point of the work with the recurrence of a line ("dona eis requiem") that is heard in both the Introit and the Agnus Dei.

The sheet of sketches itself deserves attention. It is surprising to find that the "Amen" sketch comes before the "Rex tremendae" sketch, although the latter belongs to an earlier movement. There can be no doubt that the "Amen" sketch (lines 3–5) was written first. Furthermore, the "Rex tremendae" sketch (lines 6–9) can only have been written in the immediate context of writing down the short score, as the chord of D major articulated by two eighth notes with which the sketch starts (bar 7) must already have been notated in the autograph score (Ex. I.5). From this it is possible to reconstruct two processes that went on simultaneously: Mozart sketched polyphonic and other technically tricky passages (such as "Rex tremendae"), and he also sketched thematically or formally significant expositions (such as the "Amen" fugue). The implications of this observation for the movements Mozart did not have time to write (from the Sanctus on) are obvious and will be discussed below. Sketches for these movements are likely to have been confined to specific musical elements: thematically difficult opening phrases and complicated polyphonic passages destined for positions in mid-movement.

The single sheet of sketches also demonstrates another central feature in the conception of the Requiem: the fact that Mozart treats the four-part vocal writing as the chief substance of his work and reduces the importance of the instrumental element to a minimum. It is entirely in keeping with his usual procedure in composing large-scale works (observed from the early part of his residence in Vienna, at the latest) to concentrate on the essential musical substance (the solo part in a concerto, for example, or the vocal part in an aria) when first working through a piece. Close study of the autograph sections of the Requiem score shows that the four-part vocal writing is at the center of Mozart's planning and execution. This is similar to the process that can be observed in his working out of polyphonic structures (from the "Haydn" Quartets on): Mozart thinks of the

EXAMPLE I.5. Sketch: Rex tremendae, bars 7ff.

four-part texture as a whole, allowing it to develop in periods and scarcely high-lighting any individual melodic part for quite long stretches.[91] This is a crucial difference between the musical character of the Requiem and that of the church music Mozart composed in Salzburg, and it also creates a clear difference of style and texture between the Requiem and the C-minor Mass K 427 of 1783; the earlier works rest on a less homogenous vocal foundation, while the orchestral writing has correspondingly more weight and substance.

The earliest piece in which this transparent yet compact style of four-part writing comes to the fore is Mozart's Corpus Christi motet "Ave verum corpus" K 618, dated 17 June 1791. Although aspects of the Requiem such as declamatory gesture, textures, and integration of forward- and backward-looking stylistic elements are varied and defined far more strongly than in the "Ave verum corpus," the Requiem plainly develops the compositional orientation Mozart had first explored in the motet (Ex. I.6).[92] Indeed, it is as if Mozart consciously decided to open up new avenues for sacred music (a genre in which he had done no regular work since leaving Salzburg), just as he had worked intensively since the mid-1780s on new forms in other genres (opera, symphony, concerto, quartet,

91. Cf. Finscher, "Aspects of Mozart's Compositional Process."

92. Alfred Einstein wrote of K 618 that it is "so well known that the mastery with which it is fashioned, the 'second' simplicity, the perfection of modulation and voice-leading, lightly introducing polyphony as a final intensification, are no longer perceived. Here, too, ecclesiastical and personal elements flow together. The problem of style is solved" (*Mozart*, 352).

EXAMPLE I.6.   Motet "Ave verum corpus" K 618

EXAMPLE I.6. *(continued)*.

quintet, trio, duo, and solo). In that sense, the choruses of the "Ave verum corpus" and the Requiem ("so flowing, so noble and so full of expression"[93]) can also be said to be among the "classicist" initiatives that Mozart was not to be allowed to pursue;[94] it was by chance that these were, biographically speaking, "last works"; aesthetically speaking, however, they are far from being "late works."[95]

It is of some relevance, especially in view of the liturgical function of these works, to recall that Mozart had been appointed honorary Capellmeister at Vienna Cathedral in May 1791 (Doc. 2). The numerous unfinished pieces of church music demonstrate that he had been making the effort to do more in that field since 1789 or 1790.[96] The commission for the Requiem was probably therefore all the more welcome for the chance it gave him to tackle a work that would naturally attract attention, in a genre new to him, and in a new manner. It was not for nothing that E. T. A. Hoffmann cited Mozart's Requiem as the supreme example of sacred music in his celebrated and influential essay "Alte und neue Kirchenmusik," written in 1814, more than twenty years after Mozart's death:

93. The epithets are those used by Niemetschek of the choruses in *Tito* (*Leben des Kapellmeisters Mozart*, 73f.; *Life of Mozart*, 82), but he also refers to the "dignity and solemnity" of the "Ave verum corpus" and the Requiem (77; 86).

94. Blume takes the directly opposite view and criticizes the "uniformity" of the instrumentation in the Requiem as unlike Mozart: "Here, in the Requiem, another, unMozartean conception of the nature of church music was at work, a soberer, more rational, more joyless one. The tendency of the classicistically inclined waning century to regard as noble innocence and calm absence of passion in late Mozart what is in reality passion compressed and turned inward, the tendency that preferred *Tito* to all other operas of Mozart, finds here its church-music reflection" ("Requiem but No Peace," 160; cf. also n. 98, below). The aesthetic concepts of "simplicity" and "quiet nobility" are praised as characteristic of *Tito* by Niemetschek (*Leben des Kapellmeisters Mozart*, 73; *Life of Mozart*, 81), but they apply equally well to Sarastro's sphere in *Die Zauberflöte* (The March of the Priests, "O Isis und Osiris," etc.), "Ave verum corpus," and the Requiem, where they indicate a fundamentally new element in Mozart's style.

95. Cf. Wolff, "Mozart 1784."

96. See the dating revisions in Tyson, *Mozart*, 26ff. The following are among works that can now be given a date in the period 1787–91 (Anh. = a number assigned in a Köchel-Verzeichnis appendix): Kyrie in G, K Anh. 16 (196a); Kyrie in C, K Anh. 13 (258a); Kyrie in C, K Anh. 15 (323); Kyrie in D, K Anh. 14 (422a); and the Gloria in C, K Anh. 20 (323a). The large (not fragmentary) Kyrie in D Minor K 341 (368a), the autograph of which is lost, obviously also belongs to this group. See the editions in NMA I/1, vol. 6 (1990), which include Maximilian Stadler's completions in some instances.

Mozart's transcriptions of works by Georg Reutter the younger belong to the same period: Kyrie in D, K 91 (186i); "De profundis" K 93 (Anh. A22); "Memento Domine David" K Anh. 22 (93a).

In the last half of the eighteenth century increasing enfeeblement and sickly sweetness finally overcame art; keeping step with so-called enlightened attitudes, which killed every deeper religious impulse, it eventually drove all gravity and dignity from church music. Even music for worship in Catholic churches, the masses, vespers, passiontide hymns etc., acquired a character that previously would have been too insipid and undignified even for opera seria. . . . Mozart's masses, which he is known to have composed to a prescribed pattern on paid commission, are almost his weakest works. In one church work, however, he revealed his innermost feelings; and who can remain unmoved by the fervent devotion and spiritual ecstasy radiating from it? His Requiem is the sublimest achievement that the modern period has contributed to the church. Compelling and profound though Haydn's settings of the High Mass frequently are, and excellent though his harmonic development is, there is still hardly one of them that is completely without playfulness, without melodies quite inappropriate to the dignity of church style.[97]

Hoffmann also emphasizes the preeminence the Requiem gives to the vocal writing, in contrast to the greater gloss of the orchestral writing which is characteristic of Haydn's masses and is found, too, in Mozart's C-minor Mass K 427.

The primacy of the voice had an effect on the principles the composer adopted for his orchestration. To conclude that the prescribed instrumentation (two basset horns, two bassoons, two trumpets, one trombone, kettledrums, strings, and organ) is incomplete, and to deplore the absence of flutes, oboes, and clarinets as irreconcilable with Mozart's late style, is to misunderstand his intentions.[98] The reticence of the colla parte accompaniment—that is, the orchestral writing which is subordinate and non-obbligato in character, above all in the fugal passages[99]— should no more be undervalued than the a cappella passages, or even the apparently old-fashioned choral cadences with open fifth (such as the final notes of the Kyrie and "Rex tremendae"). It is in the passages added by Eybler and Süssmayr that a greater propensity toward obbligato accompaniment emerges. Interestingly, Stadler describes Süssmayr's work on the Agnus Dei as "scored in the manner of Haydn" (Doc. 24b).

97. E. T. A. Hoffmann, *Musical Writings*, ed. D. Charlton, trans. M. Clarke (Cambridge, 1989), 370.
98. Cf. n. 94, above, Blume's objections to the Requiem's alleged "uniformity."
99. Similar to what can be observed in, for example, the Mass in C Minor K 427.

This is not the place to dwell on the orchestration problems that Mozart bequeathed to Eybler and Süssmayr in the movements he had completed in short score.[100] Of greater urgency is the question of how far the Sanctus and Agnus Dei—that is, the movements that are entirely the work of Süssmayr—represent Mozart's plan and conception for them or whether at least individual musical ideas reflect his.

Both the Sanctus (with the Hosanna and Benedictus) and the Agnus Dei betray an especially high degree of technical unevenness and a large number of mistakes in the voice leading, as Mozart scholars recognized at an early date. But if the vocal substance is separated from the instrumental cladding in these movements, an astonishing congruence between the compositional conception here and that in the sections composed by Mozart comes to light. Not only that, but we also discover significantly fewer musical errors.[101] The first five bars of the Sanctus, for example, present an impeccable piece of vocal writing, which moreover displays a conspicuous relationship in melody and harmony to the vocal opening of the Sequence (Ex. I.7).[102]

The problem in the Sanctus begins with the false relation caused by the C$\sharp$ in the tenor (bar 5) and the C$\natural$ in the bass (bar 6) and with the parallel open fifths between the sopranos and first violins (bar 4). The clash of A- and C-major chords (bars 5 and 6) is crude and un-Mozartian.[103] It is conceivable, however, that Süssmayr misinterpreted a Mozartian suggestion—however it was conveyed—which might have led to bar 6 sounding as in Ex. I.8 (bass enters simultaneously with the other voices). In other respects there are no really horrendous problems with the vocal writing—except for the fact that, at ten bars, the Sanctus is far too short by comparison with other masses by Mozart.

It is conceivable that Süssmayr misunderstood ideas sketched by Mozart and that his misunderstanding could have led to the unusual, indeed absurd, key

---

100. Hess, "Ergänzung des Requiems," is the first work to examine the uneven quality and mistakes in Süssmayr's orchestration in detail. Foremost among recent attempts to improve on the 1792 orchestration of the Requiem are Franz Beyer's "corrected" version of the Süssmayr score (Zurich, 1971; 1979) and Richard Maunder's new orchestration, which sets Süssmayr's scoring aside altogether (Oxford, 1988). Both these versions take as their starting point Mozart's late practices in orchestration, particularly as illustrated in the two 1791 operas, *Die Zauberflöte* and *La clemenza di Tito*. This fails to take into account the fact that the analogy is inappropriate and introduces an alienating operatic style into the Requiem's sound-world.

The suggestions proposed by Beyer (cf. also Beyer, "Zur Neuinstrumentation des Mozart-

Dies irae

Sanctus

EXAMPLE I.7. Dies irae and Sanctus: incipits

EXAMPLE I.8. Sanctus: bars 5–7

Requiem") are in this respect far less radical as a whole than Maunder's. Maunder discusses the reasons in favor of a wholly new scoring in a separate monograph (*Mozart's Requiem*). For all the questions raised by Maunder's edition (see below, n. 130), his book sets out some crucial insights on the subject of Mozart's counterpoint, although the presentation is very condensed (Chap. 3).

101. My thanks are due to Robert Levin, who was the first to make the observations that lead to this view and has discussed them with me. Cf. also Levin, "Zur Musiksprache," and his new edition of the Requiem.

102. Since the figured bass at the start of the "Dies irae" harks back to the "Requiem" incipit (see also Ex. I.7), the Sanctus, too, appears to be connected with the opening movement, albeit indirectly.

103. The c′ in the bass in bar 5 was changed to c♯′ even in the Breitkopf first edition, but that does not eliminate the problem altogether. In the first half of the bar c♯′ would be better—and more Mozartian—than the augmented second c′. Furthermore, in consideration of the homophonic structure of the vocal harmony, the bass voices would do better to enter at the same time as the other voices, on the third beat; the timbres of the first half of the bar would then be orchestral.

change (D major to B-flat major) at the Hosanna repeat. The orchestral transitional figure, which links the B-flat major Benedictus (bars 50ff.) with the repeat of the Hosanna, is a typical modulatory figure and could easily effect a return to D major (by way of D minor; see Ex. I.9).[104] But Süssmayr does not exploit the modulatory potential of this figure, leaves the link (bars 50–53) in B-flat major, and is thereby forced to repeat the Hosanna in that key. As a result the Sanctus differs from all the other sections of the Requiem in being harmonically open-ended.

Similar misinterpretation of Mozart's ideas could also be the reason for some of the awkward writing in the Benedictus. The substance of the vocal parts and the movement's formal disposition, with vocal duet set against vocal quartet, seem as a whole to be completely unproblematical. But there can be no comparison qualitatively between the two-part vocal writing in the introduction (bars 4ff.) and the lumbering orchestral writing that accompanies it (setting aside consideration of the often-remarked melodic resemblance to a piece in the notebook Mozart wrote for his pupil Barbara Ployer, K 453b).[105] One of the failings of the accompaniment here is that it anticipates the vocal material, which is completely at variance with Mozart's practice in his draft score. On these grounds (in addition to more substantial objections to the second half of the movement), Richard Maunder refuses categorically to accept the Benedictus as a composition that could have any basis in ideas formed by Mozart.[106] Yet if Süssmayr's clumsiness is overlooked, the orchestral introduction is Mozartian from beginning to end. Distribution of the opening motive between two different instrumental groups with an echo effect (strings and basset horn or basset horn and bassoon) would certainly be closer to Mozart's manner of composition than Süssmayr's treatment of the material is (Ex. I.10).

Compared with the Sanctus and Benedictus, the Agnus Dei[107] offers a far better

104. This figure is used in a modulatory function in Tamino's scene with the Speaker in *Die Zauberflöte* (Act I, scene 15, bars 68f., 75f., 82f.).

105. Abert, *W. A. Mozart*, 724; see also Part II, n. 31, and facsimile of Mozart's entry in the exercise book for Ployer in Requiem Catalog, 263.

106. Cf. Maunder, *Mozart's Requiem*, 47–57.

107. Cf. the essentially positive assessment of this movement in Handke, "Lösung der Benedictusfrage," and Marguerre, "Mozart und Süßmayr." It seems doubtful whether the reminiscences of motives in other Mozart works that can be found in the Agnus Dei, the Hosanna, or the Benedictus have any real relevance to the question of authenticity in the Requiem (cf. Moseley, "Mozart's Requiem," 218f.).

EXAMPLE I.9. Benedictus: bars 50ff.

oder *8va bassa*

EXAMPLE I.10. Benedictus: bars 1f.

balance in the quality of the vocal and the instrumental writing.[108] The manner of combining the highly rhetorical, homophonous declamation of the text by the voices with the contrasting shape of the orchestral motive is directly reminiscent of the technique used in the "Domine Jesu." The appearance of the "Requiem" theme in the bass part has often been mentioned by commentators (Ex. I.11): it, too, supports the supposition that it is based on a Mozartian draft of some kind, perhaps a vocal sketch, the function of which was not more precisely defined but which probably already included the instrumental "motivic idea" (in Süssmayr's phrase) in the form of the violins' sixteenth-note figure (bars 1ff.).[109]

A - gnus De - i, qui tol - lis

EXAMPLE I.11. Agnus Dei: bars 1ff.

108. Cf. also Martin, "Das 'Agnus Dei' in Mozarts Requiem," although—like Handke, "Lösung der Benedictusfrage"—he does not distinguish between levels in the vocal and instrumental writing.
109. Even A. B. Marx, who was in agreement with Weber on the topic of Mozart's responsibility for the material of the Agnus Dei, remarked: "If Mozart did not write it, well, so be it, the person who did write it was Mozart" (*Berliner musikalische Zeitung* [1825]: 379).

It seems certain—especially in view of the quality of the vocal writing—that Mozart left behind sketches and drafts, not only for the Agnus Dei, but also for the Sanctus (including the Hosanna) and Benedictus. Such "scraps of paper" (Doc. 22), in addition to what Mozart had played and sung but not written down, could have given Süssmayr important guidance.[110] It is true that in his letter to Breitkopf & Härtel (Doc. 17) Süssmayr claimed these movements as his own work. His actual words "ganz neu von mir verfertigt" (wholly composed by me), do not, however, contradict what we can safely assume the situation to have been, for what Mozart left of these movements cannot have been as much as a draft score. Even if Süssmayr had sketches or other material on which to base his work, the real task of composition was still his.[111] The outcome was a unique and curious mixture of amazingly good ideas and the less successful execution or development of those ideas, not to mention the guidelines that may have been only half-understood or wholly misunderstood. In any event, Süssmayr's additions to Mozart's work amount to a far from homogenous score.

How Süssmayr set about completing the Requiem could be far more accurately judged if his sketches or first, fuller drafts had survived.[112] The fair copy of his score is all that exists now, but there must have been earlier versions, which might have made it possible to establish his methods in some detail. A working draft would probably reveal differences between material derived from Mozartian originals and wholly new material, by the very manner in which these materials were written down. Süssmayr had no doubt acquired many skills that made him a useful assistant and was an experienced composer, but he was not truly a master. In Constanze's eyes he was just Mozart's pupil, and that was clearly the reason why she did not entrust the unfinished Requiem to him from the first. Years later she told Stadler of how much helping Mozart with the Requiem taught Süssmayr and quoted Mozart himself telling his pupil, "Ey, there you are again,

110. Cf. also the testimony of Mozart's pupil Ignaz von Seyfried, written 16 October 1825: "According to what Süssmayr said to me, on repeated occasions, he found everything up to the "Hostias" worked out, the rest—more than probably—in draft form. . . . Although this does not altogether harmonize with what he wrote in his letter to Br. and Härtel, I would nevertheless like to declare myself in favor of the former" (*Cäcilia* 4 [1826]: 296).

111. The phrase "neu verfertigen" is equivalent to "compose" in the sense of "putting elements together to make something new," and those elements can be original or borrowed. Stadler, for one, admitted that it could not be proved "whether Süssmayr used some of Mozart's ideas [in composing the Sanctus, Benedictus, and Agnus Dei], or not" (Doc. 22).

112. Süssmayr gave his composing score of the Sanctus (and possibly the Agnus Dei, too) to Constanze Mozart, who still had it in 1800 (Doc. 16n). It is now lost.

like a dying duck in a thunderstorm; you won't understand that for a long time," which has the undeniable ring of truth (Doc. 28).

What about the possibility that Süssmayr took elements that originated with Mozart and integrated them into the sections of the Requiem that are his own composition? The existence of sketches, even if they related to only two movements, compels us to look again at another of the remarks Constanze made to Stadler, referring to Mozart's untidiness with his papers: "Let us suppose that Süssmayr did in fact find some fragments by Mozart (for the Sanctus, etc.), the Requiem would nevertheless still be Mozart's work" (Doc. 28). On an earlier occasion she told Stadler that "a few scraps of paper with music on them were found on Mozart's desk after his death, which she had given to Herr Süssmayr. What they contained, and what use Süssmayr made of them, she did not know" (Doc. 22). Süssmayr himself told of Mozart, like a master craftsman, talking to the assistant who had given him such valuable help with the two operas composed in 1791. It seems clear that the repetition of the "Kyrie" fugue at the end of the work, at least, went back to something Mozart had said (Docs. 16a, 17).[113]

We do not know for certain what was on the "scraps of paper," but most likely they contained the kind of musical constructions that are typical of Mozart's sketches in general, notably the one surviving sheet of sketches for the Requiem: complicated contrapuntal developments (see Exx. I.1, I.2) which he wanted to work out fully on paper rather than in his head alone. One of the outstanding differences, however, between the sections of the Requiem composed by Süssmayr and those by Mozart is that the former avoid virtually every kind of contrapuntal profundity. The only exception is the Hosanna fugue: elsewhere, the movements by Süssmayr contain only two examples of contrapuntal working at all, namely, bars 24–28 of the "Lacrymosa" and bars 10–13 of the Benedictus (recurring at bars 23–25, 33–34, and 38–39). Both of these are passages for which Mozart most likely left some sketches which Süssmayr was incapable of interpreting and using to the full.[114]

While the "Hosanna" fugue, in spite of its recalcitrant subject, comes close to presenting a textbook example of a regular, almost pedantic fugal development, the polythematic "Amen" fugue, to judge by Mozart's sketch, would have been

113. The testimony of Constanze Mozart (Doc. 16a) is independent of Süssmayr's statement (Doc. 17) and predates it.

114. Fischer is illuminating on the problematical voice leading in bars 24–28 of the "Lacrymosa" (Fischer, "Das 'Lacrimosa,'" 15f.). Cf. also the discussion below, Part II, p. 111 (Ex. II.15 and n. 63).

quite out of the ordinary. We do not know whether Süssmayr knew the sketch, but if he did he must have recognized the inherent difficulties and studiously avoided them. It is unlikely that he would have treated comparable sketches any differently: musical ideas of a general character were welcome to him, but he had neither the time, the interest, nor the technical equipment to meet contrapuntal challenges.

Original and Imitation: Horn Rondo and Requiem

If there is only circumstantial evidence for supposing that Mozart left "scraps of paper" relating to the Requiem and that Süssmayr used them, the proof that Süssmayr found drafts of other material among Mozart's papers after his death and made use of them is more direct. There is, for example, Mozart's unfinished autograph score of the Rondo for Piano and Orchestra K 386, which was discovered a few years ago inside a bundle of Süssmayr's autographs and indicates that the confusion of Mozart's and Süssmayr's manuscripts and papers was assuredly not accidental.[115] It adds to the significance of the fact that toward the end of Süssmayr's fair copy of the Requiem (Codex a[2], fols. 17–20—concluding fugue; see Table 1) there appears the same music paper, with twelve staves, that Mozart had used for part of his autograph score.[116] But clearly Süssmayr did more than help himself to Mozart's unused music paper; he also busied himself with the musical material that he found.

As Stadler was to do later, Süssmayr worked to complete pieces left unfinished by Mozart, very probably at the suggestion or request of Constanze.[117] A valuable example of an attempt by Süssmayr to write in Mozart's style is provided by a Concerto Rondo in D Major for Horn, which allows us to make direct comparisons that are germane to the study of the Requiem score. The piece was composed by Süssmayr, but he made lavish use of material by Mozart. It is only recently that the question of the date of Mozart's unfinished Horn Concerto in D Major K 412 (386b) has been satisfactorily solved with the conclusion that it

---

115. Tyson, *Mozart*, 262ff.
116. Paper type 1 (see above, n. 84).
117. Plath, "Über Skizzen zu Mozarts Requiem," 451.

is from the year 1791.[118] Curiously enough, we possess two different versions of the concerto's rondo finale, in two separate manuscript sources: (1) a draft score by Mozart, with the horn part complete but the string accompaniment complete only up to bar 40 and thereafter notated only occasionally; (2) a complete score by Süssmayr, which was long thought to be a Mozart autograph and cataloged accordingly as an authentic work, K 514.[119]

The two versions of the rondo, Mozart's incomplete draft K 412 and the complete version K 514, now revealed as the work of Süssmayr, have important things in common, but the differences are equally telling.[120] In particular, the orchestral accompaniment in K 514 shows that Süssmayr's version can in no way have been based on Mozart's draft version. It is only necessary to look at the second violin, viola, and bass parts and compare Süssmayr's rudimentary and mechanically repeated figuration with Mozart's thoroughly flexible and interesting accompaniment (Exx. I.12, I.13).[121]

What is the relationship between the two versions? Tyson thinks that Süssmayr had Mozart's version in front of him but consciously ignored it.[122] Franz Giegling argues that Süssmayr had had a brief sight of Mozart's score but had then worked from memory.[123] However, the fact that the two versions coincide exactly in the horn part, while the striking differences are to be found only in the orchestral part, points to a third explanation: as he had done on other occasions, Mozart may have written out a separate copy of the horn part as well as the version with the accompaniment sketched in.[124] This would probably have been done in order to rehearse the work with the horn player Joseph Leutgeb, for whom the concerto was intended and who is known to have attended a performance of *Die*

118. It used to be dated 1782. Clearly, the reason it is not to be found in Mozart's autograph catalog of his works is that it was unfinished. Cf. Tyson, *Mozart*, 246–61.

119. The two manuscript sources are (1) Biblioteka Jagiellonska, Cracow, Mus. ms. autogr. W.A. Mozart KV 412/417; and (2) Institute of Theatre, Music, and Cinematography, St. Petersburg, Fonds N-2/1007.

120. Cf. the discussion in Levin, *Who Wrote the Four-Wind Concertante?*, 151–54.

121. The same kinds of differences can be seen between Eybler's and Süssmayr's scoring of the wind parts in the Sequence of the Requiem (see above, Exx. I.1 and I.2).

122. Tyson, *Mozart*, 253ff.

123. NMA V/14, vol. 5, Preface, p. xvii.

124. Cf., for example, the Violin Sonata K 454 (comments in K⁶, p. 492). On the important question of the limited range of the horn part, due to consideration for the aging Joseph Leutgeb, see Levin, *Who Wrote the Four-Wind Concertante?*, 151–54.

EXAMPLE I.12.   Süssmayr: Horn Rondo K 514, bars 1–11

EXAMPLE I.13.   Mozart: Horn Rondo K 412, bars 1–11

Zauberflöte with Mozart on 8 October 1791.[125] Süssmayr must have used a horn part without accompaniment as the basis of his own score (see Table 2, where this hypothetical manuscript, entitled A, is reconstructed), without having known Mozart's draft score, for if he had had Mozart's score in front of him, he would have used the orchestration too. As it is, he followed only the solo part, and slavishly at that, line by line (see Table 3). He used everything he found and reproduced it in the same order—including two passages in A minor, the first of which Mozart cut in his draft score (Table 3, MS. B, line 4).

TABLE 2.   Mozart, Rondo K 412. Reconstruction of the Horn Part (MS. A), Including Extraneous Material

Stave	Bars	Content
1	9–16	Rondo subject, D major
2	21–26	A major
3	28–40	D major (Violin I in bar 29)
4	48a–51a	A minor
5	—	Lamentatio (psalm tone), Dorian (D minor/F major)
6	67–79	A minor
7	88–91	A major

TABLE 3.   Concordance of Süssmayr's Rondo K 514 and Mozart's draft K 412*

Rondo K 412 (MS. B) (March–November 1791)		Rondo K 514 (MS. C) (dated 6 April 1792)	
Stave	Bars	Stave	Bars
1	9–16	1	9–16
2	21–26	2	25–30
3	28–40	3	32–44
4	cut	4	59–62
5	not included	5	70–79 (Lamentatio)
6	67–79	6	84–96
7	88–91	7	109–12

* Staves and bars refer to MS. A. (Table 2).

125. Bauer-Deutsch IV, No. 1195.

Manuscript A might also, however, have included material that did not relate to the concerto, including at the very least the liturgical cantus firmus from the Lamentatio, which appears abruptly in K 514 (bars 70–79; Ex. I.14). The hypothesis is supported by the fact that Mozart's drafts and sketches often show work for several compositions mixed up on the same sheet of paper.[126] That would be one explanation for the unexpected incursion of the Lamentatio in Süssmayr's horn rondo (MS. C), while it is absent from Mozart's rondo (MS. B; see Table 3). This passage was always thought odd and has been explained as an "instrumental joke" of Mozart's;[127] now we know that K 514 is not by Mozart at all; we should perhaps read it as an example instead of Süssmayr's unthinking aping of something he had misunderstood.[128]

The Dorian cantus firmus brings the tonal range of the Requiem into the Rondo in D Major K 514, where it disrupts the harmonic disposition of the rest of the piece—which already suffers from the disproportionately long A-minor episode. It does, however, draw attention to another connection with the Requiem. The quotation from the Lamentatio, a modified version of the first psalm tone, is the same as that used as cantus firmus by Michael Haydn for the line "Te decet hymnus" in the Introit of his C-minor Requiem (Ex. I.15). Mozart knew that work well, having taken part in its performance in Salzburg Cathedral in

EXAMPLE I.14. (a) Lamentatio = 1st psalm tone
              (b) Tonus peregrinus = 9th psalm tone

126. Cf. Konrad, *Mozarts Schaffensweise*, 104–106, 339ff. Plath, "Das Skizzenblatt KV 467a," discusses an exemplary case; see also Fig. 1 (sketches for *Die Zauberflöte*, Requiem, etc.).

127. Grau, "Ein bisher übersehener Instrumentalwitz." An example of the instrumental use of melodies from Lamentations, which is justified both tonally and expressively, is found in Haydn's Symphony No. 26 in D minor ("La lamentatione").

128. Robert Levin (*Who Wrote the Four-Wind Concertante?*, 151–54) mentions the possibility that Süssmayr's quotation of the Lamentatio melody is an allusion to Mozart's death, but he does not make the connection with the Requiem.

Te de - cet hy - mnus De - us in Si - on,   et ti - bi red - de - tur vo - tum in Je - ru - sa - lem

EXAMPLE I.15.   M. Haydn: Requiem in C Minor (1st psalm tone)

1771 at the funeral of Archbishop Schrattenbach, and he introduces a liturgical cantus firmus at the identical line in his own Requiem.[129] He may originally have thought of using the same psalm tone that Michael Haydn had used and made a note of it with that purpose in mind (on the horn part he was working on at the time; see Table 2) but later changed his mind and used the ninth psalm tone, the so-called *tonus peregrinus*.

This excursus on Süssmayr's work on the D-major horn rondo yields little more than circumstantial evidence of the former existence of Requiem sketches and drafts. At the same time—and this is of far greater importance—the Rondo K 514 of the spring of 1792 provides an exact parallel to the Sanctus and Agnus Dei of the Requiem: both times Süssmayr was faced with the task of composing something new on the basis of unfinished materials, left out of order and sometimes not intended to belong together. In both cases he clung slavishly to everything that could serve as a guide—and in both cases the product was a piece of music that used an essentially Mozartian vocabulary but not the grammar and idiom that alone would have characterized the speech as Mozart's own.

The survival of material that permits the comparison of the two horn rondos gives a welcome insight into Süssmayr's working methods and his creative psyche. Even if we assume that the material relating to the Sanctus and other unwritten sections of the Requiem was less extensive than what had been written down of the horn rondo, the analogy is nonetheless cogent. The problems that afflict the Requiem movements from the Sanctus to the Agnus Dei, with their intermittent flares of brilliant musical ideas, imperfectly integrated because the composer lacked the technique to master them, have exact counterparts in the Horn Rondo K 514. Even though the Mozartian material in Süssmayr's sections of the Requiem cannot be defined as precisely as it can be in the rondo, its existence cannot be ruled out. It makes it a little easier to trust Mozart's closest friends and their

129. See Part II, p. 65.

often baffling actions, above all their vehement and stubborn defense of the authenticity of the Requiem as a work admitted to be incomplete but claimed as Mozart's spiritual property, even in the passages completed by others.

Epilogue

Study of the manuscript sources of the Requiem according to musicological principles allows the clear distinction of work in Mozart's own hand and that in the hands of the other composers who undertook to finish it. Stylistic criticism following the same principles also yields a certain amount of insight into the working methods of the most important of those composers: Franz Xaver Süssmayr. As a result we can draw some important general conclusions about the genesis of the work, but we still have no definitive solutions to such crucial problems as the precise designation of Mozart's contribution to the score from the Sanctus onward. This aporia is particularly frustrating when it is a question of performing the Requiem with the legitimate aspiration of allowing as much purely Mozartian music as possible to be heard, mixed with no more non-Mozartian material than is absolutely necessary. The boundaries between the Mozartian and the non-Mozartian are and remain uncertain. Where the essential matter had already been set out by Mozart—in the movements up to the Offertory (excepting the "Lacrymosa" from bar 9 onward)—the instrumentation and other additions made by Eybler and Süssmayr are clearly visible and easily emended, when necessary.[130] It is with the later movements that we face the insoluble dilemma of either emending too much, and so running the risk of discarding

---

130. Franz Beyer did this carefully and persuasively in his edition (1971; 1979); see in particular the account he recently gave of himself (Beyer, "Zur Neuinstrumentation des Mozart-Requiems"). It can be objected, however, that Beyer stays too close to Süssmayr in the "Dies irae" and overlooks the often superior versions of Eybler.

On Richard Maunder's edition, see Bauman, "Requiem, but No Piece," as well as the reviews by Barry Cooper (*Journal of the Royal Musical Association* 114 [1989]: 248–51) and Stanley Sadie (*Notes* 46 [1990]: 1052–55), and the replies by Maunder and Sadie in *Notes* 47 (1990): 583–87. Sadie refers to the paper I read at the 1987 conference of the American Musicological Society in New Orleans (Wolff, "Composition and Completion of Mozart's Requiem") when he concludes: "Maunder's models are cleverly chosen: chiefly Mozart's music of 1791 and his earlier church music. Yet the style of his principal ones, *Die Zauberflöte* and *La clemenza di Tito*, is not the style of the Requiem, as far as we have it. Each work of this late period is in some way new and individual, and none more markedly so than the Requiem, with its unique and austere wind coloring, and its handling of counterpoint generally. When no model is valid, we had best be content with what we have: Mozart's intention perceived, however hazily, and realized, however inadequately, by Franz Xaver Süssmayr."

Mozartian material, or interfering too little, and thus distorting Mozart's intentions. But Mozart's intentions are very largely a matter of hypothesis.

An essential feature of the surviving manuscript sources of the Requiem—sketches and drafts of the score alike—is that Mozart wrote down the vocal parts *first,* and in some places that is *all* he wrote. Thus the vocal parts constituted the nucleus—the germ—of all the rest of the musical material. In view of these stylistic premises and Mozart's verifiable intentions, analytical attention must necessarily focus in particular on the construction of the elements contained in the vocal parts; in the case of the movements for which no draft by Mozart exists, however, we are thrown back on Süssmayr's score. This priceless historical document is more than the only surviving, accessible record of what Süssmayr composed; it is also the only source that offers the opportunity to discover the ideas that originated with Mozart: basic musical elements, motives, fragments, forms, and techniques. Rejecting Süssmayr's score out of hand, as has been done, most drastically by Maunder in his edition, means rejecting the chance of preserving what traces there are of Mozart's original material.[131]

For that reason alone, Süssmayr's score would deserve preservation.[132] The bottom line is that it represents the decisive historical, textual, and musical documentation of the work—in particular of all that which Mozart himself was no longer able to execute in more than rudimentary form. To the attentive listener, moreover, Süssmayr's score offers an aesthetic dimension that no later edition can match, not least on account of its history. The manuscript that was delivered to Count Walsegg has remained to this day the last witness—the only surviving and incorruptible witness—of the confusion that reigned in the days immediately before and after Mozart's death. And this score is unique in representing and

131. Robert Levin prepared a new and totally rethought completion of the Requiem, one that not only includes an "Amen" fugue (after Mozart's sketch) but also critically evaluates the movements by Süssmayr (Sanctus through Agnus Dei), thus reinforcing their documentary value. Now as ever, I am convinced that the attempt to approach Mozart on the basis of that type of analytical understanding is well worth making, so long as it is fully understood that it is only an attempt and that it will not be the last—for the next person to make the attempt will also have to go back to Süssmayr's score.

132. It is in this spirit that we must regard the decision of Johannes Brahms to use Süssmayr's version of the score, untouched, in his edition of the work for the original Mozart-Ausgabe. Brahms wrote: "The editor was never in any doubt that his sole concern must be to give as true and reliable a picture as possible of how Mozart left his work, and of how his pupil finished it after his death, and to that end to reproduce exactly the two manuscripts in which the work has come down to us" (AMA-Supplement, Revisionsbericht zu Serie XXIV, No. 1, 1877, 55–56).

embodying in its physical fabric the original and essential musical truth of the unfinished work. In its often abrupt opposition and imperfect union of the finished and the unfinished, it draws us spellbound into the situation of the last days of 1791: into the oppression weighing upon Mozart's family and friends as they looked on the unfinished Requiem and faced the responsibility of dealing with their daunting musical legacy—only too conscious that they could not do it.

FIGURE 1. Autograph sketch leaf (Staatsbibliothek zu Berlin (Stiftung Preussischer Kulturbesitz), Haus I; Mus. ms. autogr. W. A. Mozart: zu KV 620), fol. 2r

FIGURE 2. Autograph score (Österreichische Nationalbibliothek, Vienna; Mus. Hs. 17561a), fol. 1r: Requiem

FIGURE 3. Autograph score, fol. 11r: Dies irae (supplemental instrumentation by Joseph Eybler)

FIGURE 4. Autograph score, fol. 33r: Lacrymosa

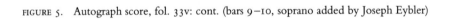

FIGURE 5. Autograph score, fol. 33v: cont. (bars 9–10, soprano added by Joseph Eybler)

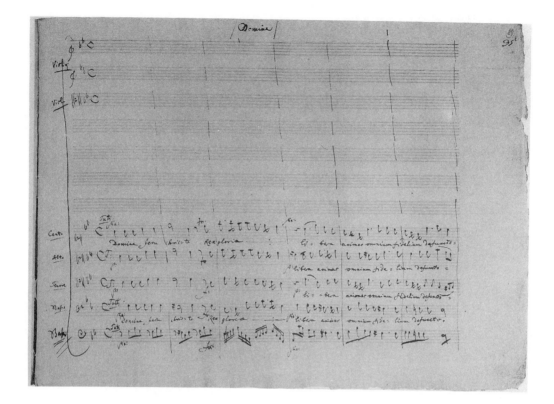

FIGURE 6. Autograph score, fol. 35r: Domine Jesu Christe

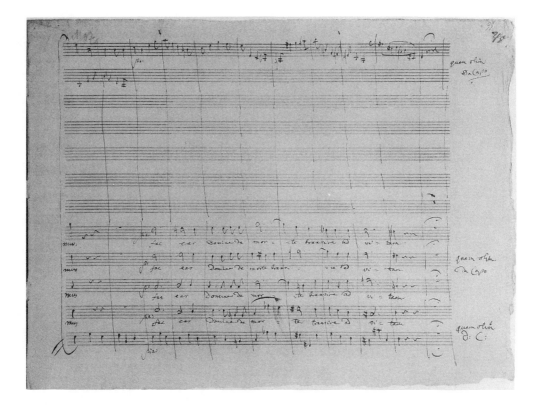

FIGURE 7.   Autograph score, fol. 45r: Hostias (condition before the mutilation of this last page of Mozart's autograph; cf. Nowak 1958)

FIGURE 8. Maximilian Stadler's score (Österreichische National bibliothek, Vienna; Mus. Hs. 4375), fol. 1r: Domine Jesu Christe

FIGURE 9 (*above*). Franz Xaver Süssmayr's score (Österreichische National bibliothek, Vienna; Mus. Hs. 17561b), fol. 24r: Domine Jesu Christe

FIGURE 10 (*opposite*). Organ and choir loft of the St. Michael's Church (Michaelerkirche) in Vienna, site of the Requiem performance at Mozart's exequies on December 10, 1791.

CHAPTER TWO

Musical Aspects

The Concept, Structure, and Character of Mozart's Requiem

Mozart's music is no easier to encompass and describe than are the creative statements of other great masters. It is possible, however, at least to some extent, to explain the construction of a work of art—how it was made and what was made—in such a way as to give a better understanding of the work and of the composer's intentions. That is the purpose of the following part of this book. It contains neither detailed analyses of individual movements nor a comprehensive critical discussion of the work and its style within its historical context, either in the late eighteenth century in general or in Mozart's oeuvre in particular. Rather, it raises considerations that help to plot connections and expressive details in the musical structure of the Requiem and its individual movements.

Background, Text, Formal Layout

The commission handed to Mozart by the mysterious "Grey Messenger"—an envoy, as has long been known, of Count Walsegg—would not have included any individual stipulations as to the form of the mass: of that we can be reasonably sure. The fee of 50 ducats, too, would not support a hypothesis that a particular format or other special conditions were requested. This means that the composer was under no obligation to depart from the usual norms, either with respect to the performing forces and the technical standards to be expected of them or, more important, with respect to the formal layout.[1] Mozart decided in favor of

1. Cf. below, p. 71.

something at once pragmatic and consciously original: rather than a grand, large-scale work suitable only for the occasion for which it was commissioned, he conceived a concise overall form with brief individual movements, on the lines of a missa brevis et solemnis, which would make the work suitable as a repertory piece.[2] At the same time, he gave it an individual sonority, texture, and musical language intended to make it stand out from the tradition of the requiem mass as a genre.

The mass for the dead, or missa pro defunctis, developed as a special type of the polyphonic mass from the late fifteenth century onward and became one of the most assiduously cultivated types of liturgical-musical works composed for solemn and special occasions. The earliest reference to the composition of a cyclical requiem mass is found in the will of Guillaume Dufay, the Franco-Flemish composer who died in 1474; he wrote the music for his own exequies, but it is believed lost. The earliest surviving requiem mass, also composed before the year 1500, is by Dufay's younger contemporary Johannes Ockeghem. From the seventeenth century on, especially in Italy, in the Habsburg domains, and also in France, it increasingly became the practice to compose and perform requiem masses to mark the deaths of prominent people, notably in court circles.[3] The solemn Requiem Mass composed late in 1771 by Michael Haydn on the death of Sigismund Christoph von Schrattenbach, Prince-Archbishop of Salzburg, was a work of great musical merit, and its performance was an exceptionally important event in the life of the young Mozart. He and his father Leopold took part, as members of the archiepiscopal chapel, when the funeral was celebrated in Salzburg Cathedral early in January 1772.[4]

Since the early Middle Ages, the variable and invariable sung sections (Proper and Ordinary) of the Roman rite of the mass for the dead had undergone alterations and enlargements: the Sequence had been the last addition to the Ordinary,

2. This type of mass setting was cultivated in Salzburg, in particular, from the middle of the eighteenth century on; cf. Senn, "Abbé Maximilian Stadler," 14, and MacIntyre, *Viennese Concerted Mass*, 6. The term "missa brevis," in use since the sixteenth century, denotes a brief setting of the five sung sections of the mass, while "solemnis" denotes a setting for feast days, using trumpets and timpani in addition to the normal instrumentation of the "missae mediocres" on ordinary days.

3. On the history of the genre, see above all Robertson, *Requiem;* Albert Seay, "Requiem," *MGG,* 11: cols. 297–302; James W. Pruett, "Requiem Mass," *New Grove, 15:* 751–55; Schnerich, *Messe und Requiem;* Jaksch, *H. I. F. Biber, Requiem à 15;* MacIntyre, *Viennese Concerted Mass.*

4. Jaksch, *H. I. F. Biber, Requiem à 15,* contains an informative catalog of requiem masses of the seventeenth and early eighteenth centuries, both published and unpublished (pp. 131–35); on the Salzburg tradition, see also Chafe, *Church Music of Biber,* 108–17. On Michael Haydn's relations with the Mozarts, see Croll, "Johann Michael Haydn"; on Michael Haydn's sacred music, see Hintermaier, "Michael Haydns Requiem," and Schmid, *Mozart und die Salzburger Tradition.*

in the fourteenth century. One of the aims of the liturgical reforms following the Council of Trent (1545–63) was to put a stop to the proliferation of regional and local variants. From 1570 on, in accordance with the Missal of Pius V, the following texts were prescribed for use in the musical sections of the requiem mass:

I. Introit

Requiem aeternam dona eis, Domine: et lux perpetua luceat eis.[5]

Eternal rest give unto them, O Lord: and let perpetual light shine upon them.

Te decet hymnus, Deus, in Sion, et tibi reddetur votum in Jerusalem.[6]

A hymn, O God, becometh Thee in Sion; and a vow shall be paid to Thee in Jerusalem.

Exaudi orationem meam, ad te omnis caro veniet.

Hear my prayer: all flesh shall come to Thee.

. . . Requiem aeternam . . .

. . . Eternal rest . . .

II. Kyrie

Kyrie, eleison.
Christe, eleison.
Kyrie, eleison.

Lord, have mercy upon us.
Christ, have mercy upon us.
Lord, have mercy upon us.

III. Gradual

Requiem aeternam dona eis Domine: et lux perpetua luceat eis.

Eternal rest give unto them, O Lord; and let perpetual light shine upon them.

In memoria aeterna erit justus; ab auditione mala non timebit.

The just shall be in everlasting remembrance: he shall not fear hearing evil.

IV. Tract

Absolve, Domine, animas omnium fidelium defunctorum ab omni vinculo delictorum.

Absolve, O Lord, the souls of all the faithful departed from every bond of sin.

Et gratia tua illis succurrente, mereantur evadere judicium ultionis.

And by the help of Thy grace may they be enabled to escape the avenging judgement.

Et lucis aeternae beatitudine perfrui.

And enjoy the happiness of everlasting life.

5. IV Ezra 2: 34–35. The Fourth Book of Ezra is one of the pseudoepigrapha of the Old Testament.
6. Psalm 64 in the Vulgate (Psalm 65 in many Protestant versions).

V. Sequence[7]

1. Dies irae, dies illa,
   Solvet saeclum in favilla:
   Teste David cum Sibylla.

   Day of wrath! O day of mourning,
   See fulfilled the prophets' warning;
   Heaven and earth in ashes burning.

2. Quantus tremor est futurus,
   Quando judex est venturus,

   Cuncta stricte discussurus!

   Oh, what fear man's bosom rendeth
   When from heaven the Judge descendeth,
   On whose sentence all dependeth!

3. Tuba mirum spargens sonum
   Per sepulcra regionum,
   Coget omnes ante thronum.

   Wondrous sound the trumpet flingeth,
   Through earth's sepulchers it ringeth,
   All before the throne it bringeth.

4. Mors stupebit et natura,
   Cum resurget creatura,
   Judicanti responsura.

   Death is struck and nature quaking,
   All creation is awaking,
   To its Judge an answer making.

5. Liber scriptus proferetur,
   In quo totum continetur,
   Unde mundus judicetur.

   Lo! the book exactly worded,
   Wherein all hath been recorded;
   Thence shall judgement be awarded.

6. Judex ergo cum sedebit,
   Quidquid latet, apparebit:
   Nil inultum remanebit.

   When the Judge His seat attaineth,
   And each hidden deed arraigneth,
   Nothing unavenged remaineth.

7. Quid sum miser tunc dicturus,
   Quem patronum rogaturus,
   Cum vix justus sit securus?

   What shall I, frail man, be pleading,
   Who for me be interceding,
   When the just are mercy needing?

8. Rex tremendae majestatis,
   Qui salvandos salvas gratis,
   Salva me, fons pietatis.

   King of majesty tremendous,
   Who dost free salvation send us,
   Fount of pity, then befriend us!

9. Recordare, Jesu pie,
   Quod sum causa tuae viae:
   Ne me perdas illa die.

   Think, good Jesu, my salvation
   Caused Thy wondrous incarnation.
   Leave me not to reprobation.

10. Quaerens me sedisti lassus,
    Redemisti Crucem passus;
    Tantus labor non sit cassus.

    Faint and weary Thou hast sought me,
    On the cross of suffering bought me;
    Shall such grace be vainly brought me?

7. Thirteenth-century poem attributed to Thomas of Celano (d. ca. 1250); translation by W. J. Irons. The text of the original "Dies irae" poem before it came to be used by the end of the fourteenth century as a liturgical sequence consisted of only seventeen stanzas. The eighteenth stanza ("Lacrimosa"), based on a four-line structure and a different rhyme scheme, was added later. A further appendix of two lines of seven syllables each ("Pie Jesus") with a concluding "Amen" departs from the rhyme and metric organization as well as from the first-person style (e.g., "mihi finis" in stanza 17 as opposed to "eis requiem" in stanza 19) and lets the liturgical sequence essentially end in prose form. See *Analecta Hymnica*, 54:269–75; Raby, *History of Christian-Latin Poetry*, 443–53; and Vellekoop, *"Dies irae dies illa."*

11. Juste judex ultionis,
    Donum fac remissionis
    Ante diem rationis.

Righteous Judge! for sin's pollution
Grant Thy gift of absolution.
Ere that day of retribution.

12. Ingemisco tamquam reus:
    Culpa rubet vultus meus;
    Supplicanti parce, Deus.

Guilty, now I pour my moaning,
All my shame with anguish owning;
Spare, O God, Thy suppliant groaning.

13. Qui Mariam absolvisti
    Et latronem exaudisti,
    Mihi quoque spem dedisti.

Thou the sinful woman savedst;
Thou the dying thief forgavest;
And to me a hope vouchsafest.

14. Preces meae non sunt dignae:
    Sed tu bonus fac benigne,
    Ne perenni cremer igne.

Worthless are my prayers and sighing;
Yet, good Lord, in grace complying,
Rescue me from fires undying.

15. Inter oves locum praesta,
    Et ab haedis me sequestra,
    Statuens in parte dextra.

With Thy favoured sheep O place me,
Nor among the goats abase me,
But to Thy right hand upraise me.

16. Confutatis maledictis,
    Flammis acribus addictis,
    Voca me cum benedictis.

While the wicked are confounded,
Doomed to flames of woe unbounded,
Call me with Thy saints surrounded.

17. Oro supplex et acclinis,
    Cor contritum quasi cinis:
    Gere curam mei finis.

Low I kneel, with heart-submission;
See, like ashes, my contrition;
Help me in my last condition.

18. Lacrimosa dies illa,
    Qua resurget ex favilla
    Judicandus homo reus:
    Huic ergo parce, Deus.

Ah! that day of tears and mourning!
From the dust of earth returning
Man for judgement must prepare him.
Spare, O God, in mercy spare him.

19. Pie Jesu Domine,
    Dona eis requiem.
    Amen.

Lord all pitying, Jesu blest,
Grant them Thine eternal rest.
Amen.

VI. *Offertory*

Domine Jesu Christe, Rex gloriae,
libera animas omnium fidelium
defunctorum de poenis inferni et de
profundo lacu: libera eas de ore leonis,
ne absorbeat eas tartarus, ne cadant in
obscurum: sed signifer sanctus Michael
repraesentet eas in lucem sanctam:
Quam olim Abrahae promisisti et
semini ejus.

O Lord Jesus Christ, King of glory,
deliver the souls of all the faithful
departed from the pains of hell and
from the deep pit: deliver them from
the lion's mouth, that hell may not
swallow them up, and may they not fall
into darkness; may Thy holy standard-
bearer Michael lead them into the holy
light; which Thou didst promise to
Abraham and to his seed.

Hostias et preces tibi, Domine, laudis offerimus: tu suscipe pro animabus, illis, quarum hodie memoriam facimus: fac eas, Domine, de morte transire ad vitam.
Quam olim Abrahae . . .

We offer to Thee, O Lord, sacrifices and prayers: do Thou receive them in behalf of those souls whom we commemorate this day. Grant them, O Lord, to pass from death unto life. Which Thou didst promise . . .

VII. Sanctus

Sanctus, Sanctus, Sanctus Dominus Deus Sabaoth.
Pleni sunt caeli et terra gloria tua.
Hosanna in excelsis.
Benedictus qui venit in nomine Domini.
Hosanna in excelsis.

Holy, Holy, Holy, Lord God of hosts.

Heaven and earth are full of Thy glory.
Hosanna in the highest!
Blessed is he that cometh in the name of the Lord.
Hosanna in the highest!

VIII. Agnus Dei

Agnus Dei, qui tollis peccata mundi: dona eis requiem.
Agnus Dei, qui tollis peccata mundi: dona eis requiem.
Agnus Dei, qui tollis peccata mundi: dona eis requiem sempiternam.

Lamb of God, who takest away the sins of the world, give them rest.
Lamb of God, who takest away the sins of the world, give them rest.
Lamb of God, who takest away the sins of the world, give them rest eternal.

IX. Communion

Lux aeterna luceat eis, Domine: Cum sanctis tuis in aeternum: quia pius es.

Requiem aeternam dona eis, Domine: et lux perpetua luceat eis.
Cum sanctis tuis . . .

May light eternal shine upon them, O Lord. With Thy saints for ever, for Thou art merciful.
Eternal rest grant them, O Lord; and let perpetual light shine upon them.
With Thy saints for ever . . .

X. Responsory

Libera me, Domine, de morte aeterna, in die illa tremenda: Quando caeli movendi sunt et terra: Dum veneris judicare saeculum per ignem.

Tremens factus sum ego et timeo, dum discussio venerit atque ventura ira.

Deliver me, O Lord, from eternal death in that awful day: When the heavens and earth shall be moved: When Thou shalt come to judge the world by fire.
Dread and trembling have laid hold on me, and I fear exceedingly because of the judgement and the wrath to come.

Quando caeli . . .	When the heavens . . .
Dies illa, dies irae, calamitatis et miseriae, dies magna et amara valde.	O that day, that day of wrath, of sore distress and of all wretchedness, that great and exceeding bitter day.
Dum veneris . . .	When Thou shalt come . . .
Requiem aeternam dona eis, Domine: et lux perpetua luceat eis.	Eternal rest grant unto them, O Lord, and let light perpetual shine upon them.
Libera me . . .	Deliver me, O Lord . . .

Antiphon

| In paradisum deducant te Angeli: in tuo adventu suscipiant te martyres, et perducant te in civitatem sanctam Jerusalem. Chorus angelorum te suscipiat, et cum Lazaro quondam paupere aeternam habeas requiem. | May the angels lead thee into paradise: may the martyrs receive thee at thy coming, and lead thee into the holy city of Jerusalem. May the choir of angels receive thee, and mayest thou have eternal rest with Lazarus, who once was poor. |

There had always been five principal sections of polyphonic settings of the mass: (1) Introit–Kyrie; (2) Sequence; (3) Offertory; (4) Sanctus; (5) Agnus Dei–Communion. Spoken sections of the liturgy would come *between* the principal sections. The Gradual, Tract, and concluding Responsory were normally sung monophonically (choraliter), less often polyphonically (figuraliter). Among the exceptions are Cherubini's requiem masses (C minor, 1816, and D minor, 1836), which include the Gradual, and those of Verdi (1873) and Fauré (1877), which both end with the Responsory "Libera me." Mozart contented himself with the five central sections of the Ordinary, ignoring the Gradual, Tract, and Responsory; in his selection and subdivision of these movements, Mozart followed what was clearly the normal practice in Salzburg and Vienna. Michael Haydn's Requiem Mass for Archbishop Schrattenbach, an important model for Mozart, is laid out in the same five sections.[8] There is no evidence to suggest that the overall layout of the Requiem, as completed by Süssmayr, departs in any way from Mozart's plans.

The prescribed layout of the five main sections of the text left the composer little room for further subdivisions, except in the Sequence, with its nineteen stanzas. The many possibilities this allowed were well exploited by different composers: Michael Haydn, and Cherubini and Verdi in their time, opted for through

8. Croll, "Johann Michael Haydn."

composition (Verdi brings back the "Dies irae" stanza after stanzas 6 and 17), while Berlioz made five groups within the whole (stanzas 1–6, 7, 8–9, 10–16, 17–19). Mozart, for his part, subdivided the Sequence to form six movements, as follows: (1) stanzas 1–2; (2) 3–7; (3) 8; (4) 9–15; (5) 16–17; (6) 18–19. The second and fourth movements, containing more of the text than the others, are given to soloists (see Table 4). Furthermore, it suited Mozart's formal intent that, liturgically, Introit and Kyrie are understood as a single section in two parts, not as two separate sections.[9] In the autograph he gave this opening two-part movement, in D minor, a common title: Requiem (Fig. 2); the Introit ends on an imperfect cadence, and the Kyrie follows directly, not on a new side of the paper. Mozart uses exactly the same procedure later, in the Offertory, to link the "Quam olim Abrahae" fugue to the preceding passages (see Table 4). Likewise, in Süssmayr's continuation, the Agnus Dei and the Communion form a harmonically integrated movement. Thus Mozart's work falls into five main parts, each variously subdivided: (1) Requiem with Kyrie; (2) Sequence; (3) Offertory; (4) Sanctus with Hosanna and Benedictus; and finally (5) Agnus Dei with Communion.

The Musical Context

The Commission for the Requiem, as such, cannot have had any particular personal importance for Mozart—apart from the always welcome prospect of the fee. As it was given to him under the cloak of anonymity, he could not have identified Countess Walsegg as the person for whom it was ordered, and he was therefore in no position to take account of the individual circumstances. Nevertheless, in view of the plans he had been making since May 1791 to get himself appointed Capellmeister at St. Stephen's, he must have been glad of the opportunity to write for the liturgical repertory. This would mark his return to his "favourite form of composition," sacred music, and enable him to refresh and improve on the knowledge of church style that he had acquired previously in his career (Doc. 1).[10] Such considerations add credibility to Constanze Mozart's statement that her husband "told her of this remarkable request [to compose the Requiem], and at the same time expressed a wish to try his hand at this type of

9. The numbering of the sections and movements in the current editions of Mozart's Requiem (including NMA) obscures the situation.

10. See above, p. 36. "Church music . . . was Mozart's favourite form of composition. But he was able to dedicate himself least of all to it. . . . Mozart could have shown his full powers in this branch of music only if he had, in fact, obtained the post at St. Stephen's Church; he looked forward to it. How well his gifts could have been used for this type of serious church music is proved by his last work, the Requiem Mass, which certainly surpasses anything that has previously been achieved in this sphere" (Niemetschek, Leben des Kapellmeisters Mozart, 77; Life of Mozart, 85–86).

TABLE 4.   Overview of the Musical Structure of the Requiem

Movement	Meter & Tempo	No. of bars	Tonality	Fugue	Tutti/Solo
Sections composed/drafted by Mozart					
1. Requiem	C Adagio	48	d → A (d^V)		T-S-T
Kyrie	C Allegro	52	d	X	T
2. Dies irae	C Allegro assai	68	d		T
Tuba mirum	¢ Andante	62	B♭		S
Rex tremendae	C	22	g → d		T
Recordare	3/4	130	F		S
Confutatis	C Andante	40	a → F (d^V)		T
Lacrymosa	12/8	8 [+20]★	d		T
Amen		[2]★	d	X	T
3. Domine Jesu	C Andante con moto★	43	g → D (d^V)		T-S
Quam olim	C	35	g	X	T
Hostias	3/4 Andante★	54	E♭ → D (g^V)		T
Quam olim	C	35	g	X	T
Sections by Süssmayr					
4. Sanctus	C Adagio	11	D		T
Osanna	3/4 Allegro	27	D	X	T
Benedictus	C Andante	53	B♭		S
Osanna	3/4 Allegro	23	B♭	X	T
5. Agnus Dei	3/4	51	d → F (B♭^{V})		T
Lux aeterna★★	C Adagio	30	B♭ → A (d^V)		S-T
Cum sanctis★★★	C Allegro	52	d	X	T

★ By Süssmayr
★★ Repeats music from the Introit (bars 19–48)
★★★ Repeats the Kyrie fugue in full

composition, the more so as the higher forms of church music had always appealed to his genius" (Doc. 9).

Contemporary literary sources explain what Mozart meant by "the higher forms of church music," in which he (and they) included the "pathetic style." Johann Christoph Adelung, for example, wrote that the pathetic style "enhances the greatness of every idea on account of the strong emotion" that it stirs.[11] And Johann Georg Sulzer, having defined the "dark emotions" which art has the power, even the duty, to arouse as "fear, terror and somber sadness," wrote:

11. Adelung, *Über den deutschen Styl*, 2: §396.

There is pathos in a work of art when it depicts objects that fill the spirit with those dark emotions. . . . In music it is prevalent above all in sacred pieces and in tragic opera, although the latter rarely rises to such heights. The dying chorus in Graun's *Iphigenia* is very pathetic; and there is said to be much pathos in the *Alcestis* of Gluck.[12]

With Mozart's operatic experience, and in view of the many opportunities the texts of the requiem mass give for expressing those darker emotions, it is easy to understand his wish "to try his hand at this type of composition" (Doc. 9).

Mozart worked in many musical genres in the last decade of his life, in several instances for the first time. Yet it was rarely the case that he did not introduce important new impetuses; many changed the course of musical history. This tendency was increasing, if anything, rather than declining in 1790–91. *Cosi fan tutte,* his last opera buffa (completed January 1790), in particular reveals a clear intensification in the inventive exploitation of the musical possibilities, while the means employed were reduced (for example, there are only six solo roles, as opposed to the eight of *Don Giovanni* or the eleven of *Figaro*). This is analogous to the intensification of thematic-motivic working alongside an increasingly simplified rhythmic-melodic profile in the String Quintets in D Major K 593 and in E-Flat Major K 614, the Piano Concerto in B-Flat Major K 595 (Mozart's last), or the Clarinet Concerto in A Major K 622; other parallels are to be found in the paring down of the traditional opera seria in *La clemenza di Tito* and in the conception of *Die Zauberflöte* as a "grosse Oper" (a "grand opera," before the birth of the genre), in spite of the absence of secco recitatives in deference to the tradition of Singspiel.[13] It is not really possible or sensible, however, to try to reduce the attitudes that can be detected in Mozart's late works to a single denominator that would inevitably cause oversimplification. Wherever we believe the emphasis should fall, we must start from the fact that Mozart's last works are biographically "late" because his life was short, but they are not "late works" in the aesthetic sense of an oeuvre transfigured, rounded off, and permeated by the wisdom of age, such as exist in the cases of Monteverdi, Schütz, Bach, Handel, Haydn, and Beethoven. It is true that there is no mistaking the onset of a new orientation in Mozart's music from 1787 onward, and most markedly from the turn of the year 1787–88 (in the Piano Sonata in F Major K 533), and it so turns out that this new orientation, with its enhanced harmonic refinement, latent

---

12. Sulzer, *Allgemeine Theorie,* 3:661.

13. In his catalog of works, Mozart described Mazzolà's reworking (for *Clemenza*) of what was originally an old Metastasian libretto as "ridotta à vera opera" (reduced to a true opera).

contrapuntalism, and formal audacity, can correctly be called his "late style." But it must concord better with Mozart's intentions if we place less emphasis on any valedictory elements in the last works and more on the increasing trend toward new initiatives—initiatives with an artistic goal the composer's fate did not permit him to pursue.

The Requiem belongs, alongside the motet "Ave verum corpus" K 618, in that category of works that spring from the conscious consideration of a new beginning: in this case Mozart's personal definition of a "higher form of church music." Significantly, he did not integrate the classical vocal polyphony of the Palestrina tradition into his new concept, although his early Bolognese academic exercise, the motet "Quaerite primum regnum dei" K 86, took that tradition as its stylistic model. In his Viennese period he did not look further back than Bach and Handel, and there is no question of his copying a stylistic model as such; rather, his intention was to integrate certain technical elements into the music in order to enrich and refine its texture and to enhance and strengthen its expressive power. The deliberate exploration of polyphony, in the manner of Bach and Haydn in particular, and exemplarily demonstrated in the combination of fugue and sonata principles in the finale of the Quartet in G Major K 387 of 1782, leads to a wholly new kind of sound image, with nothing backward looking about it. The same is true of the Requiem, even at those points where the composer acknowledges older models.

The first movement of the Requiem is the only one where the reference to an older musical model is both concrete and significant, for a large part of the musical material of the Introit comes from the opening chorus of Handel's Funeral Anthem for Queen Caroline ("The ways of Zion do mourn") HWV 264 (1737), transposed from the original G minor to D minor (see Exx. II.1a and II.1b). The Handelian material includes the instrumental introduction (including the staccato articulation), the main theme of the "Requiem aeternam" (Mozart bars 8ff. = Handel bars 10ff.), and the orchestral counterpoint (Mozart bars 20ff. = Handel bars 18ff.). Furthermore, the chorale setting in the second half of Handel's movement quotes the well-known tune of two Lutheran funeral hymns ("Wenn mein Stündlein vorhanden ist" and "Herr Jesu Christ, du höchstes Gut"), the first line of which supplies the chorale theme (Ex. II.2).[14] Mozart uses the same theme,

14. The first known occurrence of the tune is in the Dresden hymn book of 1593. In the choice of cantus firmus and style of chorale arrangement, Handel clearly took into account Queen Caroline's German, Lutheran origins (she was born a princess of Brandenburg-Ansbach) and the fact that there would be many German dignitaries attending the funeral, who would be unable to understand the English text but would recognize the German tune and appreciate its funereal associations.

EXAMPLE II.IA. Handel: Funeral Anthem HWV 264, opening chorus, bars 1ff.

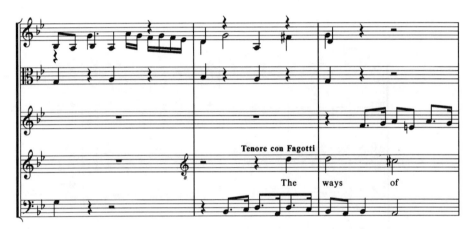

EXAMPLE II.1A.   (*continued*) Handel: Funeral Anthem HWV 264, opening chorus, bars 1ff.

EXAMPLE II.IB.   Handel. Funeral Anthem HWV 264, opening chorus, bars 51ff.
(chorale elaboration)

Wenn mein Stünd‑lein vor‑han‑den ist...
Herr Je‑su Christ, du höch‑stes Gut...

EXAMPLE II.2. Chorale melody "Wenn mein Stündlein vorhanden ist"
("Herr Jesu Christ, du höchstes Gut")

but with the introduction in bar 21 of the liturgical *tonus peregrinus* (ninth psalm tone) he enlarges the scope of the movement to make what might be called a double chorale setting.

The material of the "Kyrie" fugue comes from another work by Handel, the closing chorus of the Dettingen Te Deum HWV 265 (1743; Ex. II.3).[15] Mozart again borrows both the theme and the countersubject (and also the simultaneous setting of two texts, as in "Alleluja / We will rejoice," for "Kyrie . . . / Christe"), this time transposing the original D major modally to D minor. This procedure may have been influenced by the fact that the fugal theme appears, in the key of F minor and without a countersubject, in Handel's *Messiah* (No. 22: "And with His stripes we are healed"), of which Mozart had made a performing edition for Baron van Swieten in 1789 (K 572).[16] Incidentally, the fugue "Cum sanctis tuis" in Michael Haydn's C‑minor Requiem was also based on a variant of this familiar soggetto, and Mozart himself had also used it in a very similar fashion in the "Laudate pueri" of his Vesperae solennes de confessore K 339 (Ex. II.4). Abbé Stadler was the first to observe that Mozart chose Handel "as his model in serious vocal music" (Doc. 22) and to draw attention to Mozart's adoption of Handelian motives in the Requiem.[17]

> Just as Mozart took the motive for the Kyrie from a Handel oratorio, so too he took the motive for the "Requiem" from Handel's Anthem for the fu‑ neral of Queen Caroline, composed in the year 1737. . . . He found a very

15. Handel used it again in the same year, in No. 44 of the oratorio *Joseph and His Brethren* HWV 59.

16. The entry in Mozart's Verzeichnis reads: "In March [1789] edited Handel's *Messiah* for Baron Suiten." See also Requiem Catalog, 233–36.

17. Since Stadler, the literature on Mozart has taken surprisingly little note of this. Maunder, *Mozart's Requiem*, for example, does not even mention the Handel connection in the appropriate chapter ("Mozart's Models for the Requiem," pp. 74–94), though space is given to the far less substantial links with Florian Gassmann, Michael Haydn, and Heinrich Biber.

EXAMPLE II.3.   Handel: Dettingen Anthem HWV 265, final chorus, bars 1ff.

EXAMPLE II.4.   (a) Haydn: Requiem in C Minor
                (b) Mozart: Vesperae solennes K 339, 4th movement

apt idea for a requiem in this anthem; used it as some sheets [now lost] among his papers testified; worked it out in his own style; added the Kyrie in the manner suggested by Handel's idea; and then, when he received the commission for the Requiem, he sought out his old sketches, put everything into his new score, and developed it all in masterly style.[18]

True connoisseurs will assuredly obtain exquisite musical pleasure from the comparison of Handel's anthem and Mozart's Requiem. They will see how skillfully and beautifully both masters worked out their different chorale settings and developed the whole motive; they will admire them both and be at a loss to say which is the better. Mozart chose the so-called *tonus peregrinus* for his chorus "Te decet," and what a heavenly accompaniment he gave it! First the soprano begins it alone, followed after a brief space by all the voices, who sing it with a new accompaniment. Everything, *everything* betrays Mozart. Even the introduction of the Kyrie is glorious![19]

Stadler's account is accurate insofar as Mozart's use of Handelian material is not "borrowing," as usually understood, but limited to the selection of "motives": individual, key ideas, which he then develops independently, links with other material (e.g., Handel's counterpoint, bars 20ff., with the ninth psalm tone, bars 21ff.), and also augments with essentially new material, achieving a wholly original result. Neither the Introit nor the fugue resembles the two works by Handel in the way the material is developed or formally shaped. Mozart's unmistakable trait of reinterpreting and varying his model is apparent from the very first bars: he breaks up the strict rhythm of Handel's string chords, modifies the bass line, and transposes the oboes' contrapuntal line down to the tenor register (bassoons and basset horns). The result far outreaches Handel's original in contrapuntal complexity (see, for example, the contrapuntal stretto using Handel's motive in bars 20–25) and in refined compositional accomplishment as a whole.

The Requiem contains other ideas that may not necessarily be Mozart's own inventions. As Stadler remarks, "in the last years of his life Mozart still had such respect for the great masters that he preferred their ideas to his own."[20] But while the debt to Handel is plain to see in the opening movement, where it has considerable influence on Mozart's music, in other movements the question arises of the extent to which the material may be musical common property and its use

---

18. There is no other evidence of the existence of an earlier draft for a requiem, which might have had a connection with Mozart's fragments of sacred music from the period 1789–90.

19. Stadler, *Vertheidigung der Echtheit des Mozart'schen Requiem*, 17.

20. Stadler, *Nachtrag zur Vertheidigung*, 13; see also Doc. 22.

a matter of chance. Erich Prieger pointed out the similarity between the opening of Mozart's "Recordare" and a symphonic movement by Wilhelm Friedemann Bach, dating from about 1740–46 (Ex. II.5).[21] More recently, Hartmut Krones has argued that the "Lacrimosa" of a 1760 requiem by François-Joseph Gossec may have been Mozart's source (Ex. II.6).[22] But the similarity with the Bach is greater than with the Gossec, applying not only to the tonality but also to the writing in two different registers (the bass in bars 1–2 and the syncopated counterpoint in the upper line). The Gossec passage, on the other hand, has only the contrapunctus syncopatus in common with the Mozart: a coincidence that shows both composers using a common musical technique. In any case, such similarities apply only to very limited features of Mozart's work;[23] they also stem from the general musical vocabulary of the time and should not be interpreted as conscious imitation, let alone quotations.

Mozart's use of material from Handel's funeral anthem strongly suggests that he consciously took the tradition of funeral music and the requiem genre into account when he came to plan his own Requiem, before drafting any part of it. The examples that lay to his hand would have included Michael Haydn's Requiem of 1771 and possibly also Gossec's *Messe des morts* and Florian Gassmann's unfinished C-minor Requiem.[24] Furthermore, in building up the knowledge of church style of which he boasted (Doc. 1), Mozart would have familiarized himself with the oratorio and sacred vocal music in general (and possibly with Georg

---

21. Cf. the preface to the edition of *Sinfonia. Zur Geburtstagsfeier Friedrich des Grossen komponiert von Wilhelm Friedemann Bach* (Cologne, 1910), and Falck, *Wilhelm Friedemann Bach*, 123f. Contrary to what both Prieger and Falck say, the Sinfonia in D Minor Fk 65, the manuscripts of which use the heading "Fuga," must have been composed between 1740 and 1746 (kindly communicated to me by Peter Wollny, Cambridge, Mass.).

   Although Mozart's familiarity with the music of W. F. Bach cannot be proven by the K 404a fugues and their notoriously problematic source, the autograph score of the Sinfonia in D Major Fk 64 and a scribal copy of the Ricercata Fk 66 are of Viennese provenance and suggest a connection with Baron van Swieten's circle.

22. Krones, "Ein französisches Vorbild," 3ff., points out that the Gossec piece was published in full score in 1780 and that Gottfried van Swieten was one of the subscribers.

23. Krones, "Ein französisches Vorbild," 15, leaves it open whether Gossec was "an immediate model" or only meant "an immense addition to that fund of church-music vocabulary" from which Mozart drew, "in accordance with the usage of the time."

24. Cf. Dent, "Forerunners of Mozart's Requiem," and Kosch, "Florian Leopold Gassman." The first two movements of Gassmann's Requiem were published in *Denkmäler der Tonkunst in Österreich*, vol. 83 (Vienna, 1938). The thematic relationship between Mozart's opening movement and Gassmann's, discussed by Dent and Kosch (cf. also Maunder, *Mozart's Requiem*, 74–77), is less significant when the Handel connection is also taken into account.

EXAMPLE II.5. W. F. Bach: Sinfonia D Minor Fk 65, 2d movement (fugue)

EXAMPLE II.6. F.-J. Gossec: Lacrimosa from *Messe des Morts*

Reutter the younger's *Missa S. Caroli* in particular),[25] but it is impossible to distinguish between what he picked up in the general practice of his profession and what he learned by deliberate study.

One especially important source of Mozart's knowledge would have been the repertory—including the work of Handel—explored in the concerts promoted by Baron van Swieten and Count Esterházy, in which Mozart took part. In 1788 he directed a performance of C. P. E. Bach's oratorio *Auferstehung und Himmelfahrt Jesu* Wq 240;[26] this was not only an important and influential work but also a very recent one, having been published only in 1787. In particular, the rich variety of contrasts in the treatment of obbligato instrumental motives in the Requiem (e.g., "Confutatis," bars 1ff. and 7ff.), in a manner largely unknown in Mozart's previous work, is reminiscent of Gossec, but it recalls C. P. E. Bach far more strongly.[27] Mozart also had access to the vocal music of J. S. Bach, whose

25. Mozart transcribed some of Reutter's sacred works in or around 1788–89 (cf. Tyson, *Mozart*, 27, 142–43).
26. Mozart's version of the tenor aria "Ich folge Dir, verklärter Held" K 537d was done on this occasion.
27. Cf. Wolff, "Carl Philipp Emanuel Bach."

Magnificat BWV 243 was to be found among the scores in van Swieten's library.[28] It is true that we do not know if Mozart knew of it, or even studied it—but Bach worked the ninth psalm tone into the Magnificat, in "Suscepit Israel," as Mozart did in his Requiem. Since visiting Leipzig in 1789, when he had improved on his acquaintance with Bach's vocal music through the good offices of Johann Friedrich Doles, Bach's pupil and current cantor of St. Thomas's, Mozart himself had owned a copy of the motet "Singet dem Herrn" BWV 225, which it may be possible to regard as a key to his conception of contrapuntal vocal music.[29] Recalling the Handelian connections of the Requiem, Stadler also referred to Mozart's reception of Bach:

> Mozart inserted a chorale into this opera [*Die Zauberflöte*] that was not of his own invention; moreover for its accompaniment he took an idea of the celebrated Sebastian Bach. To save Herr Weber the trouble of writing letters to discover Bach's chorale tune, I refer him to Kirnberger's *Kunst des reinen Satzes,* Berlin 1774, page 243.[30] It should be observed that Mozart had already composed a totally different accompaniment for this very chorale, which I possess in his manuscript [K 620b (Anh. 78)].[31] But in the last years of his life Mozart still had such respect for the great masters that he preferred their ideas to his own. Anyone who compares these two versions of the chorale will see for himself the different character of this wonderful accompaniment.[32]

There is no mistaking the fact that the conception of vocal contrapuntalism that Mozart consistently realized in the Requiem goes well beyond Handel. The motivic material of bars 20–25 of the Introit, for example, is Handelian in origin, but the counterpoint that permeates the music is from Bach and the stronger

28. Staatsbibliothek zu Berlin (Preussischer Kulturbesitz), Mus. ms. Bach P40 ("Copie für Baron van Swieten," made by C. P. E. Bach's chief copyist in Hamburg, Michel).

29. Mozart's copy of Bach's motet is now in the Gesellschaft der Musikfreunde (Vienna), III 31685; the copy has a note in Mozart's handwriting on fol. 1: "NB. Müsste ein ganzes Orchestre dazu gesezt werden" (Should really have a full orchestral accompaniment written for it).

30. The reference is to the "Song of the Armed Men" in the finale of Act II, Scene 28, of *Die Zauberflöte.* This important observation by Stadler, especially the connection he makes with Kirnberger's book on composition, has been ignored in the relevant literature. See Hammerstein, "Der Gesang der geharnischten Männer," 11; and Gernot Gruber, preface to the edition of *Die Zauberflöte,* NMA II/5, vol. 19, p. xii.

31. This manuscript is among the sketches in the appendix of the Ployer exercise book, which Stadler owned at the time of writing (Österreichische Nationalbibliothck, Hs. 17559); published in the appendix of the NMA edition of *Die Zauberflöte,* II/5, vol. 19, p. 377.

32. Stadler, *Nachtrag zur Vertheidigung,* 12f.

element. That Mozart studied and was influenced by Bach is apparent on every page of the Requiem,[33] not only in the fugal passages but also in the many sections which show strict contrapuntal elaboration; for example: "Rex tremendae," bars 7ff.; "Recordare," *passim;* "Confutatis"; "Domine Jesu," bars 4ff., 21ff., and 32ff. These associations were recognized at an early date by Nissen, who regarded the Requiem as a masterpiece "which unites the power, the sacred dignity of the music of the past with the rich apparel of the music of the present."[34]

A number of the contemporary memoirs expressly state that composing the Requiem made Mozart think of his own death (Doc. 9, 10, 12). Even after making due allowance for fanciful exaggeration (combined with the effect of the legend of his poisoning), there still remains sufficient reason to believe that there is some truth in what Niemetschek wrote in 1798 (Doc. 9). Quite soon after starting to write the work, "Mozart began to speak of death, and declared that he was writing the Requiem for himself." We may also believe his sister-in-law Sophie Haibl, when she recalls in 1825: "The last thing he did was to try and mouth the sound of the timpani in his Requiem; I can still hear it now" (Doc. 10). When Mozart received the commission and began to plan and prepare the work, he can hardly have had any reason to foresee his imminent death, particularly in view of the exceptionally heavy workload he had in that autumn of 1791. But when he was struck down by a severe illness not long afterwards, he undoubtedly realized its gravity; by then he was well into the work of composition, which his illness eventually prevented him from continuing. Thus the idea of "memento mori" may have loomed larger as the moment he stopped working grew closer. A few years earlier, on 4 April 1787, Mozart had written to his father, Leopold, as he lay dying:

> I need hardly tell you how greatly I am longing to receive some reassuring news from yourself. And I still expect it; although I have now made a habit of being prepared in all affairs of life for the worst. As death, when we come to consider it closely, is the true goal of our existence, I have formed during the last few years such close relations with this best and truest friend of mankind, that his image is not only no longer terrifying to me, but is indeed very soothing and consoling! And I thank my God for graciously granting me the opportunity (you know what I mean) of learning that death is the key which unlocks the door to our true happiness. I never lie down at night without reflecting that—young as I am—I may not live to see another day.[35]

33. Cf. Emerson, "Role of Counterpoint in Mozart's Late Style."
34. Nissen, *Wolfgang Mozart's Biographie*, 2:171.
35. Bauer-Deutsch IV, No. 1044; Anderson, 907.

We cannot know precisely how and where this profoundly reflective manner of thinking and living left its mark on the music and the process of composition. We *do* know that the "pathetic style" of the Requiem is not an abstract aesthetic quality but something in which Mozart's maturest musical powers are united with a heightened need for expression—not least because his involvement in this work of all works was of the most intensely personal order.

Individual Aspects
Mozart's Score

That Mozart's Requiem survives only as a fragment is not generally obvious to the listener, because the work is performed either in its traditional form—that is, as completed by Süssmayr—or in one of the versions completed by later editors. These all have in common the fact that the fragmentary character of the original is smoothed over to the point of obliteration. Anyone who wants to discover the form of the work as it was actually written by Mozart must go either to the original manuscript sources (which already include material in hands other than his)[36] or to the edition of the autograph that was first published by Leopold Nowak in the Neue Mozart-Ausgabe;[37] a revised version of the latter is to be found in Part IV of this book. The following comments are based in essence on the musical text of Mozart's fragment.

Knowledge of Mozart's autograph is a prerequisite not only for the study of the authentic text but also particularly for the discussion of the composer's realized and unrealized intentions.[38] All the sections of the score written by Mozart himself are on twelve-stave paper, and the braces gathering the staves into systems even in those parts where the scoring is the least complete (Figs. 3–7) show that he intended to fill them all in. That is, he intended from the first that the autograph was going to be the final fair copy, even if he began by writing down only four vocal parts and a bass line with occasional figures. It is not, therefore, a draft in the sense of something provisional that would be rewritten later; it represents the first stage of Mozart's compositional process, the stage in which he set down, in the form of a particello, a final text that was musically and formally complete. That is, this skeleton score fixes (records) the process of composition. The second stage of making a full score consisted of filling in and developing and thus realizing in full the material already set down at the earlier stage.

36. The facsimile edition of the Requiem published in 1990 by Günther Brosche was the first edition to reproduce the surviving original manuscript in full.
37. NMA I/2, Abt. 2, vol. 1 (1965).
38. See also the facsimile edition (1990).

Mozart's method of writing full scores had been the same since the 1770s. There was a first stage in which he set down large stretches of the musical substance and the work's formal development in short score:[39] this comprised the melodic line of the principal voice (first violin, instrumental solo part, or top vocal line), a bass (not always fully worked out), significant accompanimental figures, and polyphonic passages. Working out the instrumentation occurred in a second stage. Whereas in Mozart's orchestral works the first stage involved setting down the principal voice and some of the subsidiary lines, in the Requiem it is a matter of the whole vocal quartet and the (partly) figured bass, with only occasional indications of the instrumentation—and then in a wholly typical form (Figs. 3–7). Süssmayr's account is quite accurate: "Mozart completed the four vocal parts and the figured bass—but of the instrumentation only indicated motivic ideas here and there" (Doc. 17).

The primacy of the vocal parts is demonstrated not only by the score in its primary state but also by the structure of the completed movements. Compared both to Mozart's late operatic scores and also to his C-minor Mass, the orchestral element is patently less significant in the Requiem, in both its accompanimental and obbligato roles. The longest purely orchestral section is the thirteen-bar introduction to the "Recordare" in the Sequence; even the opening chorus has only seven bars of instrumental introduction. For the rest, there are a large number of very brief passages, acting as introductions or coming between "paragraphs" in the text; the "Tuba mirum," "Rex tremendae," "Lacrymosa," and "Hostias" all have two-bar introductions, but the "Dies irae," "Confutatis," and "Domine Jesu" have none at all. Postludes of three or fewer bars are found following only the "Dies irae" and "Tuba mirum." The contours and structure of each individual movement always develop out of its vocal substance.

Instrumentation

Mozart did not plan a large-scale work for a great state occasion, such as the masses composed by Antonio Lotti and Johann Adolf Hasse for the Dresden court. This had a fundamental effect on the format and layout and on the performing forces for which he wrote the Requiem. His conception—as in the case of his motet "Ave verum corpus" K 618—may also have been influenced by the general conditions arising from the transition and renewal that sacred music went through following the death of Emperor Joseph II in 1790. The reforms initiated by Joseph had imposed painful restrictions on concertante Latin church music in

---

39. Cf. Wolff, Review of *Wolfgang Amadeus Mozart: Requiem.*

Austria, causing it to be in effect banned from 1783 on. For a time scarcely any new church music was written in Vienna; but after 1790 it was once again an attractive field for composers.[40] The simplicity of the musical language and outward guise of "Ave verum corpus" appears to some extent to reflect the repudiation of a style of instrumentally lavish church music, but it also looks forward to a new style that was to flower in the Requiem.

Mozart scored his Requiem for a relatively small instrumental ensemble. There are trumpets and timpani, befitting the solemn dignity of a work of this type, but no horns; there are trombones, but they serve only to support the choir. The basset horns, put to prominent use, are an unusual component, and their dark timbre is enriched by obbligato bassoons; the higher woodwinds (flutes, oboes, and clarinets) are absent; the continuo group consists of organ, violone, and cello. The orchestra is treated strictly as an ensemble; only in the "Tuba mirum" is there a short instrumental solo, for trombone, occasioned by the words. The four-part vocal writing is divided into tuttis and solos, with the lion's share going to the chorus. There are no purely solo numbers, like arias in an oratorio; only two movements are sung entirely by the soloists, but in both all four take part: in the "Tuba mirum" they sing in turn, for the most part, but in the "Recordare" they perform only as a quartet.

No demand for conspicuous virtuosity is made of either the players or the singers—unlike, for example, the Mass in C Minor K 427. The only opportunity for solo ornamentation comes at the fermata in bar 7 of "Tuba mirum"[41]—which is, in any case, the only movement to contain a short instrumental obbligato and therefore the one that comes nearest to having anything of the character of oratorio. The choral writing, in its compact, blocklike structures and its tendency to assign the melody to the top line, even in polyphonic passages, is modeled primarily on Handelian oratorio (Doc. 22);[42] the vocal solo and ripieno parts reflect, at the same time, the idea of a "classical" style of sacred music, with an attack that is comparable to Sarastro's arias and the choruses of the priests in *Die Zauberflöte*.

Only the opening movement in Mozart's fragment contains complete details of the instrumentation; in all the other movements there are substantial gaps (see Table 5). Süssmayr's attempts to make these good (mostly following Eybler's suggestions in the Sequence) are modeled on Mozart's example, but there remain

40. Cf. especially MacIntyre, *Viennese Concerted Mass*, 13–26; Otto Biba, "Church and State," in *Mozart Compendium*, 58–62; Braunbehrens, *Mozart in Wien*, 232–42.
41. Cf. the fermata in the finale of the Piano Concerto in A Major K 414 (NMA V/15, vol. 3, 65).
42. See above, pp. 74–81.

TABLE 5.   Instrumentation Specified in the Original Manuscript

Movement	Mozart	Süssmayr*
1. Requiem-Kyrie	Violini, Viola 2 Corni di Bassetto in F 2 Fagotti 2 Clarini in D, Timpani in D Canto, Alto, Tenore, Basso (T/S) 3 Tromboni (A,T,B colla parte) Organo e Basso	—
2. Dies irae	[Violini, Viole (divisi)] Canto, Alto, Tenore, Basso (T) Organo e Basso	2 Corni di Bassetto 2 Fagotti 2 Clarini, Timpani 3 Tromboni
Tuba mirum	Violini Trombone solo Basso, Tenore, Alto, Canto (S) [Organo e] Violoncello, Basso	Viola 2 Corni di Bassetto 2 Fagotti
Rex tremendae	Violini, Viola Canto, Alto, Tenore, Basso (T) Organo e Basso	2 Corni di Bassetto 2 Fagotti 2 Clarini, Timpani 3 Tromboni
Recordare	[Violini, Viola] 2 Corni di Bassetto Canto, Alto, Tenore, Basso (S) Organo e Basso, Violoncello	2 Fagotti

[ ] Not specified alongside the stave, but scored
 * Following ideas of Eybler (in part, in the Sequence) and possibly Stadler (Offertory)

areas of doubt, most notably the question of which movements should include trumpets and timpani and the extent to which the trombones should be called upon to give the chorus colla parte support (Mozart gives them a partly obbligato role in the first movement). The role of the woodwind is also inconsistent. Mozart appears to have wanted a certain degree of differentiation, especially in the Sequence (solo trombone in the "Tuba mirum," trumpets omitted from the "Recordare"), but his ultimate intentions remain debatable (should the trombones play in the "Recordare"?). There can be no doubt, however, that the Sanctus was meant to be a tutti, and Süssmayr's decision to omit the basset horns from the first Hosanna and include them in the second was perverse.

Movement	Mozart	Süssmayr★
Confutatis	[Violini, Viola] [2 Corni di Bassetto] Canto, Alto, Tenore, Basso (T) [Organo e Basso]	2 Fagotti 2 Clarini, Timpani 3 Tromboni
Lacrymosa	[Violini, Viola] Canto, Alto, Tenore, Basso [T] Organo e Basso	2 Corni di Bassetto 2 Fagotti 2 Clarini, Timpani 3 Tromboni
3. Domine Jesu	Violini, Viola Canto, Alto, Tenore, Basso (T/S) [Organo e] Basso	2 Corni di Bassetto 2 Fagotti 3 Tromboni
Hostias	[Violini, Viola] Canto, Alto, Tenore, Basso (T) Organo e Basso	2 Corni di Bassetto 2 Fagotti 3 Tromboni
4. Sanctus	—	Violini, Viola
5. Agnus Dei	—	2 Corni di Bassetto 2 Fagotti 2 Clarini, Timpani★★ Canto, Alto, Tenore, Basso (T/S★★★) 3 Tromboni Organo e Bassi

★★ Not used in Benedictus
★★★ Differentiated only in the Benedictus (T = Tutti; S = Solo)

Yet more intractable is the problem of the writing of the inner parts. In the opening movement, where Mozart had written them out in full for large stretches, there remained virtually nothing to be decided about those parts that needed to be completed (such as the mechanical colla parte accompaniment in the "Kyrie" fugue). The execution of the composer's outline in the six movements from "Dies irae" to "Hostias" gave considerably more room for maneuver, however. Stadler's estimate that "the important parts were all set out already, and Süssmayr could hardly go wrong" (see Doc. 32) seems therefore overoptimistic, especially when one looks more closely at those passages completed by Mozart.

Two examples will serve. In the first part of the opening chorus we cannot fail to notice the systematic alteration in the violin accompaniment (while the bass remains constant), which leads by stages to greater rhythmic complexity (Ex. II.7). A similar process in the "Confutatis" (bars 26ff.) leads to simultaneous rhythmic diversification in four registers: whole notes for the basset horns, half and quarter notes for the voices, eighths for the continuo, and sixteenths for the violins. Süssmayr's instrumentation lacks this kind of subtlety. He goes to work relatively schematically, for the most part; the most crass example is perhaps in the "Tuba mirum," the third stanza of the Sequence, where Mozart uses the trombone to represent the sound of the last trumpet (bars 1–18). The entry of a string accompaniment in bar 5 is an intelligent and skillfully executed idea (taken from Eybler), but Süssmayr then finds himself obliged to continue the trombone solo from bar 24.[43] Without reflection, he follows Mozart's model (trombone solo), heedless of the change taking place in the character of the music, let alone the nature of the text in the fifth stanza of the Sequence (Ex. II.8).

Styles, Textures, and Forms

The choral movements are by far the most numerous, and their formal variety and disposition are forcibly reminiscent of Handel, whose oratorios Mozart had studied with profit in the late 1780s. First and foremost of the things he took from Handel were the three principal styles or textures, which can be termed "homophonous" (or "chordal"), "cantabile,"and "imitative." The distinctiveness of each of the three styles is most clearly seen when they are juxtaposed in adjacent movements or sections of movements. Thus the imitative writing of the Kyrie is followed directly by primarily chordal declamation in the "Dies irae," while in the Offertory the polyphony of the "Quam olim Abrahae" fugue sets off the homophonous cantabile of the two versicles.

Similar contrasts exist at closer quarters, on a smaller scale. The "Rex tremendae" offers an example of a well-prepared yet sudden transition from homophony to imitative style: bars 3–5 contain separate blocks of homophony in quarter notes; bars 6–7 contain one cohesive homophonous block in dotted notes; and bars 7ff. contain dense imitative texture with mixed note values. The same type of differentiation is also found in the solo movements. In the soprano section of the "Tuba mirum" (Sequence, stanza 7), the first five bars have a pronounced

---

43. In Beyer's edition of the Requiem (1970; 1979) Süssmayr's trombone part is skillfully adapted as the basis of a part for two bassoons.

EXAMPLE II.7. Requiem: string figures

EXAMPLE II.8. Tuba mirum: bars 24ff., trombone (bassoon)

melodic flow, but homophonous declamation ensues without any mediation in bar 45 and ends in a cadence (bars 49–50) that mediates the next phase; in this (bars 51–62) the four vocal soloists offer an expanded and modified variant of the preceding homophonous segment, while the expressive melodic element passes to the violins.

Mozart's deployment of the different vocal textures gives each movement its own distinctive character, enhanced with a rich and varied interior structure; this enables him, notably, not simply to follow where the text leads him[44] but also to evolve elements that underpin the musical form. The Introit, for example, the first part of the first movement, is constructed in distinct sections:

1. imitative thematic introduction, Handelian subject I (instrumental, vocal)
2. homophonous section A
3. contrapuntal cantus firmus setting, Handelian subject II
4. cantus firmus development with chorus B, lightened by imitative-homophonous style
5. development of main subject and counterpoint (i.e., Handelian subjects I and II)
6. modified homophonous section A

Schematically expressed:

	(1)	(2)	(3)	(4)	(5)	(6)
structure	I	A	c.f./II	c.f./B	I/II	A
bar no.	1	15	20	26	33	43

The "Domine Jesu" provides another example of a construction that makes positive use of the vocal textures:

1. cantabile, melodic introduction A (bars 1ff.)
2. melody in the upper lines characterized by large intervallic leaps, above loosely polyphonic texture for the low voices (bars 7ff.)
3. loosely polyphonic reworking of the introductory material A (bars 15ff.)

44. See below, pp. 104–12.

4. imitative development of a motive (large intervallic leaps), which modulates by sequence, with continuo counterpoint C (bars 21ff.)

5. return of the cantabile introductory material A, elaborated in a canon at the fifth (bars 32ff.)

Schematically expressed:

	(1)	(2)	(3)	(4)	(5)
structure	A	B	A	C	A
bar no.	1	7	15	21	32

Merely categorizing the textures does not do justice to Mozart's musical intentions, for we are continually surprised within the individual categories by the manifold variety, which prevents any repetitiousness. This applies, for example, to the two fugues ("Kyrie" and "Quam olim Abrahae")—and to more than their structure and form. Both employ stretto from the start: a strict fugue with a constant countersubject in the earlier movement and a free fugue (without colla parte strings) in the later, where the fugal texture dissolves by stages after bar 67. Equally important are the differences in the handling of the thematic material in the two fugues and the structural consequences of those differences. The first fugue, true to its Handelian origins, follows the customary pattern of a choral fugue, in which formal integrity and stability are guaranteed; the second, by contrast, forgoes an integrated subject and thus paves the way for the gradual dissolution of the fugal texture.

The "Amen" fugue survives only as a sketch, but it is enough to make it possible to judge that its polythematicism (see Ex. I.3) indicates that Mozart planned something palpably different from the other two fugues and underlines his intention to differentiate among voices even within sections written in the same style. Within the formal scheme of the work as a whole, it is absolutely necessary for the Sequence to finish with a fugue so that there is one to end each of the five main sections; another feature of the five fugues is that their meters alternate between common and triple time (see Table 4). The "Hosanna" fugue (setting aside the weaknesses of Süssmayr's completion of it) is a decisively original conception in that it is based on a strongly shaped theme, elaborates the fundamental element of the subject of the "Quam olim Abrahae" fugue,[45] and thus provides

45. This was pointed out by Abert, *W. A. Mozart* (1955–56), 2:723.

the basis for structural stability overall (Ex. II.9). The distinctive originality of the "Hosanna" fugue is also demonstrated by the syncopated triple-meter beginning and above all by its richly contrasting internal contouring (construction in 3 + 3 bars with asymmetrical layout; syncopation at the start; regular eighth-note motion at the finish).

Mozart's approach to fugue is one manifestation of a twofold ambition to follow and build on tradition while transforming it—we might recall Nissen's comment on his uniting "the sacred dignity of the music of the past with the rich apparel of the music of the present."[46] It is therefore no accident that the entire Requiem is embedded in a stylistic framework made to order: the music of the Introit and Kyrie is the starting point, its repetition with a different text is the goal. Mozart takes tradition in the form of the Handelian model, enhances it by adding the plainchant psalm tone, and at the same time impresses the stamp of the new on it at every level of the composition. The transformation of the old into the new is already evident in the very first bars, as the polyphony is enriched by the carefully shaded play of tone color.

An important new element is at work in the variety of ways in which Mozart deploys his instruments, from straightforward colla parte (e.g., the basset horns and trombones in the Introit, bars 7ff.) to strict obbligato accompaniment (e.g., the strings in the same section, bars 20ff.). He appears to want to avoid pure a capella texture, although sometimes he gets close to it, cutting off the obbligato accompaniment at particular points, such as at "salva me, fons pietatis" at the end of "Rex tremendae" (bars 20–22). The subordination of the instrumental element is particularly noticeable when Mozart dispenses with any kind of orchestral introduction ("Dies irae," "Confutatis," "Domine Jesu"), and yet it is precisely in these places that the orchestra's special strengths are shown and its potential for differentiation is seen to be equal to that of the vocal writing. As Mozart's particello demonstrates, it is primarily—almost exclusively—the strings that he uses to develop the vocal writing; the function of the wind instruments is largely supportive (this is true even of the two pairs of woodwinds, except in a few instances such as the "Recordare"), and they do not venture far from the realm of a "Harmoniemusik."

The orchestra's essential role, apart from giving colla parte support, is to reinforce the score by adding a rhythmic dimension as well as tone color. Comparison of the string accompaniment in the "Dies irae"—tremololike and transfused with

---

46. See above, p. 84.

EXAMPLE II.9.   Osanna and Quam olim Abrahae: fugal themes

accented notes—with the tremolo in the "Confutatis" (bar 24 to the end) shows how rhythmic figuration and shifting accents can be used in different ways to develop an instrumental foil that supports the voices and intensifies the musical expression. The ways in which partly obbligato accompanimental voices are formed depend on the music's texture and can result in substantial differences that amount to a deliberate means of modification. In addition, the instruments make an independent contribution in a number of unobtrusive ways: preimitating vocal material (in extended form in the prelude of the opening movement, most concisely in the trombone solo introducing the "Tuba mirum"); presenting pointedly contrasting material ("Rex tremendae" and "Confutatis"); accommodating vocal and instrumental textures to each other.

This last technique is put to especially good effect in the prelude of the "Recordare." This is the longest purely instrumental passage in the Requiem, and it exemplifies the synthesis of vocal and instrumental counterpoint. The basset horns with their two-part syncopated counterpoint (X; see Ex. II.10) act as substitutes for human voices, while the cellos offer an opposing instrumental counterpoint (Y). In the next segment (bars 7–13) the instrumental counterpoint, now in three parts, occupies the upper register, while the "vocal" syncopated counterpoint descends to the bass. This exchange takes place strictly according to the rules of double counterpoint. On the entrance of the singers (bar 14), oblique motion (bass, bar 14) is added to the contrapuntal texture, and the weave as a whole

EXAMPLE II.10.   Recordare: counterpoints

becomes denser and extends over a wider area. The rondolike form of the movement as a whole is decisively shaped by the dialectic of the two counterpoints, X and Y, as the following analysis indicates; in particular the use of the Y material in the manner of a ritornello is a strong unifying force.

1. instrumental introduction, X/Y
2. stanza 9a, X/Y; stanza 9b, new musical idea A
3. prelude Y to stanza 10, new idea B with counterpoint Y
4. prelude Y to stanza 11a, X/Y, stanza 11b, idea A
5. prelude Y to stanza 12, new idea C, stanza 13, new idea D
6. stanza 14a, X/Y, stanza 14b, new idea E
7. stanza 15a, idea A, stanza 15b, idea F, postlude Y

Schematic outline (lower-case letters = instrumental passages)

	(1)	(2)	(3)	(4)	(5)	(6)	(7)
structure	x/y –	X/y, A –	y, B/y –	y, X/y, A –	y, C, D –	X/y, E –	A, F, y
bar no.	1	14 26	34 38	52 54	68 72 84	93 105	110 119

Harmonic Design

Many of the strands that make up the musical fabric of the Requiem—melody and rhythm, periodic structures and contrapuntalism or voice leading, the vocal and instrumental writing—could be singled out for analysis and stylistic criticism. But it would serve a useful purpose only if it were done with reference to Mozart's numerous other works, particularly those composed since the mid-1780s, for there are cross-connections and evolutionary developments that cannot be ignored. While there are still important parallels to be drawn with other works by Mozart, however, the Requiem's harmonic design is the technical element that is more original, more independent of precedent, and altogether newer than anything else in the work.

Mozart's starting point in the selection of his principal key was, we may be certain, the Dorian mode of the Sequence's "Dies irae," which thus comes to impress itself decisively on the entire Requiem, even if the medieval melody associated with the mode is never actually heard. But the mere fact that D minor is the main key is finally less important than the way in which the spectrum of D-related keys is used in the work.

Of course there are other works in D minor by Mozart. Prime examples include the quartets K 173 and K 421; the Piano Concerto K 466; Electra's aria in Act I and the closing chorus in Act II of *Idomeneo*, the Queen of the Night's Act II aria in *Die Zauberflöte*, and preeminently the overture and long stretches of *Don Giovanni*; finally the Kyrie K 341, which can be dated well into the Vienna period.[47] Whether there is a text or the expression is purely instrumental, it is the "pathetic," indeed demonic qualities of the key that Mozart brings out, but without ever exploiting their potential so systematically as he was to do in the Requiem. For all its many movements, the structure of the Requiem is never lost to sight; and as a setting of the mass for the dead its textual content provides abundant expressive references; consequently, compared to cyclic compositions in three movements (K 421 and K 466), or even *Don Giovanni*, with its far more extensive spectrum of tonalities, the work offers a wholly different range of possibilities and challenges to define D minor, together with its entire field of harmonic relations, for the purposes of a large-scale cyclic form.

In focusing on D minor in the Requiem, Mozart imposes greater restrictions on himself than in the Mass in C Minor K 427 of 1783, which has ga movement in E minor ("Quoniam").[48] Sharp-side tonalities, even the dominant A major, are excluded from the range of keys selected for the individual movements of the Requiem; the only exception to that rule is D major, the tonic major. The overall layout (see Table 6 and also Table 4) is dominated by three large D-minor structures (Introit–Kyrie, Sequence, and Agnus Dei–Communion), thrown into relief by the subdominant G minor of the Offertory and the D major of the Sanctus (assuming that that key was Mozart's choice).

The opening and closing D-minor sections stay within tight harmonic bounds throughout their two parts (B-flat major is used once only in each), but the six-movement Sequence uses a wider range of tonalities. Only its first and last movements are in the tonic, which otherwise appears only once, for maximum effect, at the climactic end of the third movement ("Rex tremendae"), in the setting of the line "salva me, fons pietatis" (bars 18ff.). This movement and one other in the Sequence ("Confutatis") start in one key and modulate to another: the former from the subdominant G minor to the tonic, and the latter from the dominant minor, A minor, to the submediant F major. The other two inner movements

47. See above, p. 36.

48. We have no means of knowing how Mozart would have organized a mass in D minor, but the Kyrie K 341, which is undated but clearly belongs in the late 1780s, could have been part of one (see Tyson, *Mozart*, 27).

TABLE 6.   Overall Tonal Design of the Requiem

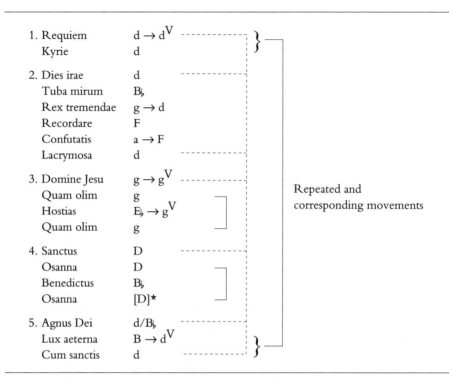

| 1. Requiem | $d \rightarrow d^V$ |
| Kyrie | d |

2. Dies irae	d
Tuba mirum	B♭
Rex tremendae	$g \rightarrow d$
Recordare	F
Confutatis	$a \rightarrow F$
Lacrymosa	d

3. Domine Jesu	$g \rightarrow g^V$
Quam olim	g
Hostias	$E♭ \rightarrow g^V$
Quam olim	g

4. Sanctus	D
Osanna	D
Benedictus	B♭
Osanna	[D]★

5. Agnus Dei	d/B♭
Lux aeterna	$B \rightarrow d^V$
Cum sanctis	d

Repeated and corresponding movements

★ Süssmayr: Repetition of "Osanna" in B♭ major
→ Movements ending on the dominant, followed by an attacca

("Tuba mirum" and "Recordare") are in the mediant and submediant keys, B-flat major and F major, so that the tonic D minor appears framed by its lower and upper thirds.

The two main sections that are not in D minor, the Offertory and the Sanctus, extend the tonal field of reference by intent. The subdominant G minor, having appeared already in the Sequence, receives a stronger accent in the Offertory. In turn, it enables its own submediant, E-flat major, a key remote from D minor, to be used in the "Hostias." But if the tonal design of the Offertory can be called logical, that of the Sanctus and Benedictus, as composed by Süssmayr, is problematical and reinforces the doubt surrounding the authenticity of the recurrence of the "Hosanna" fugue in the Benedictus in B-flat major. If it were in D major, the Sanctus would fit the overall tonal design without strain and would correspond formally to the Offertory, including the move to the submediant (B-flat major in this case) at the start of the Benedictus. Be that as it may, the tonal plan of the Sanctus enlarges the harmonic spectrum in that it turns a spotlight on the tonic major before the definitive return to D minor. The alternation of major and minor keys is interrupted for the first time in the work, leaving the major mode in sole command. The ground has been well prepared for D major's appearance by the G-minor Offertory, both movements of which end in a half cadence on the dominant D before the start of the "Quam olim Abrahae" fugue ("Domine Jesu," bar 32; "Hostias," bar 54).

Steps of a third (mediant and submediant) are preferred to the fifth as a general rule in the tonal design of the individual movements and of the larger groups. Within individual movements, the decision to make as intensive and refined a use as possible of the field of tonal relationships is an important factor. The internal harmonic progressions (see Table 7) reveal an unparalleled harmonic density—particularly in view of the relative brevity of the individual movements. The principal tonality, D minor—historically the naturally chromatic key, the "genus chromaticum"[49]—allows Mozart to modulate to every degree in the chromatic scale in the course of the Requiem. Given the unmistakable melodic role that the underlying chromaticism plays in the opening movement (cf. especially the chromatic "lamento" bass of the half cadence, bars 47–48), we cannot fail to notice that its use as a modulatory technique is introduced only gradually.

The internal harmonic structure of the Introit rests on no more than three pivotal points (F major, G minor, B-flat major), while the Kyrie, in addition to them, introduces C minor (bars 23ff.) and F minor (bars 32ff.). With the Sequence, as Table 7 shows, the harmonic framework begins to spread much wider, and wider still in the Offertory, especially in the "Hostias," which moves from its tonic E-flat major to the remote regions of F- and B-flat minor and D-flat and A-flat major. Mozart uses a wide range of modulatory techniques to create the colorful harmonic design of this movement, from abrupt shifts (bars 21–23: B-flat major to B-flat minor) to harmonic and melodic sequence (bars 27–34: D-flat major to A-flat major, F minor to C major).

The harmonic progressions within the individual movements and the intentions revealed by them increase the uncertainties surrounding the movements Mozart

---

49. Well-known examples are Sweelinck's Fantasia chromatica and Bach's Chromatic Fantasy and Fugue, among many others; the G mode (transposed Dorian), later G minor, functioned as a secondary "genus chromaticum" from the seventeenth century. Mozart was yet another composer who made a point of chromatically enriching the two keys D minor and G minor.

TABLE 7.   Internal Harmonic Progressions

Movement	Tonal spectrum and scale steps* (bar no.)
Composed/drafted by Mozart	
Requiem	**d**–F(14f)–**B**♭(19)–g(26f)–g(32)–d(34)–**B**♭(43)–**d**(46) →
Kyrie	**d**–F(16)–g(20)–c(24)–**B**♭(28)–f(33)–d(39)–**d**
Dies irae	**d**(8)–F(10)–//–**a**(19)–**c**(31)–//–d^V(40)–d(56)–**d**
Tuba mirum	**B**♭–**f**(18)–**g**(24)–**d**(29)–**B**♭(40)–//–**d**(51)–g/C(56f)–**B**♭
Rex tremendae	**g**–//–F(12)–//–**A/a**(16f)–d(18f)–**d**
Recordare	**F**–C–F(14)–C–G(26)–//–C(34)–**c**(38)–//–d(44)–**B**♭(54)–//–
	B♭(68)–c(76)–**d**(80)–a/g(85ff)–C/F(92f)–**C**(105)–//–F(118)–**F**
Confutatis	**a**–C(7f)–C/c(10)–//–**a**(16f)–**a**♭(29)–**g**(33)–F(38)–F(39) →
Lacrymosa	**d**–//(5f)–[d(9)–//–d(14)–//–**F**(19)–d(22)–//–d]
Amen	[g–**d**]
Domine Jesu	**g**–//–D/B♭(7)–c(10)–//–**c/A**♭(14f)–F/b♭(17f)–//–g(20)–//–
	D(30)–**g**(32)–//–D/g(43f) →
Quam olim	**g**(44)–//–g(67)–//–**g**
Hostias	**E**♭–B♭–E♭(10)–G/c(15f)–**B**♭(21)–b♭(23)–D♭(27)–A♭(30)–f(31)–C(34)–
	//–A/d(38f)–//–**E**♭(44)–//–D →
Quam olim	**g**(44)–//–g(67)–//–**g**
By Süssmayr	
Sanctus	**D**–**D**(10) →
Osanna	**D**–(28)–**D**
Benedictus	**B**♭–F(10)–d(15)–**F**(18)–F(23)–**B**♭(28)–E♭(33)–**F**(38)–**B**♭(46) →
Osanna	**B**♭–**B**♭
Agnus Dei	**d**–F(9f)–F(17)–E/G(24f)–**C**(31)–B♭ | d(41)–F →
Lux aeterna	**B**♭–g(8)–**g**(14)–d(16)–B♭(25)–**d**(30) →
Cum sanctis	**d**–F(47)–g(50)–c(54)–**B**♭(58)–f(63)–d(69)–**d**

* Without specifying the functions (dominants, major/minor relatives, mediants etc.), pivotal modulatory changes in bold type

// Several harmonies touched briefly during passages of rapid modulation

→ Attacca link to following movement

[ ] Not by Mozart

did not compose. The "Lacrymosa" does not correspond to the preceding movements of the Sequence in the disposition of harmonic pivotal points (especially when account is taken of Mozart's eminently chromatic opening to the movement, bars 5–8), nor do the movements that follow the Offertory (see Table 7). The Benedictus, in particular, suffers from harmonic poverty; the Agnus Dei is less unfortunate. Because of the strong contrast between the texts of these two movements, it is desirable for them to have different word–tone relationships; furthermore, it is in the tradition of the genre that the Agnus Dei should have greater modulatory variety. Apart from those considerations, the fundamentally weaker harmonic contours of the Benedictus (above all the excessive emphasis on the dominant) support the supposition that Süssmayr was following Mozart's directives in the Agnus Dei.[50]

The abundance of the modulations in Mozart's music, over both greater and smaller spans, is overwhelming, and—as the composer's outline score shows—they are developed virtually exclusively from the vocal writing. A few examples will have to serve to illustrate the various types of harmonic procedure Mozart uses:

(1)   Movement by neighboring tones. Bar 104 in the concluding part of the extensive "Recordare" initiates a series of cadences that lead to F major (bars 105, 118, 122, 126, 130). The second of these cadences is extended for longer than might be thought its share, and in a highly sophisticated manner. The dominant, C major, is clearly presented in bars 105, 107, and 109, but in other bars it is "muted" by diminished chords on the neighboring degrees B♮ (bar 106) and D♭ (bar 108); this process widens in a kind of harmonic pendulum action, marked by the notes C♮, D♭, B♮, and B♭ in the bass (bars 110–15), and this action, by means of enharmonic change (D♭ = C♯), finally allows the cadence to reach its conclusion in bar 116 with the sequence of triads: D minor, B-flat major, C major, and F major.

(2)   Stepwise alternation of major and minor. In the "Domine Jesu" Mozart works with the triadic head motive in a way that allows the melodic element (which is such a prominent factor of this movement) to become the peg on which the harmonic developments are hung. The opening section introduces three versions of the head motive, one after another, in G minor (bars 1f.), A-flat major (bars 15f.), and B-flat minor, finishing on a major third (bars 18ff.; Ex. II.11). This rising series of statements of the head motive, in alternately minor and major keys, is given to the soprano alone, but it prepares the imitative development (bars 32ff.) carried out by all four voices in descending canon at the fifth. The imitative working exploits the motive's ambivalent major/minor third (B♭/B♮, E♭/E♮, etc.) and thus extracts the quintessence of the separate major and minor versions of it.

50. The harmonic darkening (G sharp, C sharp) in the concluding bars of the Agnus Dei is surely another instance.

EXAMPLE II.11.   Domine Jesu: principal motive (bars 1f., 15f., 18f.)

(3)   Alternating harmonic rhythm. The first part of the "Hostias" is harmonically very restrained, in the context of the cantabile choral writing, moving within the range E-flat major, C minor, and B-flat major. Its middle section (bars 21–44) leads back from B-flat major to E-flat major, but the progression takes a volatile modulatory course, initiated by an abrupt shift from B-flat major to B-flat minor (bar 23). It then progresses through F major, D-flat major, A-flat major, F minor, and C minor toward a D-minor cadence (bar 38) and then, through a second chord with altered tonic C♮/C♭ (bars 40f.), to a final E-flat major. The rapid alternations of the harmonic rhythm do not disrupt the melodic flow of the vocal writing; Mozart manages this above all by using sustained notes extensively (bars 23–26, 39–42) and by confining intervallic movement in the soprano part to a limited range of stepwise progression.

(4)   Enharmonic change. The closing section of the "Confutatis" (bars 25ff.) sets the seventeenth stanza of the Sequence ("Oro supplex"), modulating in each line of the text. The first line goes from A minor to A-flat minor, the second to G minor, and the two-part third phase finally, by way of a noncadencing enharmonic modulation G♭/F♯, to F major (Ex. II.12).

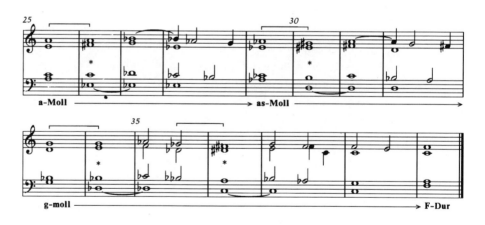

EXAMPLE II.12.   Confutatis: modulatory procedures (bars 25–39)

The chromatic-enharmonic progression moves to each next step by way of an augmented second chord (indicated by an asterisk in the example). The necessary nonmelodic tritone steps in the bass are balanced by unifying and (where appropriate) enharmonically changed cadential target notes in the soprano A (bars 25f.), A♭/G♯ (bars 29f.), G♮ (bars 33f.), and G♭/F♯ (bars 35f.). The first two modulations each take place within a four-bar period. In the interests of increasing tension, the last two take place without internal periodization, in an asymmetrical, seven-bar scheme.

Constantin Floros has pointed out that the model for this last technique may have come from the "Miserere" of the *Missa S. Caroli* by Georg Reutter the younger, Capellmeister of St. Stephen's in Vienna at the time he composed it (1734).[51] Reutter's work does indeed display a concentrated modulatory technique, based on chromaticism and enharmonic change, but it differs markedly from Mozart in detail (Ex. II.13). Nevertheless, it can be accepted that in his preparation for writing the Requiem Mozart probably studied the tradition of related vocal genres, especially mass and oratorio, and looked further afield than Handel and Michael Haydn. However, even when it can be proved beyond a shadow of doubt that this work or that served as his model, Mozart's distance from the originals always demands more attention than his closeness to them.

The emphasis given to the concluding cadences of some movements performs an important role in the overall harmonic design of the Requiem by underlining important formal divisions. Both parts of the opening movement end, after a marked caesura (bar 46 and bar 50, respectively), with an emphatic homophonic V–I cadence over two and a half bars. A IV–I cadence, over three and a half bars, differently constructed but comparable in function, and again preceded by a caesura, concludes the fugue that occurs twice in the Offertory. The half close after a caesura in the Agnus Dei (bar 45) is formed from an emphatic cadence nearly six bars long. Compared with these, the two-bar plagal ending of the "Lacrymosa" seems underemphasized and the Sanctus, ending after only ten bars, downright abrupt. These are the work of Süssmayr, and their distance from Mozart's cadences is a measure of the weakness of his movement endings.

51. Floros, *Mozart-Studien I*, 135. Reutter's mass is in *Denkmäler der Tonkunst in Österreich*, vol. 88 (1952).

EXAMPLE II.13. G. Reutter the younger: *Missa S. Caroli*

Words and Music

It would be unnecessary to say that the words and the music are inseparable in Mozart's Requiem, if the statement conveyed nothing more than a general observation that is true of vocal music of all kinds. If, however, it is said with reference to the manifold connections, from the general concept of the work down to the invention of individual musical ideas on which the words exercised an influence, then some things appear in a different light. It is clear that even in the concept of the work Mozart distinguished from the beginning between those sections of the text that belong specifically to the mass for the dead on the one hand and those that belong to the regular mass Ordinary—Kyrie, Sanctus, Hosanna, and Benedictus—on the other. In other words, the settings of the Kyrie and the Sanctus (assuming that this section is Mozartian at least in its rudiments) are what might be termed more neutral, while the musical expression in those parts of the liturgy that belong to the mass for the dead alone is incomparably more fervent.[52]

Another distinction occurs between the verse of the Sequence and the prose of the rest. The liturgical prose is treated in traditional motet style and set in accordance with the variation and irregularity of the segments of text, which are shaped by sense. The treatment of the text according to the principles of motet style begins in the Introit, which consists of six vocal segments laid out as follows[53] (the repetition of the Introit antiphon after the two psalm verses, "Te decet hymnus" and "Exaudi," is prescribed in the liturgy):

1a. "Requiem aeternam" (bars 1–14); Handelian subject I

1b. "Et lux perpetua" (bars 15–19): new musical idea A

2a. "Te decet hymnus" (bars 20–25): 9th psalm tone with Handelian subject II = solo

2b. "Exaudi" (bars 26–31): 9th psalm tone with new material B in the accompaniment = tutti

1a. "Requiem aeternam" (bars 32–42): combination of subjects I and II

1b. "Et lux perpetua" (bars 43–48): A material, followed by homophonic half close.

The funereal character of the first main subject is already present in Handel's setting of the poem "The ways of Zion do mourn" (see Ex. II.1), but it is intensified by Mozart's changes to the rhythm. Michael Haydn settled on the key word "hymnus" in the first psalm verse for psalmodic cantus firmus elaboration in his C-minor Requiem, which was undoubtedly one of Mozart's models.[54] The pregnant "lux perpetua" motive may also originate in Michael Haydn's setting of the phrase (Ex. II.14), which Haydn brought back in the last movement of the Schrattenbach Requiem to round off the work as a whole.

The influence of motet style on the segmentation of the text, including the singling out of key individual phrases or words, extends to all the other prose

---

52. There is also a variation in the text of the Agnus Dei: the words "miserere nobis" in the Ordinary of the mass are replaced by "dona eis requiem" in the requiem mass. On topical references in mass composition of the baroque era, see Jaksch, *H. I. F. Biber, Requiem à 15*, 65–80.

53. See above, p. 92.

54. See above, pp. 49–50.

EXAMPLE II.14. M. Haydn: Requiem in C Minor, opening and final choruses

sections in the requiem liturgy. The musical structure of the Sequence, on the other hand, is determined in each movement by the strophic character of the text, although, far from allowing the strict regularity of the stanza form to dominate his music, Mozart makes every effort to alleviate it. It is in the Sequence's opening movement, and especially the first of the two stanzas (bars 1–8), that he sticks most closely to the pattern of the text, with its regular trochees (alternating accented and unaccented syllables), regular periodic structure of four feet in each line, and unvarying rhyme pattern (aaa, bbb, etc.):

/. /. /. /.
Dies irae, | dies illa
solvet saeclum | in favilla:
teste David | cum Sybilla.

Corresponding bars for line 1 (2 + 2) and line 2 (1 + 1) are followed by the two-bar concluding phrase for line 3; the identical rhyme (illa / favilla / Sybilla) is highlighted by the identical formula at the end of each line (two quarter notes). The verse-governed rhythm of the vocal writing is emphasized by the irregular alternation of consonant and dissonant chords, with the caesuras spanned by instrumental syncopation (bars 2, 4, 5–6, etc.). The rest of the movement displays a similar type of declamation, although it is subjected to constant modifications. The bizarre melody of the first violins, with its virtually incessant tremolo in sixteenths, provides a weighty instrumental counterpoint while it links the two stanzas that form this movement.

These brief examples of the two different styles of treating the text reveal one common trait, namely a readiness to be guided by the text, one stage at a time. This affects not only the formal frameworks of the individual movements but even their musical substance. The invention of musical ideas to suit the character of each movement or part of a movement, in accordance with the expressive principles of "pathetic style," is especially evident in the Sequence. Individual segments of the text give Mozart, as it were, the "key" to the right kind of musical ideas for them. Naturally, the vivid imagery of the poem is especially stimulating to the composer's intention.

The gripping pictorial immediacy of the first movement of the Sequence, "Dies irae,"[55] originates in the line "Quantus tremor est futurus," from the second stanza, which suggests the fundamental musical idea (tremor = tremolo) of the whole movement; it is enhanced, in particular, by the tremolo effect of the whole orchestra playing eighth and sixteenth notes in all its registers. The two verse stanzas are sung twice in the first forty bars; from bar 41 Mozart isolates their first lines from the rest and puts them side by side. The unison delivery of "Quantus tremor est futurus" (in bars 40–42, 44–46, 48–50), with its repeated "trembling" figuration, is a striking example of the immediacy of the musical translation.

The invention and development of the musical motivic material in the remaining movements of the Sequence are triggered by certain key phrases in the text, which determine the character of the entire movement in question or at least its often decisive opening gesture. The options of developing the material homogenously or of dividing the movement into two or more sections with different expressive content depend above all on the quantity of text in each movement. In all cases Mozart's decisions about where to subdivide the Sequence were based on the imagery or expressive character of the first stanza in each of the five movements after the first.

- Second movement, "Tuba mirum" (stanzas 3–7). The first line of stanza 3 ("Tuba mirum spargens sonum") inspires the vivid effect of the unaccompanied solo trombone, which launches the movement and furnishes an obbligato throughout the rest of stanza 3.[56] But then, for the vocal opening of stanza 4 ("mors stupebit"), Mozart uses the distinctive opening motive again, transposed from B-flat major to F minor, to express the textual "quaking" in the face of death. A no less impressive effect is created by the repetitions of the "sighing" figure (suspiratio) to

---

55. "Terrifying in its beauty, fearful in its grandeur, is the painting of the Last Judgement 'Dies irae, dies illa' " (Nissen, *Wolfgang Mozart's Biographie*, 2:172).
56. "The trombone solo 'Tuba mirum spargens sonum' fills the hearer with dread" (Nissen, *Wolfgang Mozart's Biographie*, 2:172).

express despair (last line of stanza 7: "Cum vix justus"): heard first as a soprano solo (bar 45: 𝄾 ♩ 𝄾 ♪), then from the chorus, at first sotto voce without syncopation (bar 51: ♩ 𝄾 ♩ 𝄾), and finally syncopated and with dynamic contrast (bar 57: 𝄾 *f* ♩ 𝄾 *p* ♪).

- Third movement, "Rex tremendae" (stanza 8). Once again the first line ("Rex tremendae majestatis") provides the impetus for the musical invention. The use of dotted rhythms follows the baroque convention for paying homage to princes (standardized in the "French" overture), and the whole movement is Handelian in style.

- Fourth movement, "Recordare" (stanzas 9–15). This is an exceptionally long movement, setting six stanzas.[57] The first word, "Recordare," sets the tone for the development of the central musical idea, which is first presented in the orchestral prelude. The concept of thought and reflection (stanza 11 refers to the "dies rationis") suggests to Mozart intricate polyphonic elaboration, using double counterpoint, inversion, and other techniques.

- Fifth movement, "Confutatis" (stanzas 16–17). The musical invention in this movement is kindled by the second line of stanza 16 ("flammis acribis addictis"). Mozart paints the flickering flames in the intense interplay of the four-part choral writing and the unison instrumental counterpoint.

- Sixth movement, "Lacrymosa" (stanzas 18–20). The idea conceived by Mozart for the start of this movement takes up the reference to "tears and mourning" in the first line ("Lacrimosa dies illa"). Sighing and sobbing are a traditional subject for musical word-painting, and a conventional figure is elaborated with great expressiveness in both the orchestral and the vocal writing.[58] While the instruments continue to dwell on the initial motive, however, the voices move to something new after only two bars (bars 5ff.). The ascending line in the soprano, rising one and a half octaves, at first diatonically and then chromatically, underlines the main idea of stanza 18, the resurrection foretold in its second line ("qua resurget").

---

57. Constanze told the Novellos that this movement "was one of his [Mozart's] own greatest favorites" (Doc. 12).

58. "The chorus of lamentation, 'Lacrimosa dies illa' etc., most deceptively imitates a fearful quiet, broken by sobs and groans" (Nissen, *Wolfgang Mozart's Biographie*, 2:172).

This manner of composing by bringing together different but closely interrelated ideas leads to an extraordinarily dense texture with a greatly enhanced power of musical expression. In addition to deploying diverse material simultaneously, however, Mozart also uses contrasting material in succession, which, by its very disruption of musical coherence, produces a comparable intensity of expression. There is an especially striking example of this in the "Confutatis,"[59] where there is an abrupt change of rhythm at the line "voca me cum benedictis" (bars 17ff.), from the ferocity of the preceding bars to a gentleness appropriate to the "Call to the Blessed."[60] At the same time there is a new sound-image that corresponds to the baroque "bassetto" (a texture using high-register instruments for the bass line and no continuo harmony).[61] For a moment, then, we are transported to a musical Isle of the Blessed. It is followed by another new image, that of the contrite suppliant ("oro supplex"), depicted by an emphatic descending modulation (see Ex. II.12).[62]

The end of the "Rex tremendae" (bars 18ff.) provides another very similar instance of sudden structural transformation corresponding to the text and illustrating the inexhaustible variety of Mozart's formal invention. At the cry "salva me" (subito piano), a kind of antiphonal texture is created (with high and low choruses) as the instrumental accompaniment loses its contrapuntal definition and joins in the homophonous declamation of the choir (bar 20) in the prayer to the "fount of pity." All of this leads to the pure sound of an open fifth (Mozart inserts the minor third subsequently in the first violins).

The highlighting of individual portions of the text by musical means so that they stand out in their immediate context is an important feature of the Requiem, but the creation of associations across wide spans is at least equally important. Sometimes, though relatively infrequently, a correspondence between different sections of the text evokes an individual musical reference, as, for example, at the phrase "rex gloriae" in the "Domine Jesu" section of the Offertory. A dotted rhythmic figure suddenly appears in bar 3, without any preparation in the music

59. "This 'Confutatis maledictis' depicts the outbreaks of despair of the damned, in contrast to the rejoicing of the righteous; that contrast, the moment of the greatest musical splendour, bestows a grandiose effect on the music" (Nissen, *Wolfgang Mozart's Biographie*, 2:173).

60. Stadler, *Vertheidigung der Echtheit des Mozart'schen Requiem*, 23.

61. Examples in Bach's work include the arias "Aus Liebe will mein Heiland sterben" (*St. Matthew Passion*), "Jesu deine Gnadenblicke" (*Ascension Oratorio*), and "Wie zittern und wanken" (from BWV 105).

62. Nissen draws attention to the "uniquely beautiful painting in the accompaniment" at this point (*Wolfgang Mozart's Biographie*, 2:173).

immediately preceding it, and creates a direct allusion to the dotted rhythms in the third movement of the Sequence, especially the choral harmonies in bar 6, demonstrating that the "rex gloriae" is the same "rex tremendae majestatis" who was invoked earlier.

An example of a correspondence purely of musical form, without any textual cause, appears in the beginnings of the Sanctus and the Sequence (see Ex. I.7). On the other hand the text clearly generates the formal function exercised by the four fugues, which are all repeated (that is, performed twice for structural reasons). The texts of all four ("Kyrie/Christe eleison"; "Quam olim Abrahae"; "Osanna in excelsis"; "Cum sanctis tuis") are age-old, evoking the early church, the covenant of the Old Testament, and the communion of saints. Mozart had every reason, therefore, to select fugue, with its unique status in musical tradition, as the appropriate form for the setting of such texts and as the corner posts of his structural scheme (see Table 4).

Of even greater significance, however, is the way Mozart pieces together a text-generated network of associations with the aim of creating cyclic integration. Such wider relationships rest first and foremost upon certain elements of the liturgical text, between which there is a large degree of identity. The composer has no influence on where these phrases come in the text, but the repetition of key words such as "lux" and "requiem," for example, sometimes assumes strategic importance in the music's formal scheme:

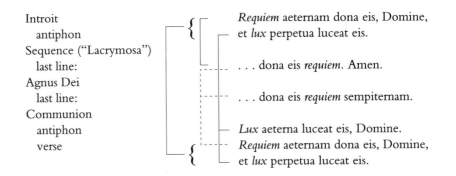

The association between the "lux perpetua" of the Introit and the "lux aeterna" of the Communion induced Michael Haydn, twenty years before Mozart, to repeat the passage from his opening chorus at the end of his Requiem (see Ex. II.14). Mozart, however, went far beyond motivic reminiscence (if we accept the probability that, in exactly repeating a large part of the opening movement, Süssmayr followed Mozart's outline). Bracketing together the opening and concluding movements gives the work as a whole a monumental frame, with a foundation in the text, where there are also associations ("dona eis requiem") to link the inner movements to the frame. Mozart's musical realization of those inner associations is especially striking in the case of the "Lacrymosa," for the harmonies of the first bar of that movement are identical to those of the first bar of the whole work.

Obviously Süssmayr was on firm ground when he allowed the main "Requiem" theme to be heard again at the end of the Sequence, too, although he shrank from melodic-contrapuntal integration, as he did from fugal elaboration of the "Amen." The strength of his position is demonstrated by the unmistakable quotation of the melody just before the end of the "Lacrymosa" (bar 26), even though it seems metrically incorrect at that particular point and certainly cannot have been meant by Mozart to assume the precise form it does (Ex. II.15).[63] Why the musical associations between the "Requiem" theme and the end of the "Lacrymosa" are not extended to the Agnus Dei (see Exx. I.5 and I.11), in spite of the correspondence in the text, is probably due to Süssmayr's failure to understand either the work's integrated conception or Mozart's principle of placing the invention and ordering of musical ideas at the service of the "unity of the material."[64] In any event, it looks as if Süssmayr at least took enough from the "scraps of paper" to have a genuinely Mozartian vocabulary at his disposal. Ultimately that is the reason for the undeniable strength of the completion of the Requiem,

EXAMPLE II.15. Lacrymosa: bars 26–28

63. This gives a concrete example of the traces of preliminary drafts or instructions that were left by Mozart and can be sensed throughout Süssmayr's completion. They are wholly eliminated by Maunder in his 1988 completion.

Wilhelm Fischer discusses the clumsy polyphony of bars 24–28 of the "Lacrymosa" and suggests a corrected version (Fischer, "Das 'Lacrimosa dies illa,' " 15–16), but he does not take the recurrence of the "Requiem" main theme into account.

64. Cf. Wolff, " 'Musikalische Gedankenfolge' und 'Einheit des Stoffes.' "

from the Sanctus onward. Its weakness is primarily structural, for those same scraps of paper will certainly not have given any clues to Mozart's architecture. That was something he always kept in his head, not on paper, and in the case of the Requiem he took it to his grave. Thus the unfinished composition and the untimely end to his life combine to make the Requiem an incomparably eloquent fragment.

CHAPTER THREE

Contemporary Documents

Genesis and Early Reception of Mozart's Requiem

Preliminaries

A coherent and comprehensive documentation of the material relating to Mozart's Requiem and the historical Requiem controversy has not been assembled to date. If it existed and if it were complete, it would require more space than is available here, although it would undoubtedly promote a better general view of the uncommonly complicated course of events. But while a more detailed documentation would strengthen the picture that emerges from the following selection, it would not change it in its essentials. There remain, furthermore, as there have always been, crucial gaps which will never be closed—what would we not give for a sight of the agreement that must have been reached by Constanze Mozart and Süssmayr (cf. Doc. 6)!

The selection takes account of disparate material drawn from original sources and more recent publications, and the attempt has been made to present it in an order that will provide some sense of narrative. Other relevant documentary material supplementing this selection is to be found above all in Bauer-Deutsch IV, Eibl VI, and the article by Plath, "Requiem-Briefe: Aus der Korrespondenz Joh. Anton Andrés 1825–1831."[1] Material about Antonio Salieri and/or the legend that Mozart was poisoned, which was already in circulation before 1800, is not included; although some of it refers to the Requiem, no concrete connections have ever been established.[2] Most of the voluminous material generated by the

---

1. This volume contains, among other things, the correspondence concerning the disposition of Mozart's musical estate; cf. also Eibl VII (index).
2. Cf. Deutsch, "Die Legende von Mozarts Vergiftung"; Bär, *Mozart;* Davies, "Mozart's Illnesses"; Hans Bankl, "Mozarts Tod—Fakten und Legenden," *Zaubertöne* (1990): 538–41.

Requiem controversy has also been passed over, notably Gottfried Weber's series of articles (1825–28) and Georg Siever's pamphlet (1829). Substantial passages from Weber are, however, quoted in Part I of the present volume, and excerpts from Maximilian Stadler's essays in response to Weber's attacks are included here because of what they say about the work's genesis (Docs. 22, 27).

Chronology

Listing together the most important known dates in the history of the Requiem and the subsequent controversy presents a succinct overview of events and allows the documents on the following pages to be placed in their context, thus helping to illuminate their content.

14 February 1791

Anna Countess von Walsegg, née Edle von Flammberg, dies.

9 May 1791

Mozart is appointed unpaid adjunct Capellmeister at St. Stephen's Cathedral in Vienna; it is also agreed that the post of principal Capellmeister will revert to Mozart in succession to Leopold Hofmann (Docs. 1–3).

17 June 1791

Motet "Ave verum corpus" K 618.

Summer 1791

Before the commission from the Bohemian Estates for the coronation opera *La clemenza di Tito* (mid-July), and at the latest before Mozart leaves Vienna for Prague (Doc. 8), Franz Count von Walsegg commissions a requiem mass for his late wife. He uses an intermediary and guards his anonymity very strictly. Mozart asks for a fee of 50 ducats and receives 25 ducats in advance (Docs. 9, 11, 16b, 16h, 20).

ca. 25 August 1791

Mozart leaves for Prague, accompanied by Franz Xaver Süssmayr, who assists in the work associated with the composition of *La clemenza di Tito* K 621 (first performance 6 September).

Mid-September

Mozart leaves Prague; written work on the Requiem begins after his return to Vienna.

30 September 1791

First performance of *Die Zauberflöte* K 620 in Vienna.

15 November 1791

Last entry in Mozart's catalog of his works: the Masonic Cantata "Laut verkünde unsre Freude" K 623 (performed under Mozart's direction on 17 November).

16–20 November 1791

Work on the Requiem resumed (Docs. 10, 12).

ca. 20 November 1791

Mozart takes to his bed with the illness that will eventually kill him.

4 December 1791

Around 2 P.M. some of the movements from the Requiem are sung through by Mozart, Süssmayr, Constanze, Schak, Hofer and Gerl (Doc. 11).

5 December 1791

Around 1 A.M. Mozart dies. He leaves an unfinished score of the Requiem, as well as some sketches and "scraps of paper" (Doc. 22; Figs. 1–7).

Before 10 December 1791

Freystädtler enters strings and woodwinds in the "Kyrie" fugue of Mozart's Requiem score (by and large merely doubling the vocal parts) in preparation for the upcoming performance.

10 December 1791

A requiem mass for Mozart is held in St. Michael's church in Vienna, at which a part or parts of the unfinished Requiem are sung (Docs. 4, 5; Fig. 10).

21 December 1791

Joseph Eybler acknowledges his receipt of the unfinished score of the Requiem, undertaking to complete it by the middle of the coming Lent (Doc. 6).

February 1792

Süssmayr finishes the score for Count Walsegg, and two copies are made for Constanze Mozart.

Before 4 March 1792

A copy is made for King Friedrich Wilhelm II of Prussia, who pays 450 florins for it (Doc. 7).

2 January 1793

First performance of the completed Requiem in the Jahn-Saal in Vienna, at a concert organized by Baron van Swieten for the benefit of Constanze and her children (*Mozart-Dokumente*, 409; *Mozart DB*, 467).

14 December 1793

Liturgical performance of the Requiem directed by Count Walsegg in the church of the Cistercian monastery (the Neuklosterkirche) in Wiener Neustadt. The count uses a copy of the score which bears the heading "Requiem composto del Conte Walsegg" (*Mozart-Dokumente*, 410; *Mozart DB*, 468). It was sung again on 14 February 1794 (Doc. 14).

20 April 1796

Performance of the Requiem in Leipzig, directed by Johann Gottfried Schicht (later Cantor of St. Thomas's; Doc. 15).

1797

Georg Nicolaus Nissen takes lodgings with Constanze Mozart (they marry 26 June 1809).

1789–99

The manuscripts left by Mozart are sorted and listed by Nissen and Abbé Maximilian Stadler.

1799

Breitkopf & Härtel of Leipzig open negotiations with Constanze over the first edition of the Requiem (Docs. 16a–n); they also bid unsuccessfully to buy those of Mozart's manuscripts which are in her possession, but they go to Johann Anton André of Offenbach in November 1799.

8 February 1800

Süssmayr writes to Breitkopf & Härtel about his part in composing the Requiem (Doc. 17).

Summer 1800

Breitkopf & Härtel publish the first edition of the full score of the Requiem.

Before 6 August 1800

A meeting in the offices of the Viennese lawyer Johann Nepomuk Sortschan, at which the sources are collated and marked by Abbé Stadler (Doc. 18).

1801

Johann Anton André publishes a vocal score.

Before 2 June 1802

Süssmayr returns autograph material to Constanze (Doc. 16n).

17 September 1803

Franz Xaver Süssmayr dies.

1812

Performing parts published by the Chemische Druckerei, Vienna.

1820

Georg Nicolaus and Constanze Nissen move from Vienna to Salzburg.

August 1825

Gottfried Weber publishes "Über die Echtheit des Mozartschen Requiem"; other articles follow, 1826–27.

22 March 1826

"A friend" gives Abbé Stadler Mozart's autograph of the Sequence up to "Confutatis" (Docs. 27, 30).

24 March 1826

Georg Nicolaus Nissen dies.

Spring 1826

Maximilian Stadler publishes his *Vertheidigung der Echtheit des Mozart'schen Requiem,* two sequels (Nachträge) follow in 1827.

Autumn 1826

André of Offenbach publishes an edition of the score of the Requiem, with a lengthy preface (Doc. 26a), and marked to distinguish Mozart's work from Süssmayr's.

11 November 1827

Franz Count von Walsegg dies.

1828

Nissen's *Wolfgang Amadeus Mozart's Biographie* is published.

1829

André of Offenbach publishes a new edition of the Sequence and Offertory in full score "after Mozart's original manuscript," with a preface.

1829–31

The Court Library in Vienna acquires a first section of Mozart's autograph (Sequence, up to "Confutatis") from Abbé Stadler (according to Doc. 12 it was deposited there in 1829).

8 November 1833

Maximilian Stadler dies.

1833

The Court Library receives a second section of Mozart's autograph ("Lacrymosa" and Offertory) from Joseph Eybler.

1838

A third section of Mozart's autograph is purchased by the Court Library for 50 ducats (the same as Mozart's original fee). This comprises the Introit and Kyrie, with additions by Süssmayr, and came from Count Walsegg's estate, having first passed to other owners.

1839

Exchange of letters about the score between Ignaz von Mosel and Constanze Nissen (Docs. 31, 32); Mosel publishes *Über die Original-Partitur des Requiem von W. A. Mozart.*

1 December 1841

Franz Jacob Freystädtler dies in Vienna.

6 March 1842

Constanze Nissen (née Weber, Mozart's widow) dies in Salzburg.

24 July 1846

Joseph Eybler, retired Court Capellmeister, dies in Vienna.

Documents

The following documents are taken from published sources, all German except the source for No. 12, but many of them have also been published before in English translation. Following the heading of each document, a parenthetical note gives the German source and either the source of the translation used here or the statement "new translation." The references are given in their short forms: for greater detail see the Bibliography, below.

The background to these texts is set out in Part I of the book, so no detailed commentary is given here. Annotation is provided either in square brackets or in footnotes, when necessary. Further information will be found in most cases in the published sources.

Mozart as Adjunct Capellmeister at St. Stephen's Cathedral in Vienna

    1. Mozart's application to the Vienna City Council, late April 1791

    (Bauer-Deutsch IV, No. 1151; new translation)

To the City Council. Humble petition of Wolfgang Amadé Mozart, composer to the Court of His Imperial Majesty, to be appointed adjunct to the present Capellmeister at the cathedral church of St. Stephen.

To the most Worshipful and Most Wise Council of the City of Vienna

    Sirs!

During the illness of Herr Capellmeister Hofmann,[3] I contemplated taking the liberty of applying for his post. My musical talent, my works, and my artistic achievements have earned me an international reputation, my name is everywhere held in esteem, and I have for several years enjoyed the honor of an appointment as composer to the Court of His Imperial Majesty here in Vienna. I hoped, therefore, that I was not unworthy of the position, and that I might receive the approbation of the learned members of the City Council.

Capellmeister Hofmann recovered his health, however, and in these circumstances, since I wish him long life from the bottom of my heart, it occurred to me that it might perhaps be of service to the cathedral and to yourselves if I was

---

3. Leopold Hofmann (1738–93) had been at St. Stephen's since 1772, having succeeded Georg Reutter the younger as Capellmeister. As Mozart had wished, after his death the nonstipendiary post of adjunct Capellmeister went to Johann Georg Albrechtsberger, who also succeeded Hofmann in 1793.

appointed adjunct to the Herr Capellmeister, who is no longer a young man. The position (without remuneration for the present) would give me the opportunity to assist that worthy man in his duties, and to earn the regard of the most wise city council for my actual performance in the office. I believe I may claim to be better fitted for it than many others, in view of the knowledge of church style that I have cultivated alongside my other accomplishments.

Your most humble servant
Wolfgang Amadé Mozart
Composer to the Court of His Imperial Majesty

2. Decree of the City Council, 9 May 1791

(*Mozart-Dokumente*, 346; *Mozart DB*, 395)

The City Council of the I. & R. Capital City of Vienna declares that Herr Wolfgang Amadeus Mozart shall in consequence of his petition be assigned as assistant to Herr Leopold Hofmann, Kapellmeister at St. Stephen's Cathedral Church, in such wise that he shall make himself liable by a legal agreement, to be deposited here, to assist the said Herr Capellmeister in his service without remuneration, to deputize for him when he cannot appear in person, and in case this post of Capellmeister shall fall vacant, to be satisfied with the salary and with all that which the City Council may decree and deem advisable.

Which is herewith imparted to the above for his information.

Jos. Georg Hörl, I & R Councillor and Burgomaster
Ex Cons. Magis, Vien. 9 May 1791.
Johann Hübner, *Secret.*

3. Announcement in the Pressburger Zeitung, 22 May 1791

(*Mozart-Dokumente*, 347; *Mozart DB*, 395)

Vienna. The Court Composer Mozart has received from the City Council here the reversion of the post of Capellmeister at St. Stephen's, which brings in 2,000 florins.

Mozart's Exequies (1791)

4. Report of the mass for Mozart's soul in St. Michael's in Vienna, from the feature "News from Vienna," in the Auszug aller europäischen Zeitungen (European Press Digest), 13 December 1791.

(Brauneis, "Unveröffentlichte Nachrichten," 166; new translation)

On 10 December, solemn exequies for the great composer Mozart were celebrated in the parish church of St. Michael,[4] at the instigation of the honest and esteemed directors of the Wiedner Theatre. We hear that Baron v. S★★ [Swieten] has undertaken the education and care of one of the composer's children.

5. From the handwritten Vienna journal Der heimliche Botschafter *(The Secret Messenger), 16 December 1791*

(*Mozart-Dokumente*, 374; *Mozart DB*, 425)

All are concerned with Mozart's widow, trying to make good her loss to some extent, and to comfort her. Thus the worthy Baron von Suitten has adopted the boy [Carl Thomas], who already plays the clavier excellently, and the Countess Thun the girl [actually the younger boy, Franz Xaver Wolfgang]. Herr Schikaneder had obsequies performed for the departed at which the Requiem, which he composed in his last illness, was executed.[5] Herr Schikaneder will give a performance of the *Zauberflöte* in the next few days for the benefit of the widow.

Completion of the Requiem score (1791–92)

6. Joseph Eybler's undertaking to complete the Requiem, 21 December 1791

(*Mozart-Dokumente*, 375; cf. Bauer-Deutsch IV, No. 1207; *Mozart DB*, 426)

The undersigned hereby imparts that Frau Constanze Mozart, widow, has entrusted him with the completion of the Requiem Mass begun by her late husband; the same undertakes to complete it by the middle of the coming Lent,[6] and at the same time guarantees that it shall neither be copied, nor given into other hands than those of the aforementioned widow.

Vienna, 21 December 1791

4. Supporting evidence is to be found in the St. Michael's Collegiate Archives (facsimile of the funeral specification in Brauneis, "Unveröffentliche Nachrichten," 166f.; see also Brauneis, "Exequien für Mozart," 8–11, and Brauneis, "Mozart's Begräbnis," *Zaubertöne* [1990]:542–47).

5. Cf. the last sentence of Doc. 8 (which is open to misunderstanding, as well as corrected by Doc. 5), and the report of Mozart's death published in the Berlin journal *Musikalisches Wochenblatt*, based on a letter dated 12 December from their Prague correspondent: "One of his last works is said to be a Requiem Mass, which was performed at his obsequies."

6. It is possible that the date set for completion was 14 February 1792, the anniversary of Countess Walsegg's death. It would be consistent with the importunity of the unknown messenger who accosted Mozart as he was about to leave for Prague (Doc. 9).

*7. Receipt for a copy of the Requiem, from the Prussian ambassador in Vienna,
Constantin Philipp Wilhelm von Jacobi-Kloest,[7] 4 March 1792*

(*Mozart-Dokumente,* Addenda, 77; new translation)

The undersigned herewith makes the following legally binding pledge to Frau
Constanze Mozart, widow, née Weber, concerning the pieces purchased from
her: *La Betulia liberata,* an oratorio, and two Corpus Christi litanies; have received
the original scores, to return them to her hands after copies have been made of
them.[8]

Vienna, 4 March 1792
pp Baron Jacobi K
Prussian Ambassador at the Court of H. I. M.

Herewith I legally surrender the rights conferred on me by the above document
to Herr Johann André of Offenbach am Main, who has purchased them from
me.[9]

Vienna, 1 January 1800   Constanze Mozart

N. B.	To copying the 4 pieces	40 fl.
	to the Requiem	450 fl.
		———
		490 fl.

7. Baron von Jacobi-Kloest had been an admirer of Mozart since at least 1784, when his name
appears among the subscribers to Mozart's academy concerts (Bauer-Deutsch IV, No. 780; see also
Mozart DB, 573–82).

8. King Friedrich Wilhelm of Prussia had instructed his ambassador, on 7 February 1792, to buy
eight works by Mozart at 100 ducats each (cf. *Mozart-Dokumente,* 386; *Mozart DB,* 440–41; and
Eibl VI, 431). On the basis of this receipt, the oratorio *La Betulia liberata* K 118, the two litanies K
125 and 243, and the Requiem can be identified. "Of Süssmayr's score, two copies were made"
as soon as it was ready (see above, Part I, n. 79); Süssmayr is also supposed to have kept a copy for
himself (Doc. 16f). Constanze "retained the right to give copies to princes" (Doc. 16c).

9. Constanze Mozart's surrender of her rights is associated with the sale of Mozart's musical estate
to André. She did not possess the rights to the Requiem (not included in "the above document").
The "N.B." portion of Doc. 7 belongs to the 1792 entry and differentiates carefully between the
copying of borrowed scores and the acquisition of a finished copy of the Requiem score.

For the copyright issue and the early circulation of Requiem copies see Docs. 16b–d and p. 27
(notes 78–79).

8. First public mention of the Requiem, in the form of an anecdote printed in the
Salzburger Intelligenzblatt, *7 January 1792*[10]

(Hintermaier, "Eine frühe Requiem-Anekdote," 436; Landon, *1791*, 160)

About Mozart—Some months before his death he received a letter without
signature, asking him to compose a Requiem, and to ask whatever fee he wanted
for it. Since this idea did not in the least appeal to him, he thought, I shall ask
so much that the amateur will surely let me go. The next day a servant came to
fetch the answer; Mozart wrote to the unknown man that he could not undertake
to do the work for less than 60 ducats, and he could not start, moreover, for two
or three months. The servant came again, brought 30 ducats instantly and said
he would enquire again in three months, and when the Mass is finished, he will
bring the other half of the money. Now Mozart had to write, which he did,
often with tears in his eyes, always saying 'I am writing a Requiem for myself';
he finished it a few days before his death. When his death was known, the servant
came again and brought the remaining 30 ducats, asked for no Requiem, and
since that time there was no further enquiry. It will actually be performed, when
it is copied, in his memory in St. Michael's Church.

9. Account based on statements by Constanze Mozart, from the first book-length biography[11]

(Niemetschek, *Leben des Kapellmeisters Mozart,* 32–37; *Life of Mozart,* 41–46)

The story of his last work, the Requiem mentioned above, is as obscure as it
is strange.

Shortly before the coronation of Emperor Leopold, even before Mozart had
received the order to travel to Prague, a letter without signature was brought to
him by an unknown messenger, which with many flattering remarks contained
an enquiry as to whether he would be willing to undertake to write a Requiem
Mass. What would be the cost, and how long would it take to complete?

Mozart, who never made the least move without his wife's knowledge, told
her of this remarkable request, and at the same time expressed a wish to try his
hand at this type of composition, the more so as the higher forms of church music

---

10. This anecdote was published in other newspapers (*Mozart-Dokumente,* 526), and it is conceivable
that Constanze Mozart herself allowed it to spread, as a means of advertising the composition and
completion of the Requiem and of avoiding awkward questions at the same time (cf. Hintermaier,
"Eine frühe Requiem-Anekdote").

11. On the mention of the Requiem in Schlichtegroll's biography (1793) see above, Part I, n. 26.

had always appealed to his genius. She advised him to accept the offer. He therefore replied to his anonymous patron that he would write a Requiem for a given sum; he could not state exactly how long it would take. He, however, wished to know where the work was to be delivered when ready. In a short while the same messenger appeared again, bringing back not only the sum stipulated but also the promise, as Mozart had been so modest in his price, that he would receive another payment on receipt of the composition. He should, moreover, write according to his own ideas and mood, but he should not trouble to find out who had given the order, as it would assuredly be in vain.

In the meantime he received a very flattering and advantageous offer to write the opera seria for the Coronation of Emperor Leopold in Prague. It was too much of a temptation for him to refuse to go to Prague to write for his beloved Bohemians.

Just as Mozart and his wife were getting into the travelling coach, the messenger appeared like a ghost and pulled at her coat. "What about the Requiem?" he asked. Mozart excused himself on account of the necessity for the journey, and the impossibility of informing his anonymous patron; in any case it would be the first task on his return, and it was only a question whether the stranger could wait so long. The messenger seemed to be quite satisfied.

While he was in Prague Mozart became ill and was continually receiving medical attention. He was pale and his expression was sad, although his good humour was often shown in merry jest with his friends.

When it was time to take his leave of his friends he was so sad that he shed tears. It seemed to be a foreboding of his coming death that produced his melancholy mood—for he was already sickening with the illness that was soon to carry him off.

On his return to Vienna he at once started on his Requiem Mass and worked at it with great energy and interest; but his indisposition increased visibly and made him depressed. His wife realised it with misgivings. One day when she was driving in the Prater with him, to give him a little distraction and amusement, and they were sitting by themselves, Mozart began to speak of death, and declared that he was writing the Requiem for himself. Tears came to the eyes of this sensitive man: "I feel definitely," he continued, "that I cannot last much longer; I am sure I have been poisoned. I cannot rid myself of this idea."

The speech fell like a load on his wife's heart. She was unable to console him, or to convince him that his melancholy imaginings were without foundation. As she felt that he was on the verge of a serious illness, and that the Requiem was getting on his over-sensitive nerves, she called in the doctor, and took the score of the composition away from him.

His health actually improved somewhat, and he was able to finish a small cantata [K 623], which had been ordered by a Society for a celebration. The splendid way in which it was performed and the applause it received gave his energies a new impetus. He became more cheerful and repeatedly expressed the wish to continue and finish the Requiem. His wife could no longer find an excuse for withholding his music.

This hopeful state of affairs was but short-lived; in a few days he became despondent once more, weaker and more listless, until he sank back in his sick-bed from which, alas, he never rose again.

On the day of his death he asked for the score to be brought to his bedside. "Did I not say before, that I was writing this Requiem for myself?" After saying this, he looked yet again with tears in his eyes through the whole work. This was the last sad sight he had of his beloved art, which was destined to become immortal.

Soon after his death the messenger arrived and asked for the composition in its incomplete state, and it was given him. From that moment onwards Mozart's widow never saw him again and never found out anything, either about the Requiem or by whom it had been commissioned. The reader can imagine that no trouble was spared in trying to find the mysterious messenger, but all efforts and attempts proved in vain.★

Mozart remained completely conscious during his illness right to the end and died calmly, although regretfully. This can be readily understood, when one considers that Mozart had been officially appointed to the post of Kapellmeister in the Church of St. Stephen with all the emoluments connected therewith since time immemorial, and had the happy prospect of living peacefully without financial worries. He also received, almost simultaneously, commissions from Hungary and Amsterdam, as well as many orders and contracts for works to be delivered at regular intervals.

This extraordinary accumulation of happy auguries for a better future, the sad state of his financial affairs as they actually existed, the sight of his unhappy wife, the thought of his two young children; all these did not make the bitterness of his death any sweeter, particularly as this much admired artist, in his thirty-fifth year, had never been a stoic: "Just now," thus he often complained in his illness, "when I could have gone on living so peacefully, I must depart. I must leave my art now that I am no longer a slave of fashion, am no longer tied to speculators; when I could follow the paths along which my spirit leads me, free and independent to write only when I am inspired. I must leave my family, my poor children, just when I would have been in a better position to look after their welfare." His death followed in the night of 5 December 1791. The doctors did not agree on the cause of his death. Countless tears were shed for Mozart, not only in Vienna, but possibly even more in Prague, where he was so much loved and admired. Every connoisseur, every music-lover felt that he was irreplaceable.

Niemetschek's note: "His widow possesses the score of this, and treasures it as a precious possession. The author speaks of the event as he has often heard it from the lips of Mozart's widow, and leaves it to the reader to draw his own conclusions. He has seen one of the notes which the 'unknown' patron wrote to Mozart. Nothing much can be gathered from it as it is very short. Mozart is requested to send the Requiem, and to state a sum for which he would compose a certain number of quartets each year. Why did the unknown 'Admirer of Mozart's talents' (thus he chose to call himself) prefer to remain anonymous? What has happened to the Requiem? No performance of the piece has been traced anywhere. Mozart's friends would be only too pleased to find an explanation, for one cannot think of any plausible reason for such mysterious concealment."

10. Memoir of Sophie Haibl, Constanze Mozart's sister: excerpt from a letter to Georg Nicolaus Nissen, 7 April 1825

(*Mozart-Dokumente*, 451; *Mozart DB*, 525–26)

My poor sister came after me and begged me for heavens' sake to go to the priests at St. Peter's and ask [one of] the priests to come, as if on a chance visit. That I also did, though the priests hesitated a long time and I had great difficulty in persuading one of these inhuman priests to do it. Then I hurried to our mother, who was anxiously awaiting me; it was already dark. How frightened the poor dear was. I persuaded her to go and spend the night with her eldest daughter, Hofer, who is now dead, and so it was; and I ran back as fact as I could to my inconsolable sister. Sissmaier was there at M's bedside; and the well-known Requiem lay on the coverlet, and Mozart was explaining to him how he thought he should finish it after his death. Then he commanded his wife to keep his death a secret until she had informed Albregtsberger of it; for the post was his by right in the eyes of God and the world. There was a long search for [Thomas Franz] Glosett, the [Mozarts' family] doctor, who was found in the theatre; but he had to wait till the play was over—then he came and prescribed *cold* compresses on his burning head, and these gave him such a shock that he did not regain consciousness before he passed away. The last thing he did was to try and mouth the sound of the timpani in his Requiem; I can still hear it now. Then Müller came from the art gallery directly and took a plaster cast of his pale and lifeless face.[12] Dear brother, I cannot possibly describe the boundless misery of his faithful wife

12. On Mozart's death-mask, see Deutsch, NMA X/32 (1961), xxi.

as she threw herself on her knees and implored succour from the Almighty. She could not tear herself from him, beg her as I did; if her grief had been susceptible of increase it must have been increased on the day after that dreadful night by people passing by in crowds, lamenting and weeping for him loudly.

11. Excerpt from the obituary for Benedikt Schak in the Allgemeine musikalische Zeitung, *1827*

(*Mozart-Dokumente,* 459f.; *Mozart DB,* 536–37)

And now for a word about the Mozart Requiem.

The story of the mysterious commissioning of it, and that the master did not complete his work, was known in Munich immediately after Mozart's death. It was known that the composition of the Sanctus and the Agnus Dei is the work of Herr Süssmayr, who may also have arranged and orchestrated many another number which had been left unfinished. But that Mozart, open, honest Mozart, accepted the fee but threw together the work itself in part from early products of his youth, and the whole without zeal, without interest, without love, simply out of necessity—not one of us would have wanted to express this strange opinion, even if it had entered into his mind.[13] And simply because it refers to this matter, we relate what the good, truth-loving Schack told us on so many occasions, long before the appearance of *Cäcilia*. Mozart, so he related among much else that is not here relevant, received fifty ducats for the composition of the Requiem, half of it paid in advance. As no urgency for this work was pressed upon him, he travelled to Frankfurt [actually Prague] in the meantime. The greatest part of his Requiem he wrote in the Laimgrube suburb, in Trattner's garden. As soon as he had completed a number, he had it sung through, and played the instrumental accompaniment to it on his piano. On the very eve of his death he had the score of the Requiem brought to his bed, and himself (it was two o'clock in the afternoon) sang the alto part; Schack, the family friend, sang the soprano line, as he had always previously done, Hofer, Mozart's brother-in-law, took the tenor, Gerle, later bass singer at the Mannheim Theatre, the bass.[14] They were at the first bars of the Lacrimosa when Mozart began to weep bitterly, laid the score on one side, and eleven hours later, at one o'clock in the morning (of 5 December 1791, as is well known), departed this life.

13. An allusion to Weber, "Über die Echtheit" (in the periodical *Cäcilia*).
14. Benedikt Emanuel Schak (1758–1826), the first Tamino in *Die Zauberflöte;* Franz Hofer (1755–96), violinist; Franz Xaver Gerl (1764–1824), the first Sarastro in *Die Zauberflöte.*

12. Excerpt from A Mozart Pilgrimage: Being the Travel Diaries of Mary and Vincent Novello in the Year 1829, *ed. Nerina Medici and Rosemary Hughes (London 1955), 128–32*

July 15th. It was about six months before he [Mozart] died that he was impressed with the horrid idea that someone had poisoned him with acqua toffana—he came to her [Constanze] one day and complained that he felt great pain in his loins and a general languor spreading over him by degrees—that some one of his enemies had succeeded in administering the deleterious mixture which would cause his death and that they could already calculate at what precise time it would infallibly take place. The engagement for the Requiem hurt him much as it fed these sad thoughts that naturally resulted from his weak state of health.

The great success of a little Masonic ode [K 623] which he wrote at this instant cheered his spirits for a time, but his melancholy forebodings again returned in a few days, when he again set to work on the Requiem. On one occasion he himself with Süssmayr and Madame Mozart tried over part of the Requiem together, but some of the passages so excited him that he could not refrain from tears, and was unable to proceed.

I was pleased to find that I had guessed right in supposing that the "Recordare" (one of the most divine and enchanting movements ever written) was one of his own greatest favourites.

She [Constanze] also confirmed the truth of his having said only three days before he died, "I am appointed to a situation which will afford me leisure to write in future *just what I like myself,* and I feel I am capable of doing something worthy of the fame I have acquired, but instead of that I find that I must die."

What glorious productions have been lost to the world by his unfortunate early death—for incomparable as his works are I have not the least doubt but that he would [have] written still finer things such as Oratorios and other extensive works (of the Epic class) had he lived.

July 23rd. Eybler has the original MS. of Mozart's Requiem beginning at the Lacrymosa and ending [with] the *fac eas* modulation into A dominant to D, part of the Offertorium, vocal parts complete with a few of the leading features of the accompaniment sketched in. I tried all I could to persuade Eybler to have a facsimile engraved of the last Page which Mozart wrote before the pen dropped from his weak hand—this would be [a] most interesting engraving to all lovers of Mozart.

July 24th. He [the Abbé Stadler] at one time was in possession of the first part of the Requiem, beginning at the "Requiem aeternam," the "Kyrie," and the

"Dies Irae" as far as the "Lacrymosa" (the latter movement and the Offertorium, "Domine Jesu Christe," the versicle "Hostias et preces tibi Domine" terminating with "fac eas in aeternum" with the direction to repeat the fugue "Quam olim Abrahae" which were the last words Mozart wrote just before he died, are in the possession of Mr. Eybler, the Capellmeister to the Chapel Royal, as I have already mentioned).

But L'Abbé Stadler has in the very highest taste (preferring the fame and reputation of Mozart to his own private gratification) sent Mozart's original score to be preserved in the Imperial Library for public reference, as the most satisfactory and incontrovertible answer to those who insinuate that Mozart did not write his own Requiem.

The "Sanctus," "Benedictus," "Agnus Dei" and "Dona eis requiem" bear such internal proofs of their having been written by Mozart that I never for a moment believed they could have been produced by another composer, especially such an obscure writer as Süssmayr of whom nothing whatever can be shewn as having the least resemblance to the style of Mozart's Requiem. My own opinion is that Mozart wrote the "Sanctus," "Agnus Dei," etc., *before* he had done the "Offertorium" and, finding his death approaching, gave directions (as his widow distinctly and decidedly asserted to me that he did) to Süssmayr to fill up the mere *remplissage* of the leading features which Mozart himself had indicated: that he also told Süssmayr to repeat the Fugue at the end, as such a mode of terminating a Mass was by no means unusual and would save time in composing another adaptation of the words, and that Mozart then went on writing the "Offertorium" till he arrived at the words "fac eas in aeternum," when the Pen dropped from his hand and he expired.

The circumstance of Süssmayr's coming forward *after* Mozart was dead and claiming the merit of having written the last part of this justly celebrated composition appeared to me so suspicious that I could not refrain from asking the widow of Mozart whether he was not possibly some envious and concealed enemy [rather] than a sincere friend and grateful pupil, and when the widow owned that although Süssmayr had a few Lessons from Mozart yet that he was also a pupil and friend of Salieri's (Mozart's bitterest foe), my suspicions were at once confirmed of his treachery, easily traced and naturally accounted for.

I hope that Mr. Eybler will follow the generous and noble example of L'Abbé Stadler and that he will also send the part which he possesses of the Requiem in Mozart's own handwriting to the same Institution, in order not only that these precious MSS. may be safely and carefully preserved, but [that] they may also be at all times accessible as documents of public reference and thus put a stop to all further dispute and cavil on the part of Mozart's jealous and mean-spirited calumniators.

I trust also that at some future day the *remainder* of this exquisite Mass will be found in Mozart's own handwriting, unless (as is but too probable) the original Copy of the "Sanctus," etc. was destroyed by Süssmayr to give some air of plausibility to the improbable falsehood he has endeavoured to propagate against the memory of his too kind and indulgent Master.

July 28th. The first part of the Requiem in Mozart's handwriting is not now to be found, but fortunately before it was sent off to the Baron who ordered it, L'Abbé Stadler made a Copy of the MS., which copy he has now presented to the Imperial Library. The sketch of the "Dies Irae" in *Mozart's handwriting* is preserved. It contains the whole *vocal score* complete of the "Dies Irae," the "Tuba mirum," "Recordare," "Rex tremendae," "Confutatis" (Query, their proper order of succession?) and the first 8 bars of the "Lacrymosa," with the proper features of the Accompaniment marked out. Here and there, where there was a symphony[15] or particular effect required, there are also figures added to the Bass, to indicate the proper chords he wanted, so that it was easy for Süssmayr or any other person who had been taught scoring by Mozart to fill in the mere *remplissage*.

The "Offertorium," beginning "Domine Jesu Christe," the Fugue "Quam olim Abrahae," the verse "Hostias" and the direction for the repetition of the Fugue "Quam olim" (which were the last words that Mozart ever wrote) were also copied by the Abbé Stadler, who has likewise presented his copy to the Imperial Library.

The original copy is in the possession of Eybler the Capellmeister of the Imperial Chapel, who I earnestly hope will follow the noble example of L'Abbé Stadler and present this interesting MS. to the Imperial Library for preservation with the rest of this inestimable work.

That the "Sanctus," "Benedictus" and "Agnus Dei" were also written by Mozart I feel not the least doubt, and I can account for the disappearance of the original score in the same manner as the commencement of the Requiem, with this unfortunate difference, however, that the Score was sent off to the Baron who ordered it *before* L'Abbé Stadler saw it or had any opportunity of preserving a copy as he had done of the Kyrie, etc.

I can only add my earnest hope that the Baron Walsegg or whoever else is in possession of this invaluable MS., will have the good feeling and honourable

15. An instrumental passage or interlude.

liberality to leave it at his death (for it is perhaps too much to expect any person to part with such a precious treasure while living) to the Imperial Library also, to do justice to Mozart's Memory and to put a stop at once to all further cavil and dispute upon the subject.

13. Entry in Constanze Nissen's diary, on the arrival of Mozart's piano from Vienna, 11 August 1829

(Bauer-Deutsch IV, No. 1438; new translation)

My dear piano, on which Mozart played and composed so much music: *Die Zauberflöte, La clemenza di Tito,* the Requiem and a cantata for the Freemasons. I have not the words to describe how happy I am to have you. Mozart loved this piano so much, and therefore my love for it is all the greater.[16]

14. "True and Detailed History of the Requiem by W. A. Mozart. From its inception in the year 1791 to the present period of 1839." An eye-witness account of Count Walsegg and the Requiem, by Anton Herzog (incorporating some information Herzog found in Stadler, Vertheidigung der Echtheit des Mozartischen Requiem, *and Stadler,* Nachtrag zur Vertheidigung)[17]

(*Mozart-Dokumente,* Addenda et Corrigenda, 101–07; most of the translation is taken from Landon, *1791,* with a new translation of matter not included by Landon)

[Publication of this report was forbidden in 1839 by the Austrian Imperial Censors, probably on the prompting of Count Dietrichstein. It came to light in 1937 but was not published for another twenty-seven years, in Deutsch, "Zur Geschichte von Mozarts Requiem."]

---

16. The instrument was a clavichord, formerly the property of the Weber family, which passed to Constanze in the summer of 1791. Mozart used it in the last six months of his life. From 1810 to 1829 it belonged to Mozart's younger son, Franz Xaver Amadeus, and then was returned to Constanze. On the occasion of Mozart's centenary in 1856 it came into the possession of the Dom-Musik-Verein in Salzburg and is now in Mozart's birthplace (Internationale Stiftung Mozarteum). The unfretted instrument has a five-octave range (F′–f′′′); its builder is unknown. Ill. in Deutsch, NMA, X/32 (1961), No. 576.

Concerning Mozart's method of composing, Niemetschek wrote: "In his mind the work was already complete before he sat down at his desk. When he received the libretto for a vocal composition, he went about for some time, concentrating on it until his imagination was fired. Then he proceeded to work out his ideas at the keyboard; and only then did he sit down and write" (Niemetschek, *Life of Mozart,* 62–63).

17. At the time of compiling this account, Herzog was schoolmaster and choirmaster in Wiener Neustadt. For more detail see Deutsch, "Der Graue Bote."

Herr Franz, Count von Walsegg, owner of the estates Schottwien, Klam, Stuppach, Pottschach and Ziegersberg, in Austria below the [River] Enns . . . lived since his marriage with Anna, *née noble* von Flammberg, in his castle at Stuppach, as a tender husband and true father to his vassals. He was a passionate lover of music and the theatre; hence every week, on Tuesdays and Thursdays, each time fully three hours' long, quartets were played and on Sundays theatre, in which latter Herr Count himself, and Madame Countess and her unmarried Madame Sister, took part, as did all the officials and the entire, numerous household, all of whom had to play roles, each according to his or her capacities. To help with the quartet-playing Herr Count engaged two excellent artists, Herr Johann Benaro as violinist and Herr Louis Prevost as violoncellist; Herr Count played the violoncello in string quartets, and in flute quartets he played the flute, and usually I played the second violin or the viola. In those days I was engaged as teacher in the Patronat-School of the Herr Count, at Klam.

So that we would not lack for new quartets, in view of so frequent productions of them, Herr Count not only procured all those publicly announced but was in touch with many composers, yet without ever revealing his identity; and they delivered to him works of which he retained the sole ownership, and for which he paid well. To name one man, Herr Hoffmeister[18] delivered many flute quartets, in which the flute part was quite easily negotiable, but the other three parts extremely difficult, which caused the players to work very hard; and that made the Herr Count laugh.

Since Herr Count never wanted to play from engraved parts, he had them beautifully copied out on ten-stave paper; but the author was never noted. The secretly organized scores he generally copied out in his own hand, and presented them for the parts to be copied out. We never saw an original score. The quartets were then played, and we had to guess who the composer was. Usually we suggested it was the Count himself, because from time to time he actually composed some small things; he smiled and was pleased that we (as he thought) had been mystified; but we were amused that he took us for such simpletons.

We were all young, and thought this an innocent pleasure which we gave to our lord. And in such fashion the mystifications continued among us for some years.

I have thought it necessary to furnish these particulars so that the origin of the *Requiem*, which has been termed mysterious, can be better judged.

On 14 February 1791, death snatched from Herr Count von Walsegg his beloved wife, in the flower of her life. He wanted to erect a double memorial to

18. Franz Anton Hoffmeister (1754–1812), composer and music publisher.

her, and he had an excellent idea. He arranged through his business representative, Herr Dr. Johann Sortschan, Court and Judicial Lawyer, in Vienna, that one of the very best sculptors in Vienna [Johann Martin Fischer, 1740–1820] should model an epitaph; and Mozart should compose a *Requiem*, for which he [the Count] as usual reserved the sole right of possession.

The first item, which cost over 3000 . . . [florins], was after a time erected in the valley with the spring near Stuppach Castle; and the remains of the lady were taken from the family vault in Schottwien and placed there.

But the *Requiem*, which was supposed to be played every year on the anniversary of Madame Countess's death, took longer than expected; for death surprised Mozart in the midst of this worthy task. What to do now? Who was going to dare to imitate a Mozart? And yet the work had to be finished; for Mozart's widow, who (as was well known) was not in the best circumstances, was to have received one hundred ducats. Whether prepayments had been effected was not precisely known to us, although there are reasons for thinking so.

Finally Süssmayr was persuaded to complete the unfinished great work, and he admits in letters to the music publishers [Brietkopf & Härtel] in Leipzig that during Mozart's lifetime he often played and sang through with him the pieces that had already been composed, namely "Requiem," "Kyrie," "Dies irae," "Domine," and so forth, and that he [Mozart] very often discussed the completion of this work and communicated [to Süssmayr] the way and the reasons of his orchestration.

From this point, and up to the dispatch of the score to Herr Count, I am obliged to turn to Herr Abbé Stadler's account, which I will quote here, because his two pamphlets may well not be in everyone's possession. He says: "The first movement, 'Requiem' with the fugue, and the second, 'Dies irae,' up to 'Lacrimosa,' were for the most part orchestrated by Mozart himself, and there was not much more for Süssmayr to do than what most composers leave for their amanuenses to do. Süssmayr's work really began with the 'Lacrimosa.' But here too Mozart had written out the violins himself; and Süssmayr only finished it from after 'judicandus homo reus' to the end. Similarly, in the third movement, 'Domine,' Mozart had written the violins' music in his score, where the voices are silent; where the voices enter he had indicated the motives for the instruments here and there, but quite clearly. He gave the violins two and a half bars to perform alone before the 'Quam olim' fugue. He wrote two bars for the violins before the entry of the voices at 'Hostias,' and eleven bars at 'Memoriam facimus,' in his own hand.

"We see nothing more from his pen after the end of 'Hostias' except [the words] 'Quam olim da Capo.' This is the end of Mozart's original autograph score. But people should not think that Süssmayr wrote out his completion of the orchestration on that. He made his own [copy of the] score, very like Mozart's. In this he copied, first, note for note, everything that was in Mozart's original manuscript, next he followed the given instructions for the orchestration meticulously, without adding a note of his own, [then] composed the 'Sanctus,' 'Benedictus' and 'Agnus Dei' himself. In such fashion the work was completed.

"Of this score there were at once made two copies. Süssmayr's manuscript was sent to the commissioner. One copy was sent to the music publisher in Leipzig for publication, the second one was retained and the parts copied from it; whereupon this marvelous work was first performed for the benefit of the widow in the Jahn rooms. Whether Mozart's original manuscript of the 'Requiem' and 'Dies irae' still exists, and where it might be, I cannot say with certainty; although I have a well-founded opinion on the subject. The 'Lacrimosa' and 'Domine' still exists, just as Mozart wrote it, untouched."

Finally Herr Abbé Stadler says, in the Postscript to his Defence, 1827, that the original manuscript of the "Dies irae" is in the possession of the principal Court Capellmeister, Herr Joseph von Eybler. Therefore Herr Count von Walsegg never received a single note of the whole *Requiem* written by Mozart's own hand. I leave it to be decided whether one dealt in an upright—I won't go so far as to say honest—fashion with Herr Count von Walsegg. He wasn't even told how far Mozart's composition went, he thought up to the "Agnus Dei."

That would explain the following circumstances: later when I had the parts copied from the published Leipzig score, for my own use, I asked Herr Count for the Organo of his *Requiem*, because it is not figured in the score, as is known, and I wanted to save myself the trouble of copying the figured bass; but he said I wouldn't be able to use his organ part for the whole piece because it had a different "Agnus Dei." I persuaded the Herr Count of the opposite, however, because every note of his *Requiem* copy was known to me; and because the "Agnus Dei," with its clever connection to the following two Mozart compositions, "Requiem" and "Cum sanctis," especially impressed me.

Herr Count sought to prove that he had a different "Agnus Dei" in his score from that of the Leipzig score in that he always said he had been a pupil of Mozart's, and had sent the score section by section to Vienna to be examined. Shortly before Mozart's death he had just sent to him the completed "Benedictus" for this purpose. After Mozart's death they found the score for the *Requiem* from the beginning up to the "Agnus Dei"; and they thought it was Mozart's composition, because their two handwritings [Walsegg's and Mozart's] were supposed to be extremely similar to each other.

Herr Count then finished the *Requiem* by adding the "Agnus Dei" and the rest; but Süssmayr had later added his own composition to fill in this part. That is how it happened that Herr Count had a different "Agnus Dei" from that in the Leipzig score. From all this one can see the extent to which the commissioner was deceived, and that he was certainly told Mozart had finished the work except for the "Agnus Dei," which was the only part composed by Süssmayr, in order to enhance the value of the work.

Can anyone blame Herr Count if he made a joke, privately, only with us his servants, and called the *Requiem* his composition, but only in front of us? Far worse liberties were taken with his property, which had cost him so dearly, as will be shown below.

I myself am convinced that Mozart would not have composed the "Sanctus" in D major and in that style; for although the text is the same as in the Mass, the circumstances of a Requiem are quite different; this is a Mass of Mourning, the church is draped in black, and the priests wear mourning robes. Dazzling music is not what is wanted. One can cry "Holy, holy" without having to add kettle-drum rolls.

The "Sanctus and Hosanna" is very similar to the same movement in Süssmayr's Mass in D. Madame Widow Mozart and her circle may not have known about the contract which her late husband made with Herr Doctor Sortschan, according to which Herr Count von Walsegg was to have been the sole owner of the commissioned *Requiem;* otherwise at the time when they delivered the score to the commissioner they would not have sent, without his knowledge and per-mission, a copy to be sold to the music publisher in Leipzig. One can imagine what an impression it made on the Herr Count, when he learned that the score of his property had appeared publicly in print in Leipzig.

Herr Count actually intended at first to take serious action against the Widow Mozart, but the matter was settled in good faith, thanks to his kind heart.

After Herr Count Walsegg had received the score of the *Requiem,* he copied the whole at once, in his usual fashion, note for note in his own very fair hand; and gave it movement by movement to his violinist Benaro, so he could copy the parts.

During this work I sat for hours at Benaro's side and followed the course of this excellent work with increasing interest; for the whole previous history of the *Requiem* was well known to me through our Senior Official Leitgeb,[19] who had

19. Franz Anton Leitgeb (1744–1812), lawyer and manager of Count Walsegg's estates in Schott-wien.

been ordered to pay out the honorarium through the gypsum office in Vienna [the Walsegg family owned gypsum works in Schottwien].

When all the individual parts were written out, preparations for performing the *Requiem* were at once set in motion. But because in the region of Stuppach not all the necessary musicians could be brought together, it was arranged that the first performance take place in Wiener Neustadt. Among the musicians, the choice of the instrumental and vocal soloists was made from among the best available; and so it happened that the soprano was sung by Ferenz [a choirboy?] from [Wiener] Neustadt, the contralto by Kernbeiß from Schottwien, the tenor by Klein of [Wiener] Neustadt, and the bass by Thurner of Gloggnitz—these were the soloists. On 12 December 1793 the general rehearsal was held in the evening, in the choir-loft of the Cistercian Abbey and Parish Church of Neustadt; and on 14 December at 10 o'clock in the morning a requiem memorial service was held in that same church, during which this famous *Requiem* was given for the first time in the fashion for which it was intended.

Herr Count von Walsegg conducted the whole. Of all the musicians who participated in it, as far as I know, and at the moment of writing, none is alive except for myself and Herr Anton Plaimschauer, at present *Thurnermeister* [leader of the city band] here in Wiener-Neustadt.

On 14 February 1794, on the anniversary of Madame Countess's death, the *Requiem* was performed in the Patronat Church of Herr Count, at Maria-Schutz on Semmering; and from this time on Herr Count made no use of it, except that he arranged it as a quintet for strings, the score of which I kept for many years.

The extent to which this glorious composition has edified the musical public of almost all Europe over the past forty-six years is well known.

That score of the *Requiem* which is supposed to be written in Süssmayr's hand was never seen by me, or anyone else, other than Herr Count, nor was it known what Herr Count did with it and the other original scores he also owned. However, the score which the Herr Count gave me to use for rehearsing the singers was in his own hand, and I would have recognized it at once.

That Herr Count wanted to mystify with the *Requiem,* as he had done with the quartets, was well known to all of us; in our presence he always said it was his composition, but when he said that he smiled.

I came out from Wiener Neustadt with his physician, Dr. Fink, to visit Herr Count in his last illness, fourteen days before his death, which occurred on 11 November 1827, and I turned the conversation to the music and the theatre of the old days, because I knew that he enjoyed talking of them, and in that context I mentioned the *Requiem*. Among other things, I asked him if he knew the pamphlets that Herr Abbé Stadler had written about it.

He said that he did, and after a little thought asked me if I knew Herr Kandler of Vienna.[20] I said that I did not know Herr Kandler personally, but had read some essays about music by him, if I was not mistaken, in the erstwhile *Vienna Musical Journal*. Hereupon Herr Count said that when he was in Baden the previous summer, Herr Kandler had approached him in order to obtain information from him about the composition of the *Requiem*. I asked if Herr Count had given him the information, to which he answered: "They now know exactly as much as they did before." Herr Kandler will probably remember this occasion. I tell this here only in order to prove that I am privy, down to the smallest details, to what happened in respect of the *Requiem* in Stuppach. That is the story up to the death of Herr Count. Following the death of Herr Count von Walsegg, his sister and residuary legatee, Madame Countess von Sternberg, sold the whole musical archives to Herr Leitner. Among these items there must have been many valuable pieces of music.

In the summer of 1838 the manorial secretary Haag died in Stuppach Castle and left his effects to the Stuppach court clerk, his residuary legatee. There was a small collection of music included. And, O miracle! They discovered the manuscript score of the Mozart *Requiem,* and they thought they saw at once that it was the original score in Mozart's own handwriting.

The affair came to the notice of His Excellency Count Moritz von Dietrichstein, and also to that of Herr Court Councillor von Mosel, and arrangements were made for the score to be sent to Vienna, so that it could be purchased by the Imperial Royal Library, where it is to be found at present, and will probably remain. How likely this score is to be the original score can be judged from what I have said above, in the event that the score in Süssmayr's hand is not taken for the original, which it might be to some extent; because Süssmayr really did compose almost half the work. I have not seen this score, but believe that it is more likely to be the one in the hand of Count von Walsegg, because it was apparently not discovered after his death among his music. As I said, I would recognize that score at a glance. If it is compared with Mozart's handwriting, which has presumably already been done, a similarity in the hands might be discerned; for Herr Count von Walsegg often said, as has been mentioned, that his own handwriting was very similar to Mozart's. Si verum est. But whether this lately discovered score is in Mozart's, Süssmayr's or Walsegg's handwriting, it neither increases nor diminishes the value of that highly esteemed work of art, in my opinion.

In conclusion, may I be permitted to draw a comparison between one art and

20. Franz Sales Kandler (1792–1831), contributor to the *Wiener musikalische Zeitung*.

another. One would suppose that a work of art executed in stone would endure for ever, while one written on paper might easily perish. And yet the opposite has turned out to be true, at least in the case of the two memorials set up by Herr Count von Walsegg to his beloved wife. The truly beautiful monument of marble and granite was so badly defaced, entirely destroyed in fact, by profane hands, perhaps in the hope of finding valuables inside, especially at the time of the enemy invasion, that the remains of the dear departed had to be disinterred and brought back to the family vault in Schottwien. Mozart's work, on the other hand, wins ever more favour in the hearts of all lovers of art, and will continue to exist as a valuable memorial to the unforgettable Mozart for as long as the good taste for classical music endures.

Peace be on the ashes of the great master, and also on his revered patron, to whose liberality we are indebted for this so valuable work of art.

From the Period of the Publication of the First Edition of the Requiem (1800)

> 15. *Announcement of the performance of the Requiem in Leipzig, 20 April 1796*[21]
>
> (*Mozart-Dokumente,* 418; *Mozart DB,* 480–81)

Madame Mozart, after being received with the greatest honour in Berlin, is now in Leipzig, prior to journeying on to Dresden, and wishes to perform here her late husband's last work, his great Requiem, surely the most diligent and masterly work of his extraordinary genius; and all friends of music, all admirers of Mozart join her in this wish. Permission has been graciously granted to use the concert hall in the Gewandhaus for the performance; and Madame Mozart flatters herself that on the coming Wednesday, the 20th April, she will once more be able to commend the memory of her deceased husband to a large audience. The piece to be performed lasts a good hour; at its conclusion Madame Mozart will sing and Herr Müller, Organist, will perform a Concerto by her husband.[22] The concert will begin, as usual, at 5 o'clock. Tickets at 16gr. are to be had of Madame Mozart at the Hôtel de Saxe, and of Herry Meyer, Librarian; from whom, as also at the entrance, printed texts may be obtained for 2 gr.

21. This was the first performance of the completed Requiem outside Vienna, apart from the two in Wiener Neustadt. See Part I, n. 49.

22. August Eberhard Müller (1767–1817), then organist of the Nikolai Kirche and later Thomas Cantor, was the editor of the first edition of the Requiem and author of *Anweisung zum genauen Vortrage der Mozartschen Clavier-Concerte* (Guide to the Performance of Mozart's Piano Concertos [Leipzig, 1796]).

The full program of the concert is to be found in *Mozart-Dokumente* (419) and *Mozart DB* (481).

A. 27 MARCH 1799

(Bauer-Deutsch IV, No. 1240; new translation)

With regard to the Requiem, I do indeed have the famous work which he wrote shortly before his death. It is on approximately the theme that you note, but not exactly the same. I know of no Requiems but this one; all others I can confidently state are not genuine. I will tell you how much of it is by himself (it is so, up to very nearly the end) when I send it to you. This is what happened. When he saw his death was upon him, he spoke to Herr Süssmeyer, Imperial Capellmeister here in the city, and asked him, if he actually died without finishing it, to repeat the first fugue in the last movement—as is usual, in any case—and told him further how to realize the ending, the major part of which had already been done in some places, in the vocal parts.

B. 25 MAY 1799

(Bauer-Deutsch IV, No. 1243; new translation)

Now I come to a very unpleasant matter which I must settle with you. In your letter of 11 March you asked me various questions about the great Requiem, *without saying* whether you had it or wanted it (although I took the latter for granted, especially in view of our previous discussions). I replied on 27 March, reserving only one piece of information, which I would give you *when I sent it to you*. In your next letter you said nothing whatever about it. And now you tell me that you have acquired 2 copies and wish to give me 20 fl.! for the loan of mine. I myself have never made it public, out of respect for the man who commissioned it and who made nonpublication a condition. If he knew that you were publishing it without any profit to me, he would certainly make a claim (not against your title in the copies, admittedly, but probably) against your right to publish it. No one in the world has a right to do that but the said man, and I myself if he consented. It would be only right that no stranger, and no one but I, should gain the principal profit from it. Furthermore, why did you not try straightaway to buy this work from me, as we agreed with regard to *all* the works I had. I want 50 ducats for the concession of the title and the loan [of my copy], and I will settle matters with the said man.

C. 15 JUNE 1799, SENT WITH A COPY OF THE SCORE

(Bauer-Deutsch IV, No. 1245; new translation)

I had always reckoned that you would acquire the Requiem from me, especially after your preliminary enquiries to me about it. Be that as it may, you have broken our agreement by doing the contrary. I could have sold it and made a decent profit for myself, after publicly asking the anonymous patron for his permission. I didn't do so, and therefore you ought to have observed reciprocity. In what way can my obligations differ from yours? How can you have more rights than I have? After the explanations you have given me, I will concede that you have a defense respecting the publication. Now, however, you also give me to understand that I have committed some crime against the anonymous patron: but that is really not the case. I made it my condition when I delivered it to him that I retained the right to give copies to princes, who, in the nature of things, would not make them public.

D. 29 SEPTEMBER 1799

(Bauer-Deutsch IV, No. 1258; new translation)

With regard to the Requiem, I must beg you not to make public the fact that you had a copy from me. When you first wrote to me about it, my intention was to seek the anonymous patron who commissioned the work, and toward whom I had certain obligations, through the newspapers, asking him to permit me, in view of the many years that had passed, to sell it for the purpose of publication. I already had permission to present copies to notabilities, and I would not have sold it to you without his permission; but then, when you assured me that you already had two copies, I accepted your offer for lending my copy to you, in order to have the known, small profit, rather than none at all. For that the anonymous gentleman cannot reproach me, since the work would have been published anyway even without me.

E. 18 OCTOBER 1799

(Bauer-Deutsch IV, No. 1260; new translation)

To my amazement I find an advertisement in the Frankfurt press, from Messrs. Gayl and Hedler, stating "that I made over to you the original score of the Requiem."

Unless you are able to give me full and proper assurances in respect of the rights of the anonymous nobleman, my obligations toward whom I have always observed—as indeed my correspondence with you testifies, notably mine of 25 May and 15 June—I shall be forced by considerations of my own honor and by my duty toward the anonymous nobleman to place a contrary statement in all newspapers where it is necessary. I can understand that this will be disagreeable for you, and I shall therefore do it with reluctance, and not before I have received your answer, but you must reply quickly. In any event, the claim that I "made over to you the original score" is directly contrary to the truth. The statement will be understood by the general public and by the anonymous patron to mean that I sold you the work, and thus have not kept my word to the anonymous patron, who has still not given me consent. This *at least you* must correct by means of another advertisement in all the newspapers where the false claim has been published.

You already know very well how things stand, but I will remind you once again. It is true that I wanted to sell the Requiem *to you* one day, but, as I informed you a number of times, not until I had placed advertisements in the press requesting permission to do so from the anonymous patron. The notice was drawn up, I take the draft now from my desk, and set it down here:

> In view of the fact that the anonymous nobleman, who commissioned a
> Requiem to be composed by the late Mozart a few months before his death,
> has still, after the passage of more than 7 years, not publicly revealed his
> identity, Mozart's widow gratefully regards this circumstance as evidence
> that the said nobleman is prepared to allow her to obtain some profit from
> the publication of the same. In the interests of gaining greater assurance for
> herself, however, and consequent upon the sentiments that the said noble-
> man has inspired in her, she regards it as her duty to request the noble gen-
> tleman, through the Viennese, Hamburg, and Frankfurt papers, kindly to
> inform her of his wishes within 3 months, after which time she will venture
> to publish the Requiem *in the complete works of her late husband.*

But then you told me that you already had 2 copies, and only wanted to borrow another copy in the interests of greater accuracy, and in order to direct some profit my way, out of regard for me. When I raised an objection, you wrote quite expressly and very coldly that you did not need my copy. Seeing that you were so determined upon publishing the work, and that you had copies, apparently several, I decided—as the anonymous patron neither would nor could have anything—to accept what you know full well was a trifling sum for the loan of my copy. Rather that than nothing at all, after 7 years in which the consciousness of my obligations prevented me from publishing the work at all, and permitted me only to allow copies to go to two or three reigning princes.

The fact that it was only on 29 September that I requested you not to let it be known that you had had the Requiem from me (really, or originally, of course) is immaterial; the request was only an excessive precaution. I ought to have been able to reassure myself with the thought that nothing would be made known that was at variance with the truth.

(Bauer-Deutsch IV, No. 1767; new translation)

I have only this to say about the Requiem. I do not perceive that I have anything to fear, from what you say, from your advertisement in answer to my advertisement, should I place it. I would publish the truth, and so would you: one truth may well stand beside another truth. I cannot deprive you in any case of the opinion that you have suddenly formed concerning my copy. I allowed it to be performed, and people in the métier made no complaints. And what if some passages in your copies are different, or better, even: does that prove that they are *authentic?* Maybe they are better, but are they by Mozart? And that's the heart of the matter. I am very eager to see the corrections that you intend to mark when you return my copy. They will put me or others in the position to judge *what could not have been by Mozart,* and I shall be greatly obliged and grateful to you for this kindness that you offer me. I hasten, while I think of it, to repay you in advance by suggesting that you could do worse than write to the Viennese Capellmeister Süssmayr on the subject. If he has a copy, as I believe he has, his is without doubt the most authentic. I am sorry for you, however, if you are correct, that you were misled by faith in me or my copy, as I must suppose, to attempt to give your edition the highest sanction in the eyes of the public by telling them, in your advertisement, that it is based on *my* manuscript. I am also sorry to learn that, if what you now say is indeed the truth, my copy was of little or no help to you: you wanted it in order to compare it with your copies, and they are now proved to be accurate. I believed that mine was accurate, as I was bound to believe it; at all events, my conscience is clear. . . .

One further thing to add to the story of my manuscript of the Requiem is that Baron Swieten—a connoisseur whom you rightly hold in high esteem—had the work performed here in 1792 [actually 1793]. Salieri himself attended the rehearsals. No one found any fault with it.

G. 30 NOVEMBER 1799

(Bauer-Deutsch IV, No. 1270; new translation)

Herewith I send you the seal that was on the letters from the man who commissioned the Requiem from my husband. The biography [Niemetschek's] mentions him and the vain search for him. This seal might be the only means of tracing him. It is only an emblem, however, which others could also have used.

H. 30 JANUARY 1800

(Bauer-Deutsch IV, No. 1278; new translation)

With some variations *all* the advertisers have announced that you will publish the Requiem *from my copy.* And that will make it hard for me to defend myself in any other way than by holding up your letters to me, in which you say the opposite to what you have told the public, namely: that you do *not* take it from my copy, because, according to your letters, it is so very bad.

However, it may console you to some extent to learn that the long-sought anonymous nobleman, who is *of very high rank,* has let it be known that a number of copies would probably satisfy him entirely, in respect of his claims. But he also mentioned the sum of 50 ducats, which was his purchase price.

I. 15 FEBRUARY 1800

(Bauer-Deutsch IV, No. 1283; new translation)

With regard to what you please to say to me about the Requiem, I refer you first of all to my letter of 30 January; for the rest I will do as you wish and not publish my justification until it is asked of me, or unless I find for some reason that I must, in order to avoid further loss or damage. In answer to the news you sent, I can tell you that the representative of the anonymous patron has not been to see me again, and that therefore *perhaps* the information I gave him on that occasion satisfied him; I too am surprised, for the anonymous patron lives not far from Vienna.

J. 7 MAY 1800

(Bauer-Deutsch IV, No. 1296; new translation)

My caution, which you call distrust—Oh, how bitterly I regret that I did not exercise far, far more of it! No matter how many copies of the Requiem you had, you would not have been in the position to publish it with honor, if you had been unable to refer to my copy, as your later letters purport to prove (there is a word I will not utter). You thought 20 fl. was sufficient recompense for it, and you claimed that you would come to an accommodation with the anonymous patron. You replied by not so much as a word when I told you he had communicated with me, and it was I alone who had to make him reparations— and you enumerated to me all that I had already had for the Requiem from various royal courts. But now I will not utter another word to you on this subject, and, as I say, I will leave it to your conscience. *En revanche,* I will thank you not to make any more of your promises, such as those listed above, which you appear to expunge from your minds the moment you have written them, for to me they can be nothing more than a mockery and an offense.

(Bauer-Deutsch IV, No. 1301; new translation)

The great delay in publishing the Requiem leads me to conclude that you took my advice to consult Süssmeyer, and found that his copy contained significant differences from *your copies*, probably to the advantage of mine. I am so pleased to have been of service to you in this matter: it is almost as good as if I had been able to let you have the original manuscript. Meanwhile I myself have received the *true* original manuscript from the anonymous patron, for scrutiny, and it would therefore be uncommonly agreeable for me to have either your edition or, since only one fascicle is to be published in the first instance, my own copy again, in order to allow me to arrange for an authoritative comparison. See if you can send it to me as quickly as possible without my incurring expense, perhaps through Traeg [a Viennese music-dealer], but not at my expense, as you did last time. The anonymous patron will not place his original manuscript in anyone else's hands, not even for comparison.

L. 16 AUGUST 1800

(Bauer-Deutsch IV, No. 1304; new translation)

I have now had your edition of the Requiem compared with the original manuscript by a connoisseur [Stadler]. He tells me that the copy you had from me corresponds fully *with the original manuscript;* the presence of several mistakes in the copy is merely the fault of the copyist; these mistakes, which caused you to declare that my copy was useless, while the 2 that you already had were excellent, could be corrected with little trouble by any person with knowledge of music, and were therefore of no serious importance.

Your said declaration notwithstanding, it is perfectly clear that your edition was based on my copy, because several of the mistakes *in my copy,* other than those you noticed, are included in your edition.

E.g, p. 10, the flat sign is missing on the bass's first note;

— 39, a sharp sign is missing in the first basset horn, on the first note of the second bar.

I have nothing more to add except that your edition would have been a little more valuable if it had included the figured bass. As for the above-mentioned mistakes, they are like mistakes in writing and printing. Where can a book or lengthy manuscript be found that is free of errors?

M. 2 JUNE 1802

(Bauer-Deutsch IV, No. 1350; new translation)

I see from the review of the Requiem in the *Musikalische Zeitung* what doubts still obtain concerning Mozart's and Süssmayer's shares in the work. I alone am in the position to resolve all the puzzles, and if my information is of value to you, the reviewers, or your prospective biographer, it is yours to command.

I will begin by saying that everything up to the beginning of the "Dies irae" is by Mozart alone, and that this his manuscript is in the possession of the anonymous patron, as I saw for myself last year. Everything else composed by Mozart himself, and hence in his handwriting, is in my keeping and is my property. Süssmayer was good enough to give it to me, unexpectedly, some considerable time ago; it had not entered my head that he must have it. This manuscript goes up to the end of "Confutatis" [Codex b (1)]. A great portion of the inner parts, and perhaps a little more besides, is not by Mozart; but everything that is not by Mozart is encircled in lead pencil, and it would in any case be obvious to a good student of handwriting. The reviewer will find there the evidence to support his astute observation that a certain passage (in "Tuba mirum," I think) was intended by Mozart not for the flutes but for the trombones.

If this copy can be of use to you, as I say, I will gladly lend it to you. Only please commission Herr Traeg or someone like him to collect it from me and return it to me in due course, so that I do not have to pay for the postage.

I think you will find that the inner parts are different from what they were in the copy that I lent you. Also I must tell you that, while Süssmayer evidently wished to give me *only* the work of Mozart, and may have believed it was to some extent his duty to give me *only* that, he also gave me the Sanctus, in which there is not a note or a word in Mozart's handwriting. Both these points would probably be worth investigating, but I wrote to ask him about the latter a long time ago, with no success, and have not spoken to him about it, as I see him but seldom.

17. Franz Xaver Süssmayr to Breitkopf & Härtel, 8 February 1800

(*Mozart-Dokumente,* Addenda et Corrigenda, 89; new translation)

Gentlemen!

Your kind letter of 24 January afforded me the liveliest satisfaction, for it showed me that you attach too much importance to the esteem of the German public to mislead that same public with works that may not be wholly attributed to my late friend Mozart. I owe too much to the teaching of that great man to stand by silently and allow a work to be published as his, when the greater part of it is mine, for I am convinced that my work is unworthy of his great name. Mozart's oeuvre is so unique and, I venture to say, so far beyond the reach of the great majority of living composers that any imitator, and especially one who claimed Mozart as the author of his work, would cut an even worse figure than the notorious raven which dressed itself in peacock's feathers.

How it came about that I was entrusted with the completion of the Requiem, the subject of our exchange of letters, was as follows. Mozart's widow foresaw, no doubt, that there would be a demand for the works her husband left behind him; death surprised him while he was yet at work on the Requiem.

The task of completing the work was therefore offered to several masters. Some were unable to undertake it because of the pressure of work; others, however, did not wish to hazard their own talent at the side of Mozart's. Eventually the task came to me, because it was known that while Mozart yet lived I had often sung and played through with him the movements that were already composed; that he had frequently talked to me about the detailed working of this composition, and explained to me the how and the wherefore of his instrumentation. The most that I can wish for is that I may have succeeded at least well enough for connoisseurs to be able to find here and there in it a few signs of his unforgettable teaching.

Of the "Requiem" [Introit] with Kyrie, "Dies irae," and "Domine Jesu Christe," Mozart completed the 4 vocal parts and the figured bass; of the instrumentation, however, he indicated only the motivic idea here and there. In the "Dies irae," his last line was "qua resurget ex favilla" [in fact, "judicandus homo reus"], and he had done the same work [there] as in the earlier movements. I finished the "Dies irae" from that line onward: "Judicandus homo reus," etc.

The Sanctus, Benedictus, and Agnus Dei were wholly composed by me; but, in order to give the work greater uniformity, I took the liberty of repeating the Kyrie fugue at the line "cum sanctis etc."

I shall be heartily glad if by conveying this information I have been able to do you a small service.

18. Frederik Samuel Silverstolpe's memoir (1800–01) of the collation of versions of the Requiem, published 1838

(Mörner, "F. S. Silverstolpes Bemerkungen," 116f.; new translation)

This first edition of Mozart's Requiem was printed, not from the original manuscript but from one of the few copies that existed in the year 1800. After the work was published by Breitkopf and Hertel, Mozart's widow wished to see it done on the basis of the said manuscript, widely rumored to be the property of a person unknown. After this wish had been advertised in the public prints, the original manuscript was laid before her in Vienna by the owner's man of business in the city, the lawyer Sortschan. It emerged that the person who had commissioned the work, and owned the original manuscript, was a Count Wallsegg, who resided on his estate of Stuppach in Lower Austria, at no great distance from Vienna.

I was present at the collation of the printed edition with the manuscript; it was actually carried out by Abbé Stadler, a man with the profoundest understanding of all branches of music, and its literature, and of so high a reputation that every composer in Vienna valued his praise. In accordance with the said manuscript, I had this my own copy marked up, firstly with the figured bass, and secondly with initials letters to denote what is demonstrably in Mozart's own hand, and what is in another hand.[23] The letter M stands for Mozart, and the letter S for Herr Süssmayer, who was often employed by Mozart to fill in parts and was called upon by the then already slowly dying master to perform the same task in the case of the Requiem.

The outcome was that, of the twelve movements making up the Requiem, three were completely executed by Mozart, as well as significant sections of two others. Five are largely by him, and probably worked out in detail and finished under his supervision. Two complete movements, and parts of two others, reveal only the handwriting of Süssmayer. To judge by the style and character in these four numbers, where the master's own pen is not to be discerned, it could be claimed that—unless they are merely fair copies of drafts which Mozart destroyed (possibly because numerous alterations had been made on them)—they were worked out in accordance either with *drafts* by himself, or with his *instructions*. But as Sanctus is one of the movements in which there is not a single note in Mozart's handwriting, what are we to say of the four consecutive fifths in bar 4: G–D, F♯–C♯, E–B, and D–A? (See page 130 in this score.) Everyone may make what he will of that. For my part, I cannot think of any reason why Mozart should have introduced these solecisms. They are not present at all in the vocal parts, but their effect in the first and second violins and the wind combined (equally when each of these is transposed) is most obtrusive. (Written in Vienna soon after the collation took place, and later copied into this book in Stockholm.)

F. S. Silverstolpe

23. Now in the Kungliga Musikaliska Akademiens Bibliotek, Stockholm.

19. Frederik Samuel Silverstolpe to his father, 22 April 1801

(Mörner, "F. S. Silverstolpes Bemerkungen," 114; new translation)

Last week and this, I have finally heard two performances of Mozart's famous Requiem, which was his last work. I have never heard church music like it before. A private person arranged for the performance in a small church in a village outside Vienna, called Neu-Lerchenfeld. A lucky chance also uncovered the fact that the Herr Anonymous, who commissioned the work from Mozart and did not wish to reveal his identity, is a Count Waldsek. Lovers of music have been trying for years to unravel the mystery of this last anecdote from Mozart's life. I have had Mozart's own manuscript in my hands, and the music was performed on this occasion from my printed copy.

20. Constanze Mozart to Johann Anton André, 9 February 1800

(*Mozart-Dokumente*, 531; *Mozart DB*, 494–95)

Dear Herr André,

There is a possibility that I might be able to obtain the original score of my husband's famous Requiem from the anonymous gentleman who commissioned it; his agent, however, mentioned to me the sum of 50 ducats. Do you wish me to expend this amount on this work? Or what is the highest price that you wish to expend on it? Up till now I had believed my copy to be a good one; but a connoisseur [Stadler] has assured me that it falls a long way short of the perfection of the original. I cannot as yet judge of the truth of this, but should it be so, it would of course be worth buying the original. As my husband did not entirely complete the work, because he died over it when it was nearly ready, I cannot be absolutely sure how much is actually written in his own hand. Meanwhile, whether it is more of it or less, this particular copy under discussion is obviously the most authentic of all. I have the honour to remain your most respectful and obedient servant

Constanze Mozart

21. Constanze Mozart to Johann Anton André, 11 October 1800

(Bauer-Deutsch IV, No. 1318; new translation)

So Breitkopf has now published the Requiem. There are a few genuine mistakes, and several—albeit not many—inaccuracies, which are always a blemish in the eyes of connoisseurs. Furthermore he has entirely omitted the figured bass. Having had the original manuscript in my power in recent days, I compared the said edition with the original, taking the greatest care, and had the above mistakes corrected in *my* copy, as well as having the complete figured bass added; both by the hand of a master, you will know who I mean [Stadler]. If such a copy can be of use to you, it is at your disposal for a fee. It would be: "with figured bass and d'après une copie corrigée sur l'original avec grand soin."

Another thing. In the copy retained by Süssmeyer (you know that he finished it) the inner parts, which are mostly by him [in fact, Eybler] are wholly different from Breitkopf's edition. A copy of it could also be put at your disposal, for a fee.

From the Period of the Requiem Controversy (1826–39)

22. From Maximilian Stadler, 1826

(Stadler, *Vertheidigung der Echtheit*, 9–16; new translation)

§3

Scarcely had nos. 10 and 11 [of *Cäcilia:* Weber, "Über die Echtheit"] appeared in Vienna when a number of people who knew and admired Mozart's work came to see me and informed me of what was in them; and, when I had enlightened them about the whole affair, they pressed me to publish my views on the subject to the musical world. It was not for me to refuse this just request, the more so because I had followed the entire course of events closely, had enjoyed a friendly relationship with Mozart himself, and moreover, after his death, had been of some service to his widow regarding the manuscripts her husband had left. She had asked me, namely, to bring some order to these manuscripts. She wanted to send them to me in my apartments, but I refused to allow her to do so, promising, instead, to visit her whenever my time permitted, and, in the presence of her neighbor, Herr von Nyssen, to go through the entire collection of music left by her late husband, to sort it, and to draw up a catalog of it. This was done in a short period of time: I read everything out, Herr von Nyssen wrote it all down meticulously, and very quickly completed the catalog. As is well known, Herr André in Offenbach later purchased all the manuscripts that Mozart left. For the rest, I cannot resist speaking of the pleasure this investigation gave me. I discovered how diligent Mozart was in his youth, how he committed to paper not only his own original ideas but also those of other masters that especially appealed to him, in order to work them up later in his own manner and transform them, as the saying is, *in succum et sanguinem*. I discovered that he constantly studied the great Handel and chose him as his model in serious vocal music. There was a large mass, which he did not fully complete but rewrote many years later as the oratorio *Davide penitente*. It is composed entirely in the style of Handel. Similarly he scored many works by his teacher Eberlin and used Eberlin's motive when he wrote his "Misericordias Domini." Finally, not to dwell overlong on this topic, I benefited from the occasion to acquire the most exact knowledge possible of Mozart's handwriting, which remained the same until his death, and which I know now as well as I know my own. Having established these facts, I come to the matter on which Herr Weber has cast doubt. I rejoice, and thank God, that He has permitted me to live long enough to bear witness to the truth, as an old man of eight-and-seventy, whose own end cannot be far off.

§4

Gottfried Weber describes Mozart's Requiem "bluntly, as the least perfect, the least finished," of all his works, and "scarcely worthy to be called a work of Mozart's at all." No, no! It is his most perfect, his most finished, as far as he was able to execute it before his death, a work genuinely and purely Mozart's. It was not cobbled together by Süssmayr from "sketches," "rough drafts," "croquis," and "snippets of paper," as Herr Weber asserts. Mozart himself wrote it out on Italian paper, with twelve staves, as a formal, orderly score. What Süssmayr stated in his letter to the music publishers in Leipzig was perfectly correct: namely, the three principal movements, "Requiem" with "Kyrie," "Dies irae" except for the last verse, "Domine Jesu," all flowed entirely from Mozart's hand, in that he had completely finished the four vocal parts and the figured bass while having indicated the motivic ideas for the instrumentation. It is most remarkable that the last words he wrote, in the "Domine" following the "Hostias," were "Quam olim da capo," as if he wished to denote that he himself was now passing into the eternal life promised by God to Abraham and his seed.

Herr Weber further alleges that the facts are in general virtually forgotten. No, again, they are still held in the liveliest recollection. There are several people still alive who have accurate knowledge of them, who, like me, have held Mozart's original manuscripts in their own hands and perused them with the warmest gratification. The first movement, "Requiem" with the fugue, and the second, "Dies irae," up to "Lacrymosa," were for the most part orchestrated by Mozart himself, and there was not much more for Süssmayr to do than what most composers leave for their amanuenses to do.

Süssmayr's work really began with the "Lacrymosa." But here too Mozart had written out the violins himself; and Süssmayr only finished it from after "judi-candus homo reus" to the end. Similarly, in the third movement, "Domine," Mozart had written the violins' music in his score, where the voices are silent; where the voices enter he had indicated the motives for the instruments here and there, but quite clearly. He gave the violins two and a half bars to perform alone before the "Quam olim" fugue. He wrote two bars for the violins before the entry of the voices at "Hostias," and eleven bars at "Memoriam facimus," in his own hand. We see nothing more from his pen after the end of "Hostias" except, as I mentioned above, "Quam olim da capo." This is the end of Mozart's original autograph score. But people should not think that Süssmayr wrote out his completion of the orchestration on that. He made his own [copy of the] score, very like Mozart's. In this he copied, first, note for note, everything that was in Mozart's original manuscript, next he followed the given instructions for the orchestration meticulously, without adding a note of his own, [then] composed the Sanctus, Benedictus, and Agnus Dei himself. In such fashion the work was completed. Of this score there were at once made two copies. Süssmayr's manuscript was sent to the commissioner. One copy was sent to the music publisher in Leipzig for publication, the second one was retained and the parts copied from it; whereupon this marvelous work was first performed for the benefit of the widow in the Jahn rooms.

Whether Mozart's original manuscript of the "Requiem" and "Dies irae" still exists, and where it might be, I cannot say with certainty; although I have a well-founded opinion on the subject. The "Lacrymosa" and "Domine" still exist, just as Mozart wrote it, untouched; the motives noted by Mozart were not continued any further. Süssmayr holds to this in his score. If the two scores are placed side by side, it becomes clear how exactly Süssmayr observed Mozart's prescription in carrying out the orchestration. I have had these original manuscripts in my hands twice in the recent past, and perused them carefully. Once again, I was saddened by "Quam olim da capo." Who can blame the fortunate owner if he will not allow it to leave his hands? How many own Mozart's original manuscripts, and preserve them carefully, like a precious treasure! I myself am fortunate enough to possess a work that I value highly, namely an exercise in composition which Mozart gave my cousin, and which she gave me in his memory. Whenever I go through those pages, I remember the great master and rejoice to see how he went to work as a teacher.

Yet, in Herr Weber's view, it is irresponsible not to publish Mozart's original manuscripts for the Requiem and incorporate them in facsimile in his *Cäcilia!* The owner will no doubt know the best course of action to take in the fullness of time and will deposit them in a place where they will be preserved for study by those who know and admire Mozart, with as much care as a valuable, albeit uncopied, painting by Raphael in a public gallery. Nothing would be easier than to arrange for a facsimile in this city where there are so many lithographic printers;

but to entrust the task to *Cäcilia,* of all things, seems most inadvisable, since the work is so lamentably misrepresented and denigrated in its pages. The celebrated Leipzig *Musikzeitung* would be a far more suitable place for it, for that has always given Mozart's Requiem the praise it deserves.

Just as I am perfectly sure of the existence of Mozart's original manuscript of the "Lacrymosa" and "Domine," so too I could set down here the name of the man who commissioned the work. But because of his wish to remain anonymous I cannot permit myself to do so in public. I do not think it at all necessary, in any case. The fact is correct. It is enough that we owe the masterpiece to his generosity. There is one thing that I think I may mention, however, namely, that the unknown patron learned at one time that the Requiem was not entirely by Mozart, who died while yet at work on it, and he therefore investigated the matter further. He sent the score in Süssmayr's handwriting that had been delivered to him to his man of business, a very famous lawyer in Vienna, in order to learn more about it. The widow was asked, but she requested me and Herr von Nyssen, who were the people best informed about the matter, to attend at the lawyer's office. We did it willingly. The score was laid before us. I indicated which movements were written by Mozart, and which by Süssmayr. The lawyer wrote down everything that was told him. The matter was settled, the score was sent back, and the unknown patron was satisfied. Meanwhile the widow received back the copy from which the Requiem was printed in Leipzig. I received it from her as a gift, and found that some—very few—errors made by the copyist had been marked in red ink, and these had been corrected before printing.

Finally, Herr Weber claims that, according to his letter, Süssmayr had found some sketches by Mozart (p. 226). I read this letter several times and could not find a single syllable about sketches. What Süssmayr says is that while Mozart yet lived he had often sung and played through with him the movements that were already composed, namely the "Requiem," "Kyrie," "Dies irae," "Domine," and so forth; further, that Mozart frequently talked to him about the detailed working and explained to him the how and the wherefore of his instrumentation.

Up till now, the subject under discussion has been the first three movements of the Requiem, which are indisputably by Mozart. Süssmayr composed the last stanza of the "Lacrymosa" ("Huic ergo parce Deus"), then the Sanctus, the Benedictus, and the Agnus Dei. Whether Süssmayr used some of Mozart's ideas in doing this, or not, cannot be proved. The widow told me that a few scraps of paper with music on them were found on Mozart's desk after his death, which she had given to Herr Süssmayr. What they contained, and what use Süssmayr made of them, she did not know.

23. *Maximilian Stadler to Georg Nicolaus Nissen, 3 April 1826*

(Bauer-Deutsch VI, No. 1413b; new translation)

Noble, honorable Herr Staatsrat and friend!

You have done me too much honor and cause for gratitude in expressing your complete approval of my essay in such amiable terms in your letter of 5 March, received on the 28th. I had assuredly no other purpose than to justify Mozart and to allay the doubts excited by Gottfried Weber's article. Herr Marx in Berlin did the same, at the same time, in the *Musikalische Zeitschrift,* which I read soon afterwards. I would imagine that Tandler sent him my essay as well. Rochlitz is said to have included an excellent review of my essay in the Leipzig *Musikzeitung.* Herr Weber, I hear, is highly displeased with me; he now claims to have done nothing more than remind people of all the things said by others long before now; but that is contradicted by the whole tone of his writing and, in particular, by the words inserted in the last note after the advertisement of the new edition of the Requiem in issue No. 11: "disjecti membra Poetae."

It is generally known that I twice carefully perused the original manuscript of the "Lacrymosa," "Domine," "Quam olim," and "Hostias" before I wrote about it. It belongs to a good friend of mine in Vienna, and I may study it again every day if I wish. But now, such a stroke of indescribable good luck! Someone came to me unexpectedly, on 22 March, and entrusted the original manuscript of the "Dies irae" up to "Lacrymosa" to my care for a limited period. I read through it, I placed it beside the other original manuscript mentioned above, and it transpired that the two fit exactly together, for each sheet is numbered. Nothing more is needed now to complete Mozart's manuscript of this work but the first movement: "Requiem" and "Kyrie." Perhaps that too will be found in time, unless perhaps it is already in the hands of Herr André.

As far as the announcement of a new edition of the Requiem is concerned, I do not know but what it might be better and safer to prepare this edition from the existing original manuscripts rather than from a copy that has been collated with them. As I learn from André's subscription invitation, the letters M and S, which I am supposed to have used, will indicate what is by Mozart and what by Süssmayr. To tell the truth, I cannot recall it precisely, still less that I added the figured bass; that is something which, for the most part, Mozart himself observed meticulously in every tutti. It is possible that I marked those places in the music where the copyist or Süssmayr had omitted it. In any case, the letter S could not be inserted anywhere by Herr André in an edition based on the original manuscripts, which I have recently seen and carefully perused, except after the first 8 bars of the "Lacrymosa," which Süssmayr continued and finished, starting at the

9th bar. Finally an S can be set above Sanctus, Benedictus, and Agnus Dei, until the point in the Agnus Dei, at the beginning of the section in common time, at the words "lux aeterna," where the letter M should be placed, because it is only a recapitulation of the first movement. There is no call for an S in "Domine," "Quam olim," or "Hostias," because Mozart's manuscript shows as clearly as daylight that he was the composer of all three. I know that a number of people have said that the "Hostias" is not by Mozart and were mistaken, for I myself may have been one of them. But Mozart's manuscript, which I have now read through several times, has completely convinced me that he himself was the sole composer of "Domine," "Quam olim," and "Hostias."

I write this in order that Herr André may be alerted to the danger of making some erroneous claim, which would give Herr Weber the chance to make rebuttals, so that the verdict at the end would be worse than it was before. I know Herr André only too well, and I know how obstinately he clings to his opinions once formed. He visited me some years ago and claimed that Mozart had composed the entire Requiem long before his death but had done nothing to it in the period immediately before his death. Might that be true? he demanded. Similarly, others want to make out that the commission was a fiction, pure and simple, and so forth. In this manner, I might in all sincerity have said things here and there in my essay which ran contrary to such notions. But there, I was not privy to Herr André's secrets, and I wrote candidly things that I was fully convinced were true, having heard them spoken so often, without wishing to say anything false. Recently André wrote here to Herr Streicher that the "Quam olim da capo" to which I drew attention, written by Mozart after the "Hostias," was of no significance. But it is proof, first, that he himself must first have written the "Hostias," and, second, that Süssmayr did not repeat the "Quam olim" on his own initiative but in accordance with Mozart's instruction.

Last, a printer's error has crept into André's announcement, where it says that Mozart made his first concert tour "in 1746." Mozart was not born until 1756, and it should be "64."

Not long ago one of the leading music publishers confided to me that he wanted to publish a new edition of the Requiem according to the original manuscripts that have now come to light. Would not this edition be greatly preferable to André's?

Forgive this long screed. I scarcely have space left to assure you that I count myself fortunate to be able to reiterate my warmest and most sincere esteem for you, and present my profoundest respects to your lady wife.

Your most unfeigned and sincere servant and friend
Abbé Stadler

24a. Johann Baptist Streicher to Johann Anton André, enclosing remarks by Maximilian Stadler, 12 March 1826[24]

(Plath, "Requiem-Briefe," 182f.; new translation)

Now to Mozart's Requiem. . . .

Following your advertisement, and its being made known to Abbé Stadtler, he has come halfway to meet us, and I can now relate to you the following, vouched for by Abbé Stadtler.

1. First and foremost he refers you to his *Vertheidigung der Echtheit des Mozartschen Requiem* and to the *remarks in his own hand, enclosed herewith.*

2. The tale about the anonymous patron was already well known in Mozart's lifetime.

3. This tale is *completely true,* and the patron was Count Walseck, who is still alive; but this is *between ourselves.*

4. The first performance of the Requiem was given here, in the Jahn rooms, for the benefit of Mozart's widow.

5. Count Walseck received a copy of the Requiem, in which Abbé Stadtler, at Sortschen's request and in his presence, marked the passages composed by Mozart and by Sühsmayer.

6. Capellmeister Eybler of Vienna owns the original manuscript of part of Mozart's Requiem; Abbé Stadtler scrutinized it once more only recently and found that the "Hostias" was also composed by Mozart, although previously he had doubted it. See Abbé Stadtler's note No. 3.

7. It is thought by some, including Abbé S, that the remainder of Mozart's autograph manuscript fell into the hands of someone else and was destroyed. "Someone else" means either Swieten or Salieri.

8. It is not known if Sortschen had any dealings with Jacobi Klöst [Doc. 7].

9. Abbé Stadtler sends you his very best regards and wishes to warn you against allowing any new doubts to arise, thus giving Herr G. Weber the opportunity to launch a new attack.

That is what I have to tell you, but please do not make any public use of it, without first receiving written approval from Abbé Stadtler.

24b. Enclosure: Maximilian Stadler's autograph remarks

1. In "Tuba mirum," Mozart gave the accompaniment to the trombone throughout the bass solo, and it is a mistake in the first Leipzig printing to assign it to the bassoon after the first few bars.

---

24. Johann Baptist Streicher (1796–1871) was a Viennese piano builder and André's son-in-law.

2. Mozart himself noted the figured bass here and there in the organ part, but not throughout. He did so in order to indicate exactly the chords to be observed in the instrumental accompaniment, which he indicated but did not write out in full.

3. Mozart himself composed the "Hostias." This is shown quite clearly by the original manuscript of the "Domine," at the end of which he wrote his last words: "Quam olim da capo." Before the original manuscript was found, many attributed the "Hostias" to Süssmayr.

4. A skilled connoisseur of Mozart's style will have no difficulty in telling the difference in the last 3 sections of the Requiem—Sanctus, Benedictus, and Agnus Dei. It may be that Süssmayr borrowed some of Mozart's ideas, but the way they are executed is not at all Mozartian; the style is Süssmayr's and similar to his Mass in D. The Agnus Dei is scored in the manner of Haydn, and in bar 29, on the last note, the soprano and bass come together on a fifth.

25. Maximilian Stadler to Johann Anton André, 1 October 1826

(Plath, "Requiem-Briefe," 197f.; new translation)

Honored Sir and Friend!

I was delighted that you sent your son to see me. In accordance with your request, I not only made available to him the copy of the Mozart Requiem which is in my hands, and from which the Leipzig first edition was made, for him to compare with the proofs of your edition, but I also introduced him to Herr Capellmeister Eybler, who kindly showed him the original manuscript of Mozart's "Lacrymosa," "Domine," "Quam olim," "Hostias," "Quam olim da capo." Furthermore, I allowed him to see Mozart's autograph score from "Dies irae" up to [the start of] "Lacrymosa," which is now also in my hands. At the top of the first sheet (no. 11), there is a note by Herr Nyssen: "Everything not circled in pencil is in Mozart's handwriting," up to pagina 32. Essentially, the circling matches the M and S marked here and there in your copy. I have no doubt, therefore, that Herr Nyssen himself inserted those letters in the copy which you have, instead of the pencil marks. I, at least, know nothing of those letters, and I never set eyes on a bottle of red ink in Widow M's house. So the good lady was in error in attributing the letters to me. Equally, she was also in error in naming Süssmayr as the composer of the "Hostias," which Mozart himself drafted fully in his original manuscript of the "Domine," adding "Quam olim da capo" at the end of it. Had the lady not made Herr Eybler a gift of the "Lacrymosa" and "Domine" at such an early date, she could easily have seen for herself from the original manuscript that Mozart, not Süssmayr, composed the "Hostias."

I copied the "Requiem" and "Kyrie," and the whole "Dies irae" up to "Lacrymosa," in my own hand, from Mozart's original manuscript score, before the printing of the Leipzig edition, which was made from a copy of Süssmayr's score. With Herr Eybler, I laid this copy of the "Dies irae," made by me at so early a date, beside the newfound original manuscript, and discovered that they correspond note for note. The very same thing would be found in the case of the "Requiem" and "Kyrie," if the original manuscript of those ever came to light. I would have copied the "Lacrymosa" and "Domine" in the same way, had the Widow Mozart still had those movements in her possession.

The fact that Count Wallseeg commissioned the Requiem from Mozart was known to me immediately after Mozart's death. I have also always known about the count's intentions, and all the other alleged mysteries. From time to time, without soliciting it, I have received news of the count's family circumstances. But it is unseemly and inexcusable to divulge secrets, and therefore I did not take the liberty so much as to reveal the name of the patron. Someone else did so, however. The patron is still alive, and even if he was dead, I should still consider it impertinent to disclose to the world at large matters relating to family circumstances and personal affairs, and much of it merely gossip.

What is certain is that Mozart himself worked out the first 3 movements up to the Sanctus etc. with much effort, and diligence, and love. Men of good repute are ready to testify publicly that they encountered Mozart engaged in this work, and full of enthusiasm for it, shortly before his death: as little as three days before, when his complete exhaustion forced him to lie back in his sickbed, from which he never rose.

Mozart's original manuscripts, and the music therein, which is acknowledged as magnificent by all true connoisseurs, are the only true guarantors of this work. All the rest is irrelevant. Everyone who studies these manuscripts carefully is bound to acknowledge that Mozart alone was the composer, and Süssmayr did no more than could have been done by any experienced amanuensis with some skill in thoroughbass. Everything essential springs from Mozart.

Finally, I implore you kindly to tell me of the contradictions that you say you have found in my *Vertheidigung*. I will gladly revoke them. I am not one of those people who refuse to give up an idea, once they have taken it into their heads. I beg you to make no public use of what I have written you thus far in confidence, as a friend. Farewell, and hold me in your esteemed friendship,

as your most sincere admirer,
Abbé Stadler mpia

26a. Johann Anton André's preface to his edition of the score

(Offenbach, 1827; new translation)

[The letters from Constanze Mozart Nissen, Georg Nicolaus Nissen, and J. Zawrzel, which André printed as footnotes to his own text, are printed below as Docs. 26b–f.]

I lay before the public herewith the edition of the Mozart Requiem which was announced about a year ago but was delayed in its appearance, as I explained in my most recent public advertisement, dated 28 December.

I believe it is of primary importance to reiterate here how and when I came to be the owner of the documents on which this edition is based, and the causes why I now make them known.

In November of the year 1800, I set in train the preparation of a vocal score of the Mozart Requiem that would be as faithful as possible to the original score, for publication by my company (Firma Johann André). Having a year previously purchased from the composer's widow all the original Mozart manuscripts left in her possession, I now had reason to ask Frau Mozart whether she could not also supply me with Mozart's original manuscript of the Requiem.

I received from her the answer printed below (No. 1) [Doc. 26b]. (I mention only, as clarification of the phrase "with my copy or with Breitkopf's edition," which occurs in the first few lines, that the said copy, which Frau Mozart had had collated with the manuscript in Herr Dr. Sortschen's hands, was a printed copy of the Br. & Härtel edition; it is that copy which Frau Mozart calls "her copy or the Breitkopf edition" in this letter.) The articles mentioned in this letter were not actually sent until later, with the letter of 26 January 1801, the relevant passage of which is printed below (No. 2) [Doc. 26c].

The material sent consisted, as stated:

1) of a copy of the Br. & Härtel edition of the score of the Requiem, in which, in accordance with the comparison and indications made by Herr Stadler, the letters M and S were used throughout to show what was by Mozart and what by Süssmayr; it should be noted that those passages marked in lead pencil with M or S, and enclosed accordingly by circles or brackets, were as indicated by Herr Stadler, while the figured bass (wholly absent from the printed edition) was added in red pencil, also by Herr Stadler. (Both the lead-pencil initials and brackets and the red-pencil figured bass had been painstakingly gone over at an early date in red ink—in order, doubtless, to prevent erasure and also to make everything clearer to see; there are, nevertheless, places where the lead-pencil and red-pencil marks still show through.) All of this is plain on the copy in question, which is still in my possession.

Apart from the markings mentioned above, it is also particularly worthy of mention that, inside the front cover, written in the hand of Herr von Nissen, there is the remark: "Hostias, Sanctus, Benedictus, Agnus Dei by S[üssmayr], except for the repeats."

2) of the original Mozart draft, in score, from pages 11 to 32, containing the five numbers "Dies irae" (No. 2), "Tuba mirum" (No. 3), "Rex tremendae" (No. 4), "Recordare" (No. 5), and "Confutatis" (No. 6). At the time I compared the said manuscripts with the Stadler markings on the collated copy but now greatly regret that I returned those manuscripts shortly afterwards, without retaining a proper facsimile of them.

I then went ahead with the vocal score, as planned, without making any public use of the information concerning the authenticity or inauthenticity of the work, which had come to my knowledge through this comparison, for it had been entrusted to me under the seal of secrecy; since then, rather, those data have remained preserved in my library for more than a quarter of a century.

Even when, after the passage of so much time, this same question of authenticity or inauthenticity was raised in issue No. 11 of the periodical *Cäcilia,* I still did not contemplate making publicly known the facts confided to me by Mozart's widow and felt obliged to refuse Herr Gottfried Weber's request to do so, as my letter, printed on page 287 of *Cäcilia* No. 16, proves.

Shortly afterwards, however, I received the letter printed below (No. 3) [Doc. 26d], from Mozart's widow, by then the wife of Herr Staatsrat von Nissen, in which she herself asks me to publish an edition of the collated copy that she had sent me 25 years previously, in order to settle the dispute.

Confirmation of the content of this letter, as well as that of the earlier letters, is given by the letter from Herr Staatsrat von Nissen, which is also printed below (No. 4) [Doc. 26e].

The course of events which I have related here, with the support of the documentary evidence, constitutes my legitimation for publishing the present edition. This edition is nothing other than a most exact printed reproduction of the copy mentioned several times in the foregoing, which was enhanced by the figured bass added by Herr Stadler, marked with the letters M and S, and moreover collated and corrected in a number of places according to the original manuscript; in this edition the letters M and S are also reproduced exactly, in a style designed to make them as clear as possible to the reader.

Moreover, before allowing this edition to be printed, I commissioned my son Carl to use the opportunity of his visit to Vienna last autumn to call on Herr Stadler at his house, in order to look at the manuscripts of the Requiem which

Herr Stadler had recently assured me he possessed and to make once again the most thorough comparison between them and the information I had been given by Mozart's widow. The few disparities between the copy collated 25 years ago and the manuscript shown my son last year are to be found, indicated by special markings, on pages 132–34, page 66, and pages 86–89 of the present edition. Thus my edition possesses the further advantage of indicating the more up-to-date information that Herr Stadler has recently made known.

So much by way of general introduction. In addition, I have the following comments to make on individual passages and numbers within the work.

With references to No. 1 ("Requiem" with "Kyrie"), the letters M and S will not be found anywhere in the entire number, insofar as these letters are also absent from the entire number in the collated copy, as they must be of necessity, since the original draft of this number was not in Frau Mozart's possession at that time, according to her statement in the letter No. 1 [Doc. 26b].

In any case the manuscript of this entire number, as of the other numbers, was only a draft, as is proved by the statement in Süssmayr's celebrated letter:

> Of the "Requiem" with Kyrie, "Dies irae,"★ and "Domine Jesu Christe,"
> M. completed the four vocal parts and the figured bass; of the instrumenta-
> tion, however, he noted only the motivic idea here and there. In the "Dies
> irae" his last line was "qua resurget ex favilla," and he had done the same
> work as in the earlier movements. The "Dies irae" from that line—"judi-
> candus homo reus"—onward, the Sanctus, Benedictus, and Agnus Dei were
> wholly composed by me.

This statement surely compensates, at least to some extent, for the absence of the letters M and S in this number.

With reference to the "Tuba mirum" (No. 3), on page 32 of the present edition, the continuation of the solo melody begun by the trombone is repre-sented as a bassoon solo from bar 6 to bar 18. Recently, however, Herr Abbé Stadler has attested that this melody is continued by the trombone, not the bas-soon, and I too seem to recall that that was what I saw in the manuscript at the time [i.e., in 1800], but I did not correct it in the collated copy for the sole reason that it was of no significance for my purpose (the vocal score) at that date; but now I believe that the ascription, in all editions to date, of this melody to the bassoon is erroneous and based on a mistake. I have marked this dubious passage with the symbols of a hand pointing forwards and backwards.

Further, in respect of the same number, I have to state that the 11 bars for bassoon, page 33, which I have marked with the same symbols and an NB, are also not by Mozart, according to the comparison undertaken by my son, and must therefore also have originated with Süssmayr.

In the "Lacrymosa" (No. 7) of the collated copy, the letter S is not marked until bar 9 in several of the parts, and for that reason the same occurs in the present edition. According to the comparison recently undertaken by my son, however, Süssmayr's work, in respect of the instrumentation, actually starts in bar 3, and only the first two bars of the violins and violas, and the following six bars of the voices, are by Mozart. This new emendation is indicated by means of a special parenthesis and the printing of the letters M and S alongside.

For the rest, it remains the sober fact that Mozart's draft went only as far as bar 8 of this movement, and that is where he ended the work which he left unfinished at his death.

The "Hostias" is marked as Süssmayr's work in the collated copy, and this finds further confirmation in Herr von Nissen's remark inside the cover. For that reason the reader will find that this number is marked with an S in the present edition, in conformity with the collated copy. However, I have been assured recently by my honored friend of many years, Herr Abbé Stadler, that it is the work of Mozart himself, to the same extent as those that precede it, and he showed my son the manuscript in his possession to support his statement. I have therefore, as a sign of my faith in his words, marked these passages, too, by special parentheses and the letters M and S alongside, in accordance with his present attribution of them to Mozart or Süssmayr.[†]

If, incidentally, the two said numbers "Domine" and "Hostias" (Nos. 8 and 9) are indeed by Mozart, then all I can suppose is that these two pieces—following as they do the "Lacrymosa," in bar 8 of which Mozart ceased his work—must be earlier compositions, perhaps used only after his death, in order to complete the Requiem left unfinished from the "Lacrymosa" onward.

All the preceding assumptions appear to be resoundingly confirmed, moreover, by the following remarks on the history of the Requiem's composition.

First and foremost, even at the start of the whole history, I personally was never able to believe a word of the story of the mysterious commission, which is like a fairy tale in all its many variants. My own theory, which I formed at an early date, was as follows:

At about the same time as Mozart's widow sent me the above-mentioned score, I also received another document, according to which, as early as March 1792— that is, very soon after Mozart's death—the late King of Prussia, Friedrich

Wilhelm II, a great connoisseur and venerator of the art of music, had acquired a copy of the Requiem through the agency of his then ambassador in Vienna, and had paid 450 imperial gulden = 100 ducats for it.

This suggested to me the notion that that transaction could have been the origin of the fairy tale about the fictitious commissioning of the Requiem for 100 ducats.

For the time being I allowed the truth or nontruth of the entire business to rest; at all events, it was never mentioned again between me and Frau Mozart.

It was not until last spring that the more credible history of the events came to my knowledge by chance. Happening to be in Amsterdam at the time, I encountered the first oboe at the opera in that city, Herr J. Zawrzel, who had formerly been a musician in the service of Count von Waldseck, when he lived at his castle of Stubbach, 3 hours from Wiener Neustadt. From him I learned that this same count was the anonymous person who had commissioned the Requiem, and that it was his major-domo who had conveyed the commission to Mozart in the summer of 1790 [sic], paid the fee that Mozart requested (said to be only 50 ducats, incidentally), and made it a condition at the same time that Mozart should not only furnish the composition as soon as possible but also never publish it.

After Mozart's death, Süssmayr, a friend of the household, was asked by the widow to help to look through and sort the manuscripts the composer had left, which, as is well known, were in anything but good order. While doing so Süssmayr found the manuscripts of the Requiem, and upon his asking what this unfinished requiem was, the widow remembered that the work had been commissioned from her late husband, and paid for in advance, and she asked Süssmayr to finish it. The letter printed below (No. 5) [Doc. 26f] gives fuller details.

This story strengthens me in my suspicion that Mozart, anxious to complete the commission quickly, brought out the draft of a composition in the genre that he had started at some earlier date, and used it for the work in question (as he had done in more or less similar fashion with his great Mass in C Minor, begun in 1783 but not finished, which he used two years later in his cantata *Davide penitente*).

I also believe that I am right in my suspicion that the work started earlier went as far as the point in the "Tuba mirum" (No. 3) where the bass solo with bassoon (trombone) obbligato ends, in bar 18.

For it is only from that point, only from the entry of the tenor solo "Mors stupebit," that I believe I hear those magical sounds that give Mozart's later compositions their uniquely individual character, and which I fail to hear, on the whole, in everything before that point, except for the glorious introduction of

No. 1, whereas they continue to resound unmistakably not only throughout the rest of this number (No. 3) but also in the following movements, up to and including bar 8 of the "Lacrymosa" (No. 7), from bar 9 of which, as is well known, Süssmayr's work begins in full.

And even if the next two movements, "Domine" (No. 8) and "Hostias" (No. 9) are indeed by Mozart, though they come later than the above-mentioned last bar that he wrote, yet I maintain that what I have just said supports my theory, set out above, that these numbers too, at least, could certainly be merely earlier works by the master whose later works were so sublime, and they were used after his death to complete the Requiem.

I have already, in earlier public utterances, expressed my opinion that those said earlier compositions must have been written before 1784; I would make the following remarks in support of my view:

From February 1784 onwards, Mozart kept a thematic catalog in which he entered in his own hand everything he composed; this was published by my company in 1805, and a second edition has just appeared. But Mozart was also accustomed to enter compositions in this catalog even when all that he had written was a draft; that is proved by, for example, the aria entered there as No. 111, of which I own the original manuscript, and which is nothing more than a draft, such as Mozart customarily wrote for vocal compositions with orchestral accompaniment: that is, he wrote out only the vocal part, and usually the instrumental bass also, in full in his draft, but of the remaining parts he noted only the motivic ideas here and there.

Finally, as for the manner of Süssmayr's completion of the Requiem, it seems to me that the simple explanation we have from Herr Zawrzel, who knew Süssmayr well, is far more credible than the one given by Süssmayr in his famous letter to Br. & Härtel. For it is surely obvious that Mozart would have executed the unfinished remaining sections of his work in one tenth of the time it would have taken him to explain to Süssmayr how the work was to be carried out and finished, in as much detail as Süssmayr would have had us believe. Every practiced composer will confirm what I say from his own experience.

All the information contained in these pages should suffice to allow the question of the authenticity of the Mozart Requiem to be decided with little hesitation or difficulty (even by that part of the general public which is not well-enough acquainted with the immortal composer's muse to recognize those movements of the composition which are by Mozart himself) on the celebrated principle of *ex ungue leonem*. It remains for me only to add that the letters cited here, the copy of the score sent me by Frau Mozart, the original manuscript of Mozart's diary, in which the aria sketch mentioned above is entered as a composition of 17 September 1789, and this same autograph sketch itself, are available for anyone to see in my own house.

Offenbach am Main, 31 December 1826   Ant. André

---

* To avoid any possible misunderstanding, I point out that S. does not list the individual movements of the "Dies irae" singly here and that he refers to Nos. 2, 3, 4, 5, 6, and 7 of this present edition, which together constitute the "Dies irae" as Süssmayr understands it.

† In the present edition, the repeat of "quam olim" after the "Hostias" is printed out, whereas in the manuscript shown my son there are only the written words "quam olim da Capo." This is because the present edition, as already stated, is an entirely faithful reproduction of the collated printed copy, in which the repeat is printed in full.

26b. From Constanze Mozart, Vienna, 26 November 1800

(Full text in Bauer-Deutsch IV, No. 1322)

It is impossible for either you or me to lay our hands on the complete original score of the Requiem. Doctor (Lawyer) Sortschen, who lives in Vienna, on Unter den Tuchlauben, sent it back to the anonymous owner, and it was only in S[ortschen]'s house that I was permitted to look through it and collate it with my copy or with Breitkopf's edition. The consequence is not only that my copy of the Breitkopf edition is now more accurate than that edition itself but also that the other emendations undertaken by a skilled hand even make my copy more correct than the original manuscript. I will make this my copy over to you, and then you will be able to state truthfully that your vocal score is based on a copy that has been painstakingly compared with the (true) original, and corrected accordingly. I said above that my copy is better than the original manuscript: you know, between ourselves, that not everything is by Mozart, namely many inner parts, and therefore you will not be scandalized by the many mistakes made in his name in the original manuscript. But I will do even more for you. Namely, I will procure for you "Dies irae," "Tuba mirum," "Rex tremendae," "Recordare," "Confutatis," and "Sanctus" and confide the following secret to you: the anonymous patron has the original manuscript of everything that precedes the "Dies irae." From there onward, Mozart wrote only the principal voices in "Dies irae," "Tuba mirum," "Rex tremendae," "Recordare," and "Confutatis" and did little or nothing of the inner parts; these were done by another, and, in order that two different handwritings should not be mixed up together, he also copied

Mozart's work. Now you know for certain everything in the Requiem that is by Mozart. It is what I said above, and in addition there are the mere repeats later in the work. The Sanctus that I will send you is the original manuscript of the person who wrote that movement, as he did the remainder. Another point is that the inner parts of the movements that I will send you are different from what they are in Breitkopf's edition; in the latter they are the same (apart from the small corrections) as they are in the anonymous patron's original manuscript. The person who completed the score must therefore have done them twice, and you can choose between the two, as you think fit. Thus the Sanctus is entirely by the person who completed the work, but only what is ringed in pencil in the other movements. You can thus even say in all truth that your vocal score is based on the original manuscript itself in 6 numbers (there are only 12 in all).

Hear is a list of what you will receive:

1) Capriccio, to be returned to me.
2) The corrected and collated copy of the Requiem.
3) The original manuscript of the above-mentioned 6 movements of the Requiem, which must be returned to me.★

signed: C. Mozart

★ Please note, in this context, that Herr von Nissen already took care of the correspondence about Mozart's estate, in the name of the composer's widow, later his wife, and even signed some letters in her name. The same is the Herr von Nyssen referred to on p. 15 of Herr Stadler's pamphlet. (*A. Andrê*)

26c. From the same

(Full text in Bauer-Deutsch IV, No. 1326)

Vienna, 26 January 1801

I send you herewith:

- The Requiem;
- The Capriccios, to be returned to me;
- The Leitgeb Quintet;
- Several movements of the Requiem in the original manuscript, from pag. 11 to pag. 32, to be returned to me.

signed: C. Mozart

(Full text in Bauer-Deutsch IV, No. 1404)

Salzburg, 1 January 1826

In your position, dear Herr André, I think I would settle part of the question that has arisen concerning the Requiem: I would publish the work in two different types, one for Mozart's handwriting, the other for Syssmayr's. Then no one could doubt that what was represented as being in his hand was by him.

signed: C. Nissen

p.p. Nissen

26e. From Herr Staatsrat von Nissen

(Full text in Bauer-Deutsch IV, No. 1413)

Salzburg, 16 March 1826

The Abbé [Stadler] attached such extraordinary importance to marking the score at the time, and displayed such zeal in the matter, that his whole deportment at the time is still vivid in my memory, which is very poor when it comes to matters and circumstances that are not of a kind to leave an impression. It is therefore inconceivable that he could have vouched for the authenticity of an inaccurate, incomplete copy as he is said to have done. Without taking the greatest pains his work would have been worse than without purpose, it would have been contrary to the purpose. I (and who is not with me in this?) regard the copy marked by him—a copy that went from him and so furnished, from his hands into mine and from my hands directly into yours, virgin so to speak—as more authentic, and thus surely more complete and accurate, than any other: even than an original manuscript, ten years old, which has been leafed through at home and on journeys by any number of people, who knows? perhaps even lent out for hours at a time, albeit only from one room to the next; which may have suffered fate's slings and arrows, and was always subject to accidents that were never visible or discoverable in their reality by the owners of the hands, formerly two and later four, which were its usual resting place, thanks to their ignorance, unless revealed by obvious mutilation; the music, tested by experience, was available in parts for public use.

You know that what I lent you was the reunited, original score.

You were reared in the same school as Abbé Stadler: you know Mozart's handwriting as perfectly as he, I venture to say even more perfectly, if the superlative "perfect" can take a comparative.

That I have always been convinced of the completeness and accuracy of this marked copy is proved by the suggestion I made you recently that you should publish it, in which enterprise I could not consider the use of any copy but this.

signed: Nissen

26f. From Herr J. Zawrzel

(Plath, "Requiem-Briefe," 189f.)

Amsterdam, 25 July 1826

Most esteemed Herr André,

You wish to know how Count Walseck spelt his name; as I never saw his signature, not even on the pieces of music that were alleged to be his compositions, I spelt his name according as it was pronounced.

It was August 1790 [sic] when the count sent for me. It was very soon after the countess's death. A young cellist in the count's service, who was knowledgeable about composition, told me that the count was himself composing a Requiem for the countess and had made good progress with it. He took me to the count's study to see the Requiem. I studied it carefully and found that it was complete up to the Sanctus, and very prettily written. My attention fell on the basset horns, and I told the count that instruments of that kind were not to be found in [Wiener] Neustadt. He answered that when he had finished the whole Requiem, he would send for basset horns from Vienna.

In October I came to Vienna. You yourself know that in the meantime Mozart had composed *Die Zauberflöte* and *Titus,* thought no more of completing the Requiem, and attended Emperor Leopold's coronation, in Frankfurt and in Prague, where a short time later he fell ill and died. There was great confusion in the house. Süssmayr, who was a friend of the household, was asked to sort the music, which lay in disorder in a heap, and so the Requiem was found. Süssmayr asked: "What is this Requiem, which is not finished?" Madame Mozart recalled that a gentleman had ordered the Requiem, paid what Mozart asked in advance, received what was ready from time to time, and, having come in vain on a few occasions, had stayed away for a long time. Now you can guess why nothing was heard from the count after Mozart's death; his identity would have been revealed, and he could not longer have pretended to his household to be the composer of the Requiem etc.

signed: Zawrzel

27. From Maximilian Stadler, 1827

(Stadler, *Nachtrag zur Vertheidigung,* 8–11; new translation)

To give Herr Weber his due, it must be admitted that he shows a readiness to be enlightened. In No. 11 [of *Cäcilia*], p. 215, he writes: "It would, incidentally, be of the very greatest interest to see the originals of the oft-cited Mozart manuscripts from which Süssmayr worked, for that would not only shed light on the matter as a whole but also, in particular, it would make it possible to see what was from Mozart's pen and what from Süssmayr's."

Herr Weber cannot bring himself to believe that Mozart left the first three movements of his Requiem in the form of a well-ordered score, written in his own hand, and will talk only of single sheets. But I demonstrated in my first essay that "Lacrymosa" bar 8, "Domine" with "quam olim," "Hostias," "quam olim da Capo," really exist in a score in Mozart's hand, which I have myself often studied. Now, however, I can and must add that, before the work was published in Leipzig, from a copyist's copy, I made a copy for myself, from the original copy—from the original score, from Mozart's own manuscript—of the "Requiem" and "Kyrie" and the whole "Dies irae" with all its sections up to "Lacrymosa," as scored, and I have kept it carefully to this day, as a document of the greatest importance. Furthermore, I was at last fortunate enough to receive the original manuscript of Mozart's score of the whole "Dies irae" up to "Lacrymosa," from a friend, in Holy Week of this year. The "Requiem" and "Kyrie," which I copied for myself from the original manuscript in score, consists of 5 folios; each sheet has its own number, from 1 to 10 inclusive, in Mozart's hand. The original manuscript of the "Dies irae," which is now in my hands, consists of 11 folios, numbered from 11 to 32. The "Lacrymosa" starts on sheet 33; "Domine," "quam olim," "Hostias," "quam olim da capo" are on sheets 34 to 45 and are in the possession of First Court Capellmeister Joseph Eybler. All these folios, truly, are not sketches, handed over to Süssmayr, as Herr Weber believes. Süssmayr never used the word "sketches." They are a complete score, written in Mozart's own hand. Each individual movement is worked out from beginning to end by Mozart himself, so that Süssmayr could not have added anything of his own, still less spoiled any of it. Any amanuensis possessed of only a little know-how could have done exactly what Süssmayr did—who had, moreover, enjoyed Mozart's written and oral guidance: which was nothing other than to continue the accompaniment here and there, as Mozart had indicated but not written out in full everywhere. All the passages criticized by Herr Weber, for example the melody in the "Tuba mirum," the "Confutatis," and so on, were composed by Mozart himself. If that "Dies irae" cannot be called a complete score, then every piece a composer hands to an amanuensis must be called a sketch, not a score. No sooner did I have the original manuscript of the "Dies irae" in my hands than I made haste to show it to true connoisseurs of Mozart's handwriting, who recognized it at once, at the first glance, admired Mozart's certitude in the working, figured bass and so forth, rejoiced heartily at the find, and gave me their assurance that everything I had said about it in my *Vertheidigung* was indeed exactly as I had said. These were: Herr Beethoven, Herr Eybler (First Court Capellmeister), Herr Gänsbacher (Cathedral Capellmeister), Herr Hofrat von Mosel, Herr Hofrat von Kiesewetter, Herr Baron von Doppelhof-Dier, Herr von Smezcall, the Herren Streicher, Treitschke, Gyrowetz, Haslinger, Carl and Joseph Czerny, Leidesdorf, Kandler, the two Court Organists Sechter and Assmayr, and, among many others, the son of Mozart who was here in Vienna, Wolfgang Amadé.

Everyone who wants a sight of it for himself will find me ready to show it to him, at any time. Should Herr Weber wish to peruse this splendid document in person, or nominate a good and trusted friend to do so on his behalf, his wish will gladly be granted. If Herr Weber still declares himself unsatisfied, then, truly, he is past all help. Let him rejoice in his error, while everyone else rejoices in what we know to be the truth. Let him twist and turn his "torso" as much and as long as he likes, I will join Mozart's true admirers in constant, delighted admiration of the original.

28. *Constanze Nissen to Maximilian Stadler, 31 May 1827*

(Bauer-Deutsch IV, No. 1419; new translation)

My dearly beloved friend!

You should have had an answer from me long ago, had I not solemnly promised my husband, of blessed memory, not to utter a word in the debate about the Requiem, in order not to bring all these creatures about my ears. But now I can do no less than tell you, and all Mozart's friends, the true story of the Requiem, which is as follows: Mozart had never so much as started a requiem, and often said to me that he undertook this work (the one commissioned by the anonymous gentleman) with the greatest of pleasure, because it [i.e., sacred music] was his favorite genre, and he would do it and compose it with such diligence that his friends and enemies alike would study it after his death: "if only I live long enough, for this must be my masterpiece and my swan song." And he did indeed work at it very diligently; but as he felt himself growing weak, Süssmayr often had to sing through what had been written with him and with me, and thus Süssmayr learned a lot from Mozart. I can still hear Mozart saying to Süssmayr, as he often did: "Ey, there you are again, like a dying duck in a thunderstorm; you won't understand that for a long time." Then he would take the pen and write, I suppose, important passages that were too much for Süssmayr.

The one reproach that can be made against Mozart is that he was not very tidy with his paper and sometimes mislaid something that he had started; rather than spend a long time looking for it, he would write it again; thus it came about that a thing could be written twice, and yet be no different from what he had mislaid, for once he had drawn an idea up out of the turmoil of his thoughts it was a solid as a rock and was never altered, as can be seen in his scores, which are so beautifully, punctiliously, and cleanly written, with not one note altered, for sure.

Let us suppose that Süssmayr did in fact find some fragments by Mozart (for the Sanctus, etc.), the Requiem would nevertheless still be Mozart's work.

My asking Eybler to finish it came about because I was annoyed with Süssmayr at the time (I don't remember why), and Mozart himself had a high opinion of Eybler, and I thought that anyone could finish it, since all the important passages had been set out already. And so I sent for Eybler and told him of my wish, but since he declined at once with fair words, he never laid hands on it.[25] This is the truth, I can assure you, my dear friend, as a women of honor! If Herr André says he received letters and other documents from me containing evidence that Mozart did not write this work just before his death, but much earlier, what a barefaced lie!

29. Maximilian Stadler to Johann Anton André, 19 October 1828

(Plath, "Requiem-Briefe," 200f.; new translation)

Highly esteemed Sir and friend!

My answers in response to your questions of 27 September, received 6 October, are as follows.

To the first, I am confident that you will have received the "Lacrymosa" and "Domine" by now, which I copied from the manuscript directly after your departure and gave to Herr Streicher.

Second, the folios of the manuscript are not folded together but follow one another separately.

---

25. This statement is not correct, as Doc. 6 demonstrates.

Third, you cavil at the octave made by the 2d basset horn and 2d bassoon, but I see nothing wrong with it, for it is covered by the other instruments and the finest ears will not detect it in performance. Mozart sought to give the accompaniment, too, a natural singing line, and thus the 2d basset horn sings with the reinforcement of the E in the cadenza, and at the same time this prepares the following 7th. That is how I copied it from Mozart's manuscript, without the least hesitation, and it would never have entered my head that Süssmayr could have laid a finger on even the smallest part of the "Requiem" up to the "Kyrie," where he continues with the instruments accompanying the voices as indicated by Mozart, for all the orchestration is so celestially beautiful, a true Mozartian masterpiece, which must arouse rapture in every connoisseur who hears it. No: Mozart wrote it, not Süssmayr.

Fourth, if Mozart's widow now claims that the patron did not receive the "Requiem" and "Kyrie" in Mozart's manuscript, how was she able to write, in the letter Herr André printed alongside his Preface: "The anonymous patron (Count Wallseg) has the original manuscript of everything that precedes the 'Dies irae'"? Is it not the "Requiem" and "Kyrie" which precede it?

For the rest, I would thank you once more for Mozart's quartets, which have given me so much enjoyment, and I commend myself, confident of your greatly valued friendship, as

your most sincere admirer and friend,
Abbé Stadler mp

30. Maximilian Stadler to Ignaz von Mosel, 29 March 1829

(Eibl VI, No. 1413a; new translation)

Highly esteemed Sir!

I thank you most heartily for the letter from the editors of *Cäcilia,* returned herewith. I saw from it that my essay on Mozart's Requiem was still unknown to them; also that at the same time they wish I had not been moved, as they suppose, by a highly mistaken and misdirected zeal to say things which could lead to my appearing compromised. Of that, however, there is not the least fear. For what I wrote was done with mature reflection, without passion, without the least wish to offend anyone, but simply from love of the truth, to which I can testify with the more certainty because I am far better informed about the matter than Herr André with all his confidences. According to Herr Weber, the only way the matter can be decided is by seeing the originals, Mozart's manuscripts themselves. Now, in my essay I showed that I had twice painstakingly studied the "Domine," "Quam olim," and "Hostias" and may see them again every day in the owner's house. What I said in my essay all tallies exactly with the original, to the last note and syllable. Finally, I was fortunate enough of late to receive Mozart's manuscript of the entire "Dies irae" up to "Lacrymosa," with the "Domine" as well. Someone who had received it as a gift brought it to me on 22 March last year; and it matches what I said in my essay. I was delighted and showed it to many connoisseurs, who were now even more convinced than before that my essay was right. Neither André nor even Mozart's widow can lay these two original manuscripts before the world, because they are here in Vienna. Perhaps there is a possibility that the first movement, "Requiem" and "Kyrie," will also come to light, and then everything will be settled at last. It may perhaps be in the hands of Herr André. I no longer have any clear recollection of what Herr André says about a printed copy of the Requiem which he had from the widow, and which I am supposed to have compared with the original manuscript and marked with M & S. The letters may perhaps have been inserted by someone other than me. It all happened under the seal of secrecy. It is possible that I added the figured bass in a printed copy which did not have it. But Mozart himself wrote in the figured bass where necessary and, as the original manuscripts show, with great exactitude, especially in the tuttis!

The letter I received a short time ago from Herr Staatsrat von Nissen and Constanze Mozart proves that both were perfectly satisfied with my essay, and their only outstanding wish is that it should be publicized more and more widely. The allegation, finally, that Herr Weber had some other intention in the first numbers [of *Cäcilia*] than reviving the memory of what others had said is plainly contradicted by that same phrase "disjecti membra poetae."

I remain with all conceivable respect,
yours most sincerely,
Max Stadler

31. *Ignaz von Mosel to Constanze Nissen, 7 February 1839*

(Plath, "Noch ein Requiem-Brief," 97f.; new translation)

Gracious Lady!

Your son, my esteemed friend, wrote you a few weeks ago that the original score of the Requiem by your celebrated first husband, all of it written in his own hand, had been found and deposited in the Imperial Court Library. You expressed your joy at this news in a letter to him, dated 4 January.

Now, however, after the leading Viennese authorities on music and handwriting had expressed their view that the whole of that score was indeed written in the great master's hand, *manuscripts by Süssmayer* have been found, which display such an astonishing similarity to Mozart's handwriting, and an even greater resemblance to the newly discovered score, from the "Dies irae" onward, that all complete certainty has been lost as to whether the said sections of the work—and the first two, the "Requiem" and "Kyrie"—were indeed also written in the hand of your first husband or, as Abbé Stadler maintained in his writings, in that of Süssmayer.

In a published letter to the Abbé, dated Salzburg, 31 May 1827, you said among other things, honored lady, that you asked first Herr Eybler, and then, when he declined, Herr Süssmayer, to finish the Requiem, which—as you remarked—anyone could have done, "since all the important passages had been set out already." What you said then directly contradicts the letter of 4 January to your son, for, if the work still needed to be finished, the newly discovered score *cannot* be in Mozart's hand *entirely. You must* have known that finding such a thing would be *impossible,* and consequently you could not have rejoiced at the discovery.

Madam, you will understand that, since all the daily newspapers, unhappily, have already reported the discovery much too hastily, the general public must be told something reliable, worthy of the subject, and carrying the authority of the Court Library. But since comparison of the complete score with other manuscripts of Mozart and of Süssmayer is no guarantee of a completely safe result, *you alone* can shed light on the matter, for you must know whether Mozart left the work finished or unfinished and whether, in the latter case, Süssmayer finished it at your request.

I turn to you, therefore, on the instructions of my superior, His Excellency Count Moriz von Dietrichstein (who commends himself to you), and in the interests of your great husband, of yourself, and of the whole musical world, with the plea that you will give me a definitive answer *immediately,* for the announcement by the Court Library of so important a find cannot be deferred for too long, all the less so because the announcement has already been anticipated by unauthorized correspondents in all the newspapers, and it is therefore awaited by the general public.

I give you *my word of honor* that—whatever your answer may be—the respect owed to the widow of the greatest composer will in no way be diminished. Should your information arrive too late, however, or should you give me no answer at all, then I should have no choice but to publish an opinion, based on mere suppositions and probabilities, which might offend you perhaps, without my being at fault.

In the expectation of a reply at your earliest convenience, I have the honor to remain with the greatest respect, Madam,

your most sincere servant,
Ig. Fr. von Mosel mp
Imperial Court Councillor

32. *Constanze Nissen to Ignaz von Mosel, 10 February 1839*

(Plath, "Noch ein Requiem-Brief," 100; new translation)

Esteemed Herr Hofrat!

Forgive me for not wishing to cloud my son's pleasure, and therefore not telling him directly that he should not give way to his joy so entirely, inasmuch as the newfound manuscript may well be Süssmayr's, for he himself told me that he had made a copy for his own use, in which he had imitated both the notation and Mozart's handwriting so closely that it was impossible to distinguish them, and anyone would take it for Mozart's hand. I therefore believe that it is, or may be, that score.

If the score is complete, it is not by Mozart, for he did not finish it, and so it must be possible to see the additions made by Süssmayr; for in my estimation no one is capable of imitating another person's hand so perfectly that it cannot be distinguished; so much for that. And now I assure you that no one but Süssmayr finished the Requiem, which was not so very difficult, because there is someone [Stadler] who believes that the important parts were all set out already, and Süssm. could hardly go wrong. Appalling gout in my right arm prevents me writing any more. I can therefore say no more than that I remain

yours most sincerely,
Constanze von Nissen

CHAPTER FOUR

Score of Mozart's Requiem Fragment

Introduction

This edition is based on that published by Leopold Nowak in 1964–65, in the Neue Mozart-Ausgabe (NMA I/2, vols. 1–2), but it incorporates a number of not insignificant alterations, most obviously in the Kyrie. The various revisions take account of the present state of research, first and foremost, but a further consideration has been the wish to focus attention on the Requiem's status as what may perhaps be called a double fragment, and this has been done by incorporating crucial excerpts from Süssmayr's score. The "large fragment" which survives in autograph still remains a torso, even after it has been augmented by the "small fragments" concealed in, and scattered throughout, Süssmayr's score.

Mozart's Autograph Fragment

The manuscript left behind by Mozart consists of the first three main sections of the mass for the dead—Introit/Kyrie, Sequence, and Offertory (that is, lacking Sanctus and Agnus Dei/Communion)—laid out in readiness to be a full score. Except for the "Lacrymosa," of which only eight bars were written, all the movements are fully worked out with four vocal parts and a bass. Only the first movement is orchestrated in full, while in the separate movements of the Sequence and Offertory only the "motivic idea" of the orchestral accompaniment is indicated.

The following differences from the NMA edition (vol. 1, pp. 3–58) should be noted in this edition. First, the headings of the movements follow Mozart's autograph (see Figs. 2, 3, 4, and 6); headings that refer to liturgical genres and functions (Introit, Sequence, Offertory), which Mozart did not use as titles, are not used here. Second, Mozart did not number the sections of the Requiem. The numbering used here (1–5) differs from that of the NMA edition and follows the work's musical-cum-liturgical divisions. Third, NMA includes the colla parte parts of the "Kyrie" fugue, but Mozart did not write them out, and they are not included here, so that this edition restores the fugue to the state in which Mozart left it.

Süssmayr's Completion

Süssmayr's contribution consists of two discrete processes. First, he completed the instrumentation from the Kyrie to the end of the Offertory, taking in the work done before him by others (Joseph Eybler in particular but also Franz Jacob Freystädtler and probably Maximilian Stadler too)—this part of Süssmayr's work is not included in the present edition. Second, he wrote new music to complete the "Lacrymosa" and for the whole Sanctus and Agnus Dei/Communion, incorporating Mozart's intention to repeat the opening of the "Requiem"/"Kyrie," and, it may be inferred, other ideas left behind by Mozart on "scraps of paper." This new music by Süssmayr is included in the present edition, but in reduced form, and omitting the final movement with its repetition of Mozart's opening movement.

The edition of this part of the Requiem differs from the NMA edition (vol. 2, pp. 113–117, 149–67, and 170–79) in details. In order to present an appearance analogous to that of Mozart's autograph fragment, the score with Süssmayr's additions has been reduced to its compositional substance—that is, to the vocal parts and bass—while the full instrumentation is indicated only by incipits at the start of each movement. Also, the Hosanna repeat, transposed to B-flat major, has been omitted, as has the final movement's repetition of the opening movement.

This retouching of Süssmayr's score is not intended to represent the vocal lines as being by Mozart. Rather, the purpose is to enable a better and more clear-cut comparison of the original state of the Requiem, as left by Mozart, with the substance of Süssmayr's additional material. Even though Süssmayr's working score as such has not survived, we can assume that for him, as for Mozart, the vocal writing was the starting point of his composition. The quality of the vocal writing shows decisive differences between Mozart's and Süssmayr's styles and their manners of compositional elaboration. Whatever of Mozart's original ideas entered Süssmayr's completion may be judged—at least on the testimony of the surviving autograph material—to have left its mark primarily in "the four vocal parts and the figured bass" and in the indication of the occasional instrumental "motivic idea" (Doc. 17). In that belief, this edition of Mozart's unfinished Requiem focuses attention expressly on Mozart's fragmentary ideas which lie concealed in Süssmayr's completion.

1. Requiem

34
Do - na, do - na
Do - na, do - na e - is Do - mi - ne, do - na,
Re - qui - em ae - ter - - -
Re - qui - em ae - ter - - - - - - nam
Tutti
Vc.
37
e - - - - is Do - mi - ne, do - na, do - na e - is re -
do - na e - - is re - - qui - em ae - ter - - - - - - - nam, do - na e - is
nam do - na, do - na e - - is, do - na
do - na, do - na e - is, e - is Do - mi - ne,
Tutti Bassi
Vc.
Tutti Bassi

40
- qui-em ae-ter - - - nam, ae-ter - - - nam, ae-ter - - nam: et lux per-pe - tu-a,
Do-mi-ne, do - na e - is, do - na e - is, do - na: et lux per-
e-is, do - na, do - na, do - na: et lux per-
do - na, do - na e - - is, do - na e - - is, do - na: et lux per-
44
p
et lux per-pe - tu-a lu - ce-at e-is, et lux per - pe-tu-a lu-ce-at e - is.
pe - tu-a, et lux per - pe - tu-a lu - ce-at e-is, et lux per - pe-tu-a lu-ce-at e - is.
pe - tu-a, et lux per - pe - tu-a lu - ce-at e-is, et lux per - pe-tu-a lu-ce-at e - is.
pe - tu-a, et lux per - pe - tu-a lu - ce-at e-is, et lux per - pe-tu-a lu-ce-at e - is.

37
le - - - - - i - son, e - le - - - - i - - son,
son, e - le - - - i - - son, Ky - ri - e e - lei - - son, e - - le - - -
son, e - le - i - - son, Ky - ri - e, Ky - ri - e e - - le - - i -
Chri - ste e - le - - - - - - - i - - son, Ky - ri - e e -
Tutti Bassi
40
Chri - ste e - le - - - - - - - - - - - i - son, e - le - i - son, e - le - i -
- i - son, e - le - - i - son, Ky - ri - e e - le - - i - son, Ky - ri -
son, Ky - ri - e e - le - i - son, e - le - - - - - i - son, e - le - - i - son, e - le - i -
le - - i - son, e - le - - - - - - - i - son, e - le - - i - son,
Vc.
44
son, Chri - ste e - le - - - - - i - son, Chri - ste e -
e e - le - - i - son, e - le - - i - son, Chri - ste e - le - - - - - i -
son, e - le - - - - - i - son. e - le - i - son, e - le - i - son, e - le - i -
Chri - ste e - le - - - - i - son, e - le - i - son, e - le - i - son, e -
Tutti Bassi
Vc.
Tutti Bassi
48
Adagio
le - - - - - i - son, e - le - i - son, Ky - ri - e e - le - i - - son.
son, Ky - ri - e, Ky - ri - e e - le - - i - son, Ky - ri - e e - le - - i - son.
son, Ky - ri - e, Ky - ri - e e - le - - i - son, Ky - ri - e e - le - i - - son.
le - - i - son, e - le - - i - son, e - le - - i - son, Ky - ri - e e - le - - i - son.

2. Dies irae

Tuba mirum

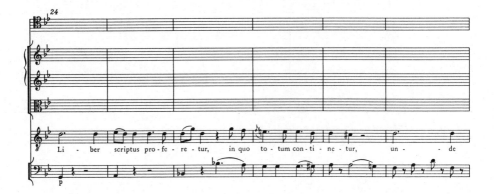

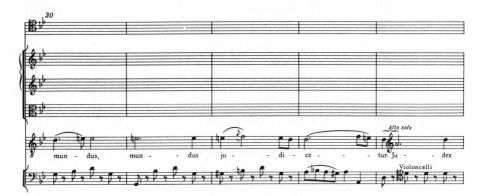

Rex tremendae

13
van-dos sal - vas gra - tis, Rex tre - men - - dae, Rex tre - men - dae ma - je -
qui sal - van - dos sal - vas gra - tis, Rex tre - men - dae ma - je -
- dae ma - je - sta - - - - - - tis, Rex tre - men - - - - - dae, Rex tre - men - dae ma - je -
men - - - - dae ma - je - sta - - - - - - tis, Rex tre - men - dae, Rex tre - men - dae ma - je -
16
p
sta - tis, qui sal-van-dos sal-vas gra - tis, Sal - va me,
sta - tis, qui sal-van-dos sal-vas gra - tis, Sal - va me,
sta - tis, qui sal-van-dos sal-vas gra - tis,
sta - tis, qui sal-van-dos sal-vas gra - tis,
Solo
p Org.: tasto solo
19
sal - - va me, fons pi - e - ta - - - - - - tis.
sal - - va me, fons pi - e - ta - - - - - - tis.
Sal - va me, sal - - va me, fons pi - e - ta - - - - - - tis.
Sal - va me, sal - - va me, fons pi - e - ta - - - - - - tis.

Recordare

79
me - us: sup - pli - can - ti par - ce De - us. Qui Ma - ri - am ab - sol - vi - sti,
me - us: sup - pli - can - ti par - ce De - us.
me - us: sup - pli - can - ti par - ce De - us. et la -
me - us: sup - pli - can - ti par - ce De - us.
86
mi - hi quo - que spem de - di - sti, mi - hi quo - que spem de - di - sti.
mi - hi quo - que, mi - hi quo - que spem de - di - sti, spem de - di - sti.
tro - nem ex - au - di - sti, mi - hi quo - que, mi - hi quo - que spem de - di - sti.
mi - hi quo - que spem de - di - sti.

Confutatis

Lacrymosa

⟨Süßmayr⟩

*) Takt 11, Violine I, 6. Note: Süßmayr schreibt es'.
**) Instrumentation bis Satzende durchgeführt.

13
ju - di-can - dus ho - mo re - us: Hu - ic er - go par - ce De - us.
Vc.
17
Pi - e Je - su, Je - su Do - mi - ne,
Tutti Bassi
Org.: tasto solo
21
do - na e - is re - qui-em, do - na e - is, do - na
do - na e - is re - qui-em, do - na e - is, do - na e - is
Tutti

3. Domine *Jesu*

Hostias

Quam olim da capo

4. Sanctus

*) Instrumentation bis Satzende durchgeführt.

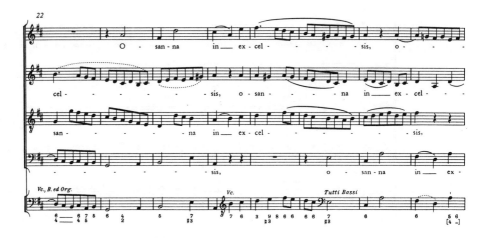

Benedictus

*) Instrumentation bis Satzende durchgeführt.

30
be-ne-di ctus qui
be-ne-di - ctus
be - ne - di-ctus qui ve-nit in no - mi-ne Do - mi-ni,
Do - mi-ni,
34
ve-nit in no - mi-ne Do - mi - ni, qui ve - nit in no - mi-ne Do - mi-
qui ve - nit in no - mi-ne Do-mi-ni, qui ve - nit in no - mi-ne Do - mi-
be-ne-di-ctus qui ve - nit in no - mi-ne Do-mi-ni, qui ve - nit in no - mi-ne Do - mi-
be-ne-di - ctus qui ve - nit, qui ve - nit in no - - mi-ne Do - mi-
cresc.
38
ni, be-ne - di - ctus qui ve - nit, be-ne - di - ctus qui ve - nit in
ni, be-ne-di - ctus qui ve - nit in no-mi-ne Do - mi - ni, qui ve - nit in
ni, be-ne-di - ctus qui ve - nit in no-mi-ne Do - mi - ni, be - ne - di - ctus qui
ni, be-ne - di-ctus qui ve-nit in no - mi-ne Domi-ni, be-ne-di - ctus qui
fp p

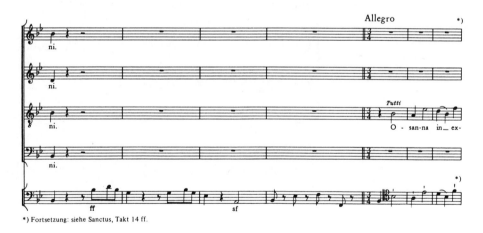

*) Fortsetzung: siehe Sanctus, Takt 14 ff.

5. Agnus Dei

*)

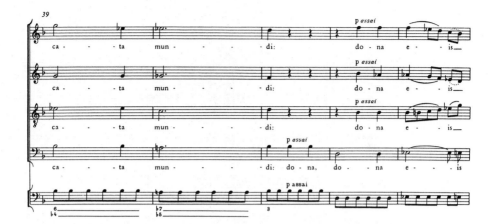

Lux aeterna

⟨Süßmayr, nach Mozarts Introitus und Kyrie⟩

*) Fortsetzung: siehe Requiem, Satz 1, Takt 23 ff.

Abbreviations

AMA *W. A. Mozarts sämtliche Werke. Kritisch durchgesehene Gesamtausgabe.* Leipzig, 1876–1905 [Alte Mozart-Ausgabe = old Mozart edition].

Anderson *The Letters of Mozart and His Family*, ed. and trans. Emily Anderson, 2 vols. 2d ed. London, 1966. 3d ed. London, 1985.

Bauer-Deutsch; Eibl *Mozart: Briefe und Aufzeichnungen. Gesamtausgabe*, ed. Wilhelm A. Bauer and Otto Erich Deutsch. 4 vols. Kassel, 1962–63 [Bauer-Deutsch I–IV]; commentary by Josef Heinz Eibl, 2 vols. Kassel, 1971 [Eibl V–VI]; index, comp. Josef Heinz Eibl. Kassel, 1975 [Eibl VII].

K Ludwig Ritter von Köchel. *Chronologisch-thematisches Verzeichnis sämtlicher Tonwerke W. A. Mozarts.* Leipzig, 1862; 3d ed., ed. Alfred Einstein. Leipzig, 1937 [= K^3]; rpt. of 3d ed., with supplement by Alfred Einstein. Ann Arbor, 1947 [= K^{3a}]; 6th ed., ed. Franz Giegling, Alexander Weinmann, and Gerd Sievers. Wiesbaden, 1966 [= K^6].

MGG *Die Musik in Geschichte und Gegenwart*, ed. Friedrich Blume. 17 vols. Kassel, 1949–86.

Mitt. ISM *Mitteilungen der Internationalen Stiftung Mozarteum.*

MJb *Mozart-Jahrbuch.*

Mozart *Compendium*	*The Mozart Compendium: A Guide to Mozart's Life and Music*, ed. H. C. Robbins Landon. London, 1990.
Mozart DB	see *Mozart-Dokumente*.
Mozart-Dokumente	*Mozart: Die Dokumente seines Lebens*, ed. Otto Erich Deutsch [= NMA X/34]. Kassel, 1961; translated into English as *Mozart: A Documentary Biography*, trans. Eric Blom, Peter Branscombe, and Jeremy Noble. London, 1965 [= *Mozart DB*]. *Addenda und Corrigenda*, ed. Josef Heinz Eibl [= NMA X/31, vol. 1]. Kassel, 1978.
New Grove	*The New Grove Dictionary of Music and Musicians*, ed. Stanley Sadie. 20 vols. London, 1980.
NMA	Wolfgang Amadeus Mozart. *Neue Ausgabe sämtlicher Werke.* Kassel, 1955– [Neue Mozart-Ausgabe].
Requiem Catalog	*Requiem: Wolfgang Amadeus Mozart 1791/1991*. Catalog of the exhibition in the Austrian National Library, Vienna (17 May–6 December 1991). Graz, 1991.
Verzeichnis	Wolfgang Amadé Mozart. *Verzeichnüß aller meiner Werke* (Mozart's Thematic Catalogue: A Facsimile. British Library, Stefan Zweig MS. 63), ed. Albi Rosenthal and Alan Tyson. London, 1990.

1. Editions of Mozart's Requiem
(editions of philological and historical significance only)

W. A. MOZARTI | MISSA PRO DEFUNCTIS | Requiem | W. A MOZARTS | SEELENMESSE | MIT | UNTERLEGTEM DEUTSCHEN TEXTE. | IM VERLAGE DER BREITKOPF & HÄRTELSCHEN MUSIKHANDLUNG | IN LEIPZIG [1800]. Without publisher's no.

W. A. Mozarti | Missa pro defunctis. | Requiem. | W. A. Mozarts | Seelenmesse, | im Klavierauszuge | mit lateinisch- und deutschem Texte. | J. André: Offenbach [1801]. Publisher's no. 1549.

Requiem | a | Canto, Alto, Tenore et Basso | II Violini, | II Fagotti, | II Corni di Bassetto o Clarinetti, | III Tromboni, | II Clarini et Timpani, | Viola, Basso e Violoncello | con Organo. | Authore. | W: A: MOZART | Vienna | Nel Magazino C: R: pr: Stamperie chimica sul Graben No 612 [1812]. Publisher's nos. 1806–1812.

*W. A. Mozarti | Missa pro defunctis | REQUIEM. | W. A. Mozart's | REQUIEM.
| Partitur. | Neue nach Mozart's und Süßmayr's Handschriften berichtigte Ausgabe |
Nebst einem Vorbericht | von | Anton Andre | . . . | Offenbach a/M, bey Joh. André*
[1827]. Publisher's no. 5018.

*PARTITUR | des | Dies irae, Tuba mirum, Rex tremendae, Recordare, Confutatis,
| Lacrymosa, Domine Jesu und Hostias, | von | W. A. MOZART'S REQUIEM,
| so wie solche Mozart eigenhändig geschrieben, und Abbé Stadler | in genauer Überein-
stimmung mit dem Mozart'schen Original copirt hat. | Nebst Vorbericht und Anhang |
herausgegeben von | A. ANDRÉ. | . . . | Offenbach a/M, bei Johann André* [1829].
Publisher's no. 5246.

Mozart, Wolfgang Amadeus. Requiem K 626, in: AMA, series 24 (supplement),
no. 1 (Leipzig, 1877); critical report by Johannes Brahms, in: AMA, series 24,
no. 1 (Leipzig, 1886): 55–56.

*Mozarts Requiem. Nachbildung der Originalhandschrift Cod. 17561 der k. k. Hofbib-
liothek in Wien in Lichtdruck* [facsimile], ed. Alfred Schnerich. Vienna, 1913; rpt.,
ed. Franz Beyer. Zürich, 1990.

Mozart, Wolfgang Amadeus. Requiem K 626, in: NMA, series I, work group 1,
section 2, vol. 1: *Mozarts Fragment;* vol. 2: *Mozarts Fragment mit den Ergänzungen
von Eybler und Süßmayr,* ed. Leopold Nowak. Kassel, 1965.

Mozart, Wolfgang Amadeus. Requiem K. 626, ed. (instrumentation) Franz Beyer. Zürich, 1971; 2d ed., 1979 [based on Süssmayr's completion].

Mozart, Wolfgang Amadeus. Requiem K 626, ed. Richard Maunder. Oxford,
1988 [new completion].

Mozart, Wolfgang Amadeus. Requiem K 626. Vollständige Faksimile-Ausgabe
im Originalformat der Originalhandschrift in zwei Teilen nach Mus. Hs. 17.561
der Musik-Sammlung der Österreichischen Nationalbibliothek (*Documenta Musicologica,* II/27), ed. Günter Brosche. Graz and Kassel, 1990.

Mozart, Wolfgang Amadeus. Requiem K 626, ed. Robert D. Levin. Neuhausen-
Stuttgart, 1993 [new completion].

2. Writings on Mozart's Requiem
(including the major standard works discussing the Requiem)

Abert, Hermann. *W. A. Mozart.* Leipzig, 1919–21; 7th ed., 2 vols., Leipzig,
1955–56.

Bauman, Thomas. "The Objective Fallacy: On Editing Mozart's Requiem." *MJb* (1991): 494–98.

———. "Requiem, but No Piece." *19th-Century Music* 15 (1991): 151–61.

Beyer, Franz. "Mozarts Komposition zum Requiem." *Acta Mozartiana* 28 (1971): 27–31.

———. "Zur Neuinstrumentation des Mozart-Requiems: Eine Werkstattbetrachtung." In *Musikalische Aufführungspraxis und Edition: Johann Sebastian Bach, Wolfgang Amadeus Mozart, Ludwig van Beethoven*, ed. Diethard Hellmann and Günter Weiss, 81–121. Regensburg, 1990.

Biba, Otto. "Par Monsieur François Comte de Walsegg." *Mitt. ISM* (1981): 34–50.

Blume, Friedrich. "Requiem but No Peace." Trans. Nathan Broder. *Musical Quarterly* 47 (1961): 147–69; rpt. in *The Creative World of Mozart*, ed. Paul Henry Lang, 103–26. New York, 1963.

Brauneis, Walther. "Exequien für Mozart." *Singende Kirche* 37 (1991): 8–11.

———. "Unveröffentlichte Nachrichten zum Dezember 1991 aus einer Wiener Lokalzeitung." *Mitt. ISM* (1991): 165–68.

———. " 'Dies irae, Dies illa'—'Tag des Zornes, Tag der Klage': Auftrag, Entstehung und Vollendung von Mozarts 'Requiem'." *Jahrbuch des Vereins für Geschichte der Stadt Wien* 47/48 (1991–92): 33–48.

———. "Mozarts Nachruhm." *Wiener Geschichtsblätter* 47 (1992): 1–21.

Croll, Gerhard. "Eine zweite, fast vergessene Autobiographie Abbé Stadlers." *MJb* (1964): 172–84.

———. "Briefe zum Requiem." *MJb* (1967): 12–17.

———. "Johann Michael Haydn in seinen Beziehungen zu Leopold und Wolfgang Amadeus Mozart." *MJb* (1988–89): 97–106.

Dalchow, Johannes, Gunther Duda, and Dieter Kerner. *Mozarts Tod 1791–1971*. Pähl, 1971.

Dent, Edward J. "The Forerunners of Mozart's Requiem." *Monthly Musical Record* 37 (1907): 124–26, 148–50.

Deutsch, Otto Erich. "Der Graue Bote." *Mitt. ISM* (1963): 1–3.

———. "Die Legende von Mozarts Vergiftung." *MJb* (1964): 7–18.

———. "Zur Geschichte von Mozarts Requiem." *Österreichische Musikzeitschrift* 19 (1964): 49–60.

Eibl, Josef. "Weitere Briefe zum Requiem." *Mitt. ISM* 23 (1975): 7–16.

———. "Süßmayr und Constanze: Bemerkungen zu einem biographischen Detail in dem vorausgehenden Beitrag von Dieter Schickling." *MJb* (1976–77): 277–80.

Fischer, Wilhelm. "Das 'Lacrimosa dies illa' in Mozarts Requiem." *MJb* (1951): 9–21.

Gärtner, Heinz. *Mozarts Requiem und die Geschäfte der Constanze Mozart.* Munich, 1986. *Constanze Mozart: After the Requiem*, trans. Reinhard G. Pauly. Portland, Ore, 1991.

Handke, Robert. "Zur Lösung der Benedictusfrage in Mozarts Requiem." *Zeitschrift für Musikwissenschaft* 1 (1918): 108–30.

Hess, Ernst. "Zur Ergänzung des Requiems von Mozart durch F. X. Süßmayr." *MJb* (1959): 99–108.

Hintermaier, Ernst. "Eine frühe Requiem-Anekdote in einer Salzburger Zeitung." *Österreichische Musikzeitschrift* 26 (1971): 436–37.

———. "Michael Haydns Requiem." *25. Mozartwoche 1980: Programmbuch*, 146–47. Salzburg, 1980.

Jahn, Otto. *W. A. Mozart*, 4 vols. Leipzig, 1856–59; 2d ed., 1867; *The Life of Mozart*, trans. Pauline D. Townsend, 3 vols. London, 1882.

Kecskeméti, István. "Süßmayr-Handschriften der Nationalbibliothek Széchényi in Budapest." *MJb* (1959): 206–18.

———. "Beiträge zur Geschichte von Mozarts Requiem." *Studia musicologica 1961* (Budapest, 1961): 147–60.

Kerner, Dieter. "Ist das Requiem Mozarts Schwanengesang?" *Schweizerische Musikzeitung* 100 (1960): 70–75.

———. "Das Requiem-Problem." *Neue Zeitschrift für Musik* 135 (1974): 475–79.

Krones, Hartmut. "Ein französisches Vorbild für Mozarts 'Requiem': Die 'Messe des Morts' von François-Joseph Gossec." *Österreichische Musikzeitschrift* 42 (1987): 2–17.

Landon, H. C. Robbins. *1791: Mozart's Last Year.* London, 1988.

Levin, Robert D. *The Unfinished Works of W. A. Mozart.* Senior thesis, Harvard University, 1968.

———. "Zur Musiksprache der Süßmayr zugeschriebenen Sätze des Requiems KV 626." *MJb* (1991): 475–93.

Marguerre, Karl. "Mozart und Süßmayr." *MJb* (1962–63): 172–77.

Martin, Bernhard. "Das 'Agnus Dei' in Mozarts Requiem: Eine ganzheitliche Raumstruktur." *Neues Mozart-Jahrbuch* 3 (1943): 197–229.

Maunder, Richard. *Mozart's Requiem: On Preparing a New Edition*. Oxford, 1988.

Mörner, C.-G. Stellan. "F. S. Silverstolpes im Jahr 1800 (oder 1801) in Wien niedergeschriebenen Bemerkungen zu Mozarts Requiem." In *Festschrift Alfred Orel zum 70. Geburtstag*, ed. Hellmut Federhofer, 113–19. Vienna, 1960.

Mosel, Ignaz Franz von. *Über die Original-Partitur des Requiem von W. A. Mozart*. Vienna, 1839.

Moseley, Paul. "Mozart's Requiem: A Revaluation of the Evidence." *Journal of the Royal Musical Association* 114 (1989): 203–37.

Niemetschek, Franz Xaver. *Leben des K. K. Kapellmeisters Wolfgang Gottlieb Mozart, nach Originalquellen beschrieben*. Prague, 1798; enlarged 2d ed., 1808; *Life of Mozart*, trans. Helen Mautner. London, 1956.

Nissen, Georg Nicolaus von. *Wolfgang Amadeus Mozart's Biographie*, ed. Constanze von Nissen. 2 vols. Leipzig, 1828; rpt. Hildesheim, 1972.

[Novello, Vincent, and Mary Novello.] *A Mozart Pilgrimage: Being the Travel Diaries of Mary and Vincent Novello in the Year 1829*, ed. Nerina Medici and Rosemary Hughes. London, 1955.

Nowak, Leopold. "Mozart's Requiem-Autograph wurde beschädigt." *Österreichische Musikzeitschrift* 14 (1959): 76–77.

musical aspects. "Das Requiem von W. A. Mozart: Einige Fragen und Probleme." *Österreichische Musikzeitschrift* 20 (1965): 395–99.

———. "Die Erwerbung des Mozart-Requiems durch die k. k. Hofbibliothek im Jahre 1838." In *Festschrift Josef Stummvoll*, ed. Josef Mayerhöfer and Walter Ritzer, 295–310. Vienna, 1970.

———. "Wer hat die Instrumentalstimmen in der Kyrie-Fuge des Requiem von W.A. Mozart geschrieben?" *MJb* (1973–74): 191–201.

Plath, Wolfgang. "Über Skizzen zu Mozarts Requiem." In *Bericht über den Internationalen Musikwissenschaftlichen Kongreß Kassel 1962*, ed. Georg Reichert and Martin Just, 184–87. Kassel, 1963; rpt. in *Wolfgang Amadeus Mozart*, ed. Gerhard Croll, 347–52, Darmstadt, 1977; and in Wolfgang Plath, *Mozart-Schriften*, ed. Marianne Danckwardt, 74–77. Kassel, 1991.

———. "Requiem-Briefe: Aus der Korrespondenz Joh. Anton Andrés 1825–1831." *MJb* (1976–77): 174–203; rpt. in *Mozart-Schriften*: 266–97.

———. "Noch ein Requiem-Brief." *Mitt. ISM* (1981): 96–101; rpt in *Mozart-Schriften*: 342–48.

Robertson, Alec. *Requiem: Music of Mourning and Consolation*. New York, 1968.

Schickling, Dieter. "Einige ungeklärte Fragen zur Geschichte der Requiem-Vollendung." *MJb* (1976–77): 268–76.

Schlichtegroll, Friedrich. "Mozarts Leben." In *Nekrolog auf das Jahr 1791*. Gotha, 1793; 2d ed. Graz, 1794; rpt. ed. Joseph H. Eibl. Kassel, 1974.

Schnerich, Alfred. *Messe und Requiem seit Haydn und Mozart*. Vienna and Leipzig, 1909.

Schumann, Robert. "Mozart's Originalpartitur des Requiems." *Neue Zeitschrift für Musik* 10 (1839): 10–11.

Senn, Walter. "Abbé Maximilian Stadler: Mozarts Nachlaß und das 'Unterrichtsheft' KV 453b." *MJb* (1980/83): 287–97.

Sievers, Georg L. P. *Mozart und Süßmayer*. Mainz, 1829.

Solomon, Maynard. "The Rochlitz Anecdotes: Issues of Authenticity in Early Mozart Biography." In *Mozart Studies*, ed. Cliff Eisen, 1–59. Cambridge, 1991.

Stadler, Abbé [Maximilian]. *Vertheidigung der Echtheit des Mozart'schen Requiem*. Vienna, 1826.

———. *Nachtrag zur Vertheidigung der Echtheit des Mozart'schen Requiem*. Vienna, 1827.

———. *Zweyter und letzter Nachtrag zur Vertheidigung der Echtheit des Mozart'schen Requiem, sammt Nachbericht über die neue Ausgabe dieses Requiem durch Herrn André in Offenbach; nebst Ehrenrettung Mozart's und vier fremden Briefen*. Vienna, 1827.

Tyson, Alan. *Mozart: Studies of the Autograph Scores*. Cambridge, Mass., 1987.

Weber, Gottfried. "Über die Echtheit des Mozartschen Requiem." *Cäcilia* 3 (1825): 205–29.

———. *Ergebnisse der bisherigen Forschungen über die Echtheit des Mozart'schen Requiem*. Mainz, 1826; rpt. in *Cäcilia* 3 (1825): 205–29; and 4 (1826): 257–352.

———. "Weitere Nachrichten über die Echtheit des Mozartschen Requiem." *Cäcilia* 4 (1826): 257–352.

———. "[Erläuterungen zum] Nachtrag zur Vertheidigung der Echtheit des Mozart'schen Requiem. . . ." *Cäcilia* 6 (1827): 133–53.

———. *Weitere Ergebnisse der Forschungen über die Echtheit des Mozart'schen Requiem*. Mainz, 1827; rpt. in *Cäcilia* 6 (1827): 133–53.

Wlcek, Walter. *Franz Xaver Süßmayr (1766–1803) als Kirchenkomponist*. Tutzing, 1978.

Wolff, Christoph. "The Composition and Completion of Mozart's Requiem, 1791–1792." In *Mozart Studies*, ed. Cliff Eisen, 61–81. Cambridge, 1991.

————. "A Requiem for Mozart: Some Myths Dispelled." *New York Times*, 1 Dec. 1991.

————. Review of *Wolfgang Amadeus Mozart: Requiem*. Reprint of the 1913 collotype, ed. F. Beyer; *Requiem*. Complete facsimile edition, ed. Günter Brosche." *19th-Century Music* 15 (1991): 162–65.

Worlitz-Wellspacher, Andrea. "Der Bote des Requiembestellers." *Wiener Geschichtsblätter* 45 (1990): 197–219.

3. Other Works Cited

Adelung, Johann Christoph. *Über den deutschen Styl*. Leipzig, 1785.

Bär, Carl. *Mozart: Krankheit, Tod, Begräbnis*. Salzburg, 1966. 2d ed., 1972.

Blume, Clemens, ed. *Analecta Hymnica*, vol. 54. Leipzig, 1915.

Braunbehrens, Volkmar. *Mozart in Wien 1781–1791*. Munich and Zürich, 1986; *Mozart in Vienna 1781–1791*, trans. Timothy Bell. New York, 1989.

Chafe, Eric T. *The Church Music of Heinrich Biber*. Ann Arbor, 1987.

Davies, Peter J. "Mozart's Illnesses and Death." *Musical Times* 125 (1984): 437–42, 554–61.

Einstein, Alfred. *Mozart: His Character, His Work*. New York, 1945.

Emerson, Isabelle. "The Role of Counterpoint in the Formation of Mozart's Late Style." Ph.D. diss., Columbia University, 1976.

Falck, Martin. *Wilhelm Friedemann Bach*. Leipzig, 1913; 2d ed., 1919.

Finscher, Ludwig. "Aspects of Mozart's Compositional Process in the Quartet Autographs." In *The String Quartets of Haydn, Mozart, and Beethoven: Studies of the Autograph Manuscripts*, ed. Christoph Wolff. Isham Library Papers, vol. 3, 121–33. Cambridge, Mass., 1979.

Floros, Constantin. *Mozart-Studien I*. Wiesbaden, 1979.

Gerber, Ernst Ludwig. *Neues historisch-biographisches Lexikon der Tonkünstler*. 2 vols. Leipzig, 1814.

Giegling, Franz. "Zu den Rezitativen von Mozarts Oper 'Titus.' " *MJb* (1967): 121–26.

Grau, P. Engelbert. "Ein bisher übersehener Instrumentalwitz von W. A. Mozart: Bemerkungen zu KV 412." *Acta Mozartiana* 8 (1961): 8–10.

Gruber, Gernot. *Mozart und die Nachwelt*. Salzburg and Vienna, 1985; 2d ed., Munich, 1987.

Hammerstein, Reinhold. "Der Gesang der geharnischten Männer: Eine Studie zu Mozarts Bachbild." *Archiv für Musikwissenschaft* 13 (1956): 1–24.

Hildesheimer, Wolfgang. *Mozart*. Frankfurt, 1977; trans. Marion Faber, New York, 1979.

Hoffmann, Ernst Theodor Amadeus. *Schriften zur Musik*, ed. Friedrich Schnapp. Darmstadt, 1965; *E. T. A. Hoffmann's Musical Writings*, ed. D. Charlton, trans. M. Clarke. Cambridge, 1989.

Jaksch, Werner. *H. I. F. Biber, Requiem à 15: Untersuchungen zur höfischen, liturgischen und musikalischen Topik einer barocken Totenmesse*. Munich, 1977.

Konrad, Ulrich. *Mozarts Schaffensweise: Studien zu den Werkautographen, Skizzen und Entwürfen*. Göttingen, 1992.

Kosch, Franz. "Florian Leopold Gassmann als Kirchenkomponist." *Studien zur Musikwissenschaft* (Vienna) 14 (1927): 213–40.

Lehner, Walter. "Franz Xaver Süßmayr als Opernkomponist." *Studien zur Musikwissenschaft* (Vienna) 17 (1931): 66–96.

Levin, Robert D. *Who Wrote the Mozart Four-Wind Concertante?* New York, 1988.

Lühning, Helga. "Zur Entstehungsgeschichte von Mozarts 'Titus.'" *Die Musikforschung* 27 (1974): 300–318.

MacIntyre, Bruce C. *The Viennese Concerted Mass of the Early Classic Period*. Ann Arbor, 1986.

Plath, Wolfgang. "Das Skizzenblatt KV 467a." *MJb* (1959): 114–26.

Raby, F. J. E. *A History of Christian-Latin Poetry from the Beginnings to the Close of the Middle Ages*. Oxford, 1927.

Schmid, Manfred Hermann. *Mozart und die Salzburger Tradition*. Tutzing, 1976.

Senn, Walter. "Mozarts Kirchenmusik und die Literatur." *MJb* (1978–79): 14–18.

Steptoe, Andrew. "Mozart and Poverty: A Re-examination of the Evidence." *Musical Times* 152 (1984): S. 196–201.

Sulzer, Johann Georg. *Allgemeine Theorie der schönen Künste*. 4 vols. Leipzig, 1771–74; 4th ed., 1792–99; rpt. Hildesheim, 1967.

Vellekoop, Kees. *"Dies irae dies illa": Studien zur Frühgeschichte einer Sequenz*. Bilthoven, 1978.

Wolff, Christoph. "Mozart 1784: Biographische und stilgeschichtliche Überlegungen." *MJb* (1986): 1–10.

———. "'Musikalische Gedankenfolge' und 'Einheit des Stoffes': Zu Mozarts

Klaviersonate F-Dur (KV 533 + 492)." In *Das musikalische Kunstwerk: Festschrift Carl Dahlhaus*, ed. Hermann Danuser et al., 441–54. Laaber, 1988.

———. "Carl Philipp Emanuel Bach und Wien: Zum Kontext der Orchester-Sinfonien mit zwölf obligaten Stimmen." In *Carl Philipp Emanuel Bach und die europäische Musikkultur des mittleren 18. Jahrhunderts*, ed. Hans Joachim Marx, 119–31. Göttingen, 1990.

Wurzbach, Constant von. *Biographisches Lexikon des Kaiserthums Oesterreich*. Vienna, 1856–91.

Zaubertöne: Mozart in Wien 1781–1791. Catalog of the exhibition in the Historical Museum, Vienna (6 Dec. 1990–15 Sept. 1991). Vienna, [1990].

Zelter, Karl Friedrich, and Johann Wolfgang von Goethe. *Briefwechsel*, ed. Hans-Günter Ottenberg. Leipzig, 1987.

Ziegler, Frank. *W. A. Mozart: Autographenverzeichnis*. Berlin, 1990.

INDEX OF MOZART'S WORKS

(and works attributed to Mozart)

Compositor: Impressions, *a division of* Edwards Brothers, Inc.
Text: 11/14 Bembo
Display: Bembo
Printer: Edwards Brothers, Inc.
Binder: Edwards Brothers, Inc.

Library of Congress Cataloging-in-Publication Data
Wolff, Christoph.
   [Mozart's Requiem. English]
   Mozart's Requiem : historical and analytical studies, documents, and
score / Christoph Wolff ; translated by Mary Whittall, with revisions
and additions by the author.
     p.   cm.
   Translation of : Mozart's Requiem : Geschichte—Musik—
Dokumente—Partitur des Fragments.
   Includes bibliographical references and index.
   ISBN 0-520-07709-1
   1. Mozart, Wolfgang Amadeus, 1756-1791. Requiem, K. 626,
D minor.
2. Requiems—Scores.   I. Mozart, Wolfgang Amadeus, 1756-1791.
Requiem, K. 626, D minor. 1994.   II. Title.
ML410.M9W36413 1993
782.32'38—dc20   92-39076
                                           CIP
                                           MN